改訂版

完全攻略！
TOEFL iBT®テスト
模試3回分

川手 - ミヤジェイエフスカ恩
（Megumi Kawate-Mierzejewska）

Steve Mierzejewski 共著

＊本書は、『完全攻略！　TOEFL iBT®テスト　模試3回分』（2015年3月刊）の内容を改訂したものです。

は　じ　め　に

　本書には、インターネット版TOEFLテスト、TOEFL iBT（Internet-Based Test）の試験問題を研究したうえで作成した模擬試験3回分を収録した。模擬試験3回分の問題を何回も解きながら、「問題形式」に慣れ「実力把握」「受験前の総仕上げ」、そして「速読と理解」にも焦点をあて、「英語運用能力の向上」を目指す。このような趣旨の下に、リーディング、リスニング、スピーキング、そしてライティングの4技能を測定する問題に加えて、「読んで、聴いて、それについて話す」「聴いて、話す」、さらに「読んで、聴いて、それに関するエッセイを書く」というような統合型問題（Integrated Task）、そして2023年7月から採用されたライティング・セクションの「オンライン投稿文問題」に至るまでを、本試験の構成に則して紹介している。

　具体的には、本書を使って「受験前の総仕上げ」として模擬試験を解くことで、TOEFL iBTテストの概要をつかめ、問題形式にも慣れ、試験で「英語を読むこと」にも慣れ、短時間で内容把握と要約のアウトライン作成ができるような受験準備も整い、自信をもって本番に臨むことができる。また、自己の弱点も把握でき、どこに重点を置いて今後の学習を進めていったらいいのかがわかり、本試験で高得点を獲得するための、つまり英語運用能力向上を目指すための効果的な学習方法が確立できる。

　本書は、TOEFL iBTテストの準備のためだけでなく、英語運用能力に磨きをかけるためにも役立ててほしい。模擬試験を解くことで、自信をつけ、自分に合った適切な学習方法を自分自身で見つけ出し、本番での高得点獲得にこの本を役立ててもらえれば幸いである。

2024年春
川手-ミヤジェイエフスカ 恩
（Megumi Kawate-Mierzejewska, Ed.D）

謝　辞

　皆さまのおかげで、本書の改訂新版が出せたことを、大変嬉しく思います。

　本書に関し、常に助力をくださり、そして温かく見守ってくださる方々に感謝します。

　このたびの改訂にあたりご尽力をいただいた株式会社アルク書籍編集部の佐野郁世氏、株式会社オフィスLEPSの岡本茂紀氏、共著者のSteve Mierzejewski氏、過去の増刷の際にご尽力をいただいた、菊野啓子氏、北折玲子氏、南美穂氏、伊藤文子氏、谷向佳子氏、大平健太氏、信田康平氏、そして本書作成に何らかの形で携わってくださったすべての方々。常に温かく見守ってくださるハワイ大学大学院名誉教授のDr. Gabriele Kasper。以下（敬称略）Min Lu、Peter Ross。さらに、（敬称略：五十音順）石田　正、大塚智美、故伊丹レイ子、故伊丹吉彦、板谷クリスティーナ絢子、市村佳子、大竹和孝、小原麻友美、加藤智恵、賀来　競、郭仁平、川手　暢、神田みなみ、鬼頭和也、久我俊二、熊谷　讓、小枝伸行、小山信子、坂谷佳子、篠田英春、松寿みゆき、高田幸詩朗、高野のぞみ、高橋良子、高橋　耀、武田裕子、長坂達彦、根本　斉、廣野真木、深沢清治、福本拓己、星川朗、森山慎吾、宮城典江、山下早代子、山口　学、山崎勤子、湯沢　斉、横井裕彦、横井友紀子、渡辺伸雄。

　以上に加えて、常に協力を惜しまない娘の賀来恵理香ミヤジェエフスキー、孫の恵茉、理蒼。

2024年春

川手 - ミヤジェイエフスカ 恩

（Megumi Kawate-Mierzejewska, Ed.D）

CONTENTS

目 次

TOEFL® テストとは

TOEFL（Test of English as a Foreign Language）テストとは、その名が示すように、外国語としての英語力判定テストです。アメリカの非営利教育団体 Educational Testing Service（ETS）により開発・運営されている TOEFL テストは、主にアメリカやカナダの大学院・大学・短大で、留学志願者の英語力が授業についていくのに必要な基準に達しているかを測るための目安として使われてきました。最近では、アメリカ・カナダのみならず、イギリス・オーストラリア・ニュージーランドを含む英語圏各国において、9,000 を超える大学・短大が、英語を母語としない留学生に対して、必要な英語力の基準を TOEFL テストのスコアで提示し、入学要件の一つとしています（TOEFL テストとともに他の英語力判定テストのスコアを採用している大学もあります）。

現在、TOEFL テストは、Internet-Based Test（iBT）と呼ばれるインターネットを利用した形式で実施されています。iBT は、それまでの Paper-Based Test（PBT）や Computer-Based Test（CBT）に代わって導入されたもので、アメリカでは 2005 年に、日本では翌 2006 年に実施が始まりました（なお、大学など教育機関での団体受験のみが可能な TOEFL ITP というペーパーテストが、別途、日本を含む各国で実施されています）。

それでは、TOEFL iBT の概要を見てみましょう。

● iBT の概要

iBT では、インターネットを使って世界各地で同じ日に同じ問題のテストが行われます。試験中は、すべてのセクションでメモ書きが許されるので、要点をまとめたメモを取ることが重要です。また、iBT では、かつて CBT にあったような、テストに先立ってコンピュータの使い方が説明される Tutorial の時間が設けられておらず、さらに、Writing のセクションでは、解答を必ずキーボードで入力しなければなりません。そのため、あらかじめコンピュータの操作に慣れておくことも必須です。

iBT は、大きく Reading（リーディング・セクション）、Listening（リスニング・セクション）、Speaking（スピーキング・セクション）、Writing（ライティング・セクション）の 4 つのセクションに分かれています。Reading と Listening は選択式で、選択肢や文中の語などをマウスでクリックする解答方式です。Speaking は設問に対する

自分の考えを述べたり、聴いた内容、または読んで聴いた内容に基づいて答える方式で、マイクに話し込む形を取り、Writing ではタイピングにより解答する方式が取られています。

＊2024年4月時点での情報に基づいています。

セクション	問題形式	問題の詳細	問題数	制限時間	備考
Reading	パッセージを読む	同義語を選択する問題・パラグラフ内容の把握問題・文章挿入問題・文意を置き換える問題・参照問題・作者の意図を探る問題・パラグラフ単位の意味を把握する問題・パッセージ要約問題	2パッセージ 1パッセージあたり10問	約35分	
Listening	講義を聞く（一般的な講義・教授と学生のインターアクションを通しての講義）	聞いたことそのままの理解度を問う問題（comprehension questions）・話者の含意を問う語用論的問題（pragmatic understanding）・聞いた情報を基に推論を行う問題（connecting information）	3講義 1講義あたり6問	約36分	マイク付きヘッドセットを使用
	会話を聞く（複数人数によるキャンパスでの会話）		2会話 1会話あたり5問		
Speaking	Independent Tasks	2つを比較してどちらを支持するかを述べる問題	1問	約16分	マイク付きヘッドセットを使用
	Integrated Tasks	パッセージを読み、それに関連する会話や講義を聞き、読んだものと聞いたものを踏まえて答える統合型問題・会話や講義を聞き、その内容について答える統合型問題	3問		
Writing	Integrated Tasks	230～300語のパッセージを3分以内に読み、約2分の講義を聞いた後に設問に答え、150～225語程度のエッセイを20分以内に書く問題	1問	約29分	タイピングのみで解答（手書き不可）
	Academic Discussion Tasks	問題提起と他の学生の意見を読み、自分の意見を100語以上で書く問題	1問		

iBT は主に土曜日・日曜日に実施されます。日本各地の大学・高校・専門学校などをテストセンターとしています。会場によって試験の実施日が異なるので、随時 ETS のホームページ（ETS アカウントの作成が必要）で確認する必要があります。受験希望者はオンラインにて希望のテスト日を予約できます。テスト結果は、受験の4～8日後に ETS のホームページ（ETS アカウント内）で確認できるようになっています。（Reading、Listening セクションについては、テスト終了時にスコア［非公式］が表示されます。）

● TOEFL テストのスコア

iBT のスコアは、Reading・Listening・Speaking・Writing の 4 つのセクション別に 0 〜 30 の間で算出され、その合計が全体のスコアとなります。つまり、最低スコアが 0、最高スコアが 120 です。

Reading	Listening	Speaking	Writing	Total
0-30	0-30	0-30	0-30	0-120

先に触れたように、TOEFL テストのスコアは英語圏の多くの大学で英語力の判定材料とされ、各大学・短大によって要求されるスコアが異なります。一つの目安として、アメリカの場合、コミュニティーカレッジと呼ばれる 2 年制大学では 45 〜 61、学部課程では 61 〜 80、大学院では 80 〜 100 を目標とするといいでしょう。しかし、入学のための競争が激しい学校や、高い英語能力が必要とされる専攻分野などでは、要求スコアが目安よりも高めに設定されている場合があります。

● 受験手続きについて

まず、TOEFL iBT® Information Bulletin（以下 Bulletin）と呼ばれる受験要項を入手します（p. 9 参照）。Bulletin には TOEFL テストに関する諸注意がこと細かに記されています。ETS では、Bulletin に記載されている内容を理解していることを前提に申し込みを受け付けているので、申し込みに先立って Bulletin を入手し、熟読しておく必要があります。情報のほとんどが英語で書かれているため、全部を読みこなすのは大変ですが、TOEFL テスト受験の第一歩と考えトライしてみましょう。Bulletin は、ETS が提供する TOEFL テストの公式ウェブサイトから、PDF 形式のファイルをダウンロードします。

iBT はインターネットを利用して行われるため、広いエリアでの実施が可能で、多くの会場が設けられています。これらの情報については、受験の都度、TOEFL テストのウェブサイトで必ず確認しましょう。

テストは、オンラインで申し込めます。

［申し込み］

　ETS の TOEFL iBT テスト申し込み用ウェブページにアクセスし、必要事項を登録します。

　◇ 申込期限と受験料
　　・受験日の 7 日前まで (Regular Registration) と受験日の 2 日前まで (Late Registration) で受験料が異なります。

　◇ 支払い方法
　　・クレジットカード
　　・PayPal

　◇受験日・会場変更
　　・受験日の 4 日前まで：有料で可能です。詳細は Bulletin をご確認ください。

　◇キャンセル払い戻し
　　・受験日の 4 日前まで：受験料の 50%

▧ Bulletin の入手先

> ETS のホームページ「受験申込 (会場受験)」または「受験申込 (自宅受験)」から TOEFL iBT® Information Bulletin (PDF 形式) がダウンロードできます。

※ TOEFL テストの手続きに関する情報は、随時更新される可能性があります。

本書の効果的な使い方

　本書は、問題・解答と解説、必要であればリスニングのトランスクリプトや日本語訳が確認できるように構成されているので、問題自体のレベルは本番のテストとほぼ同じでありながら、すべてのレベルの学習者に対応している。また、できるかぎり本番のテストに近い形で模擬試験を提供するために、実際の TOEFL iBT とほぼ同じ指示表現や設問、アカデミック・サブジェクトを使っている。さらに、それぞれのセクションではさまざまなトピックを網羅しているので、それらのトピックに関する知識を獲得するのにも役立つ。なお、本書は紙上で模擬試験を提供するものなので、コンピュータ操作に関わる設問指示は掲載していない。

　時間を計り、本番と同じような設定で、時間配分を決めて各テストに臨むのが、本書の基本的な使い方である。模擬試験が一つ終わったら、答え合わせをし、必要であれば解説、さらに訳例なども読む。そして、取り組んだ内容は、その都度理解しておこう。各トピックに関する背景知識を確認するためにも、一度は訳例に目を通しておくといいだろう。また、訳例の後に掲載した「重要語句」は語彙構築のために役立てよう。さらに、それぞれのトピックを各自で、インターネットなどで検索してみて内容を増やしておくと背景知識を増やすのに役立つ。

　目標設定については、単純に計算して、北米の学部課程に入りたいのであれば、本書の模擬試験で 60 パーセントから 70 パーセントの正解率を目安とし、大学院入学を希望するのであれば 75 パーセントから 85 パーセント以上の正解率を目標にするとよい（ここでの目標はやや高く設定してある）。

　次ページ以降に、模擬試験を受けるにあたっての留意点と本書の解答・解説の特色、また目標を達成するためのポイントを、各セクションごとにまとめたので参考にしてほしい。「試験を受けるにあたって」はそのまま実践してみよう。また、スピーキングとライティングにおいてまず考えなくてはならないのは、きちんとしたアウトラインを作成することである。それらのセクションに関しては、後述の説明を読み、自己採点の基準を理解しよう。なお、文中に記した「パッセージ」と「テクスト」は同じ意味で使われている。

リーディング・セクション

【試験を受けるにあたって】

① パッセージのタイトルを目で追い、背景知識があればそれを引き出す（30 秒）。

② すべての問題にざっと目を通し、問題の構成を頭に入れる（1 〜 2 分）。

③ 各パッセージに 10 問あるので、それぞれのパッセージに 16 分弱使うことを目安にしよう。1 問にかかる時間を考えながら解くのは現実的でなく、落ち着いて問題を解けないので、実際には一つのパッセージにかける時間を目安としたほうがいい。ただし、1 問 1 分くらいの配分で解いていける程度の力を付けておくといいので、問題を解きながらそのペースを身に付けるのもいい。

④ 最初の問題に戻り、問題文と選択肢を読んでからパッセージを読み、解答を選択する（コンピュータで行う本番テストでは、問題と同じ画面に表示されるパラグラフを読めば解答がわかる）。択一問題では、この作業を繰り返す。

⑤ 語彙問題では、意味がわからなかったら、その言葉が使われている脈絡から正解を推測する。ここでは、英語の統語的規則（文の構成）も役立つ。

⑥ 挿入問題では、代名詞や冠詞の使われ方に注目して理路整然とした話の流れを考える。なお、それぞれの挿入個所には便宜的にアルファベット (A) (B) (C) (D) を振ってあるが、本番ではコンピュータ作業が前提のため、アルファベットではなく■で表示される。

⑦ 要約問題では、与えられた文章につなげて、挿入問題を解く要領で考えていくといい。

⑧ 一つの問題に時間をかけすぎないようにしよう。わからない問題があったら、解を推測して最善を尽くし、取りあえず答えておいて、最後に時間があったらそこへ戻ってもう一度考えてみよう。

【解答・解説について】

使い方のポイント▶ まず、答え合わせをする。そして解説を読む。その際に原文を読み返し、日本語訳や単語の意味が知りたかったら、訳例や「重要単語」を参考にするといい。

その他の重要事項▶ 設問の指示や問題形式は本番のテストとほぼ同じなので、ここでしっかり模擬試験を解いて、自分なりの理解の仕方や問題への取り組み方法を習得し、トピックに関する知識を獲得して自信を付けておこう。

【目標点に達するために】

　まず、それぞれのアカデミック・トピックで使われる語彙を構築することが大切だ。それと同時に、大学の一般教養科目で習うようなアカデミック・トピックに精通する。そのためにも、北米の高校で教科書として使われているような書籍を読んでみよう。インターネットで「教科書の図書館」や「アメリカの教科書」などと検索してみるといい。また、アカデミック・トピックを扱っている雑誌などを読むのもいい。そして、それらを読む際に、パッセージの構成も把握し、重要な情報がどこに書かれているのかを確認しておくとよい。また、重要な情報だけを追って読んでいく練習や、読みながら主題を把握し大筋を理解していく練習、重要事項を列挙しておき内容に関する知識を増やす作業も大切である。

リスニング・セクション

【試験を受けるにあたって】

① リスニングのタイトルを見たら、背景知識があればそれを引き出す。

② 講義や会話を聴くときは、集中力を絶やさないようにする。

③ 聴きながらメモを取り、講義の簡単なアウトラインを作成する。また、会話なら重要なポイントだけを書きとめていく。メモを取ることに夢中になって会話を聴き損ねないようにするためにも、記号や略字、ひいては漢字を使うのもいい。また、メモを取るときはわかりやすく書く。

④ 講義における分類や物事の順序は設問につながるので、それらが出てきたら

それぞれの重要ポイントを書きとめておくといい。

⑤ 講義や会話で使われているリスニング・キュー（『新装版 海外の大学・大学院で授業を受ける技術』川手-ミヤジェイエフスカ 恩著：アルク刊 参照）を聴き取り、それぞれにどのような情報が続くのかを思い出し、内容理解に役立てる。つまり、うっかり集中を欠いてしまって途中からわからなくなってしまっても、リスニング・キューを聴き分けられれば、次にどのような情報が来るのか予想でき、そこから立て直すことができる。

⑥ 書き取ったメモを参考にして、設問に答えていく。

★このセクションではダウンロード音声を使います（p.20 参照）。

【解答・解説について】

使い方のポイント▶ まず、答え合わせをする。その際に、必要であればトランスクリプトを読みながら、内容も理解し、英語で考えて英語で答える練習をする。各トピックの内容が把握できたら、もう一回聴いて、確認をしておく。その際にリスニング・キューをきちんと聴くことも大切となる。

その他の重要事項▶ 解説は、トランスクリプト、訳例、解答・解説の順に掲載してある。また、それぞれの設問の解となる個所をトランスクリプトの中でも明示するという画期的な方法を取り入れた。つまり、聴いたことを英語で理解し、英語で考え、英語で答えなくてはならないので、日本語の解説はなるべく少なくして、トランスクリプトを見れば解が一目瞭然となるように工夫してある。そのうえで、さらに日本語訳が必要なら、訳例を参考にすればよい。

【目標点に達するために】

理解度を問う問題に対応するために、さまざまな分野のマテリアルを聴き、大意をつかむ練習が大切だ。また、キャンパス会話に精通するには、英語のテレビドラマなどを見て会話のトピックに関する背景知識を獲得するとともに、会話体を聴き取ることにも慣れておく必要がある。インターネットのリソースも活用しよう。

話者の含意を問う語用論的問題に対応するためには、英語で話せる環境をつく

り、実際に会話を行う中で学んでいったり、友人や英会話のチューターを介して決まった言い方のもつ含意について学んだりする必要がある。さらに、インターネットのリソースなどを検索してみるのもいいだろう。

　最後に、聴いた情報を基に推論を行う問題に対処するには、北米など英語圏の文化的事情や背景、習慣に関する知識を増やしたり、映画やドラマなどから、さまざまな状況における決まった対応の仕方を学んだりしておくとよい。また、ボランティア活動を通して英語を学ぶ方法もある。

スピーキング・セクション

【試験を受けるにあたって】
① 設問を聴きながら読み、何が問われているのかを明確にする。
② 与えられた準備時間を使って、トピック提起（設問に対する解）、理由づけや具体例、簡単なまとめという形で、返答のアウトラインを作成する。
③ アウトラインを参考に、それを文章にしながら話す。
④ トピックを適切に展開していくことが大切である。上記の②のように大きな概念から詳細に入り、その概念をサポートしていく。
⑤ 話す際には、つなぎ言葉を適切に使い、理路整然とした話の流れをつくっていく。
⑥ 統合型問題のリーディングとリスニングに関しては前項参照。
⑦ 設問を読んだら、本番と同じ時間配分で準備をし、設問に答える。そして、設問に対する各自の返答（スピーキング）を何らかの方法で録音しておくとよい。
★このセクションではダウンロードの音声を使います（p.20 参照）。

【解答・解説について】
使い方のポイント▶ まず、話す前の準備時間でつくったスピーチのアウトラインと、解説のアウトラインとを比べてみて、「話の組み立て方」が適切かどうかを吟味する。その後、録音した自身の返答を聴いてから、模範解答を見ながらその音声を聴き、話の組み立て方に焦点を当てながら自分の返答との違いを探って

みる。そのうえで解説全体を読み、それを参考に「話の構成（アウトライン）」を吟味、再考する。さらにその後、もう少し時間をかけてもう一度、納得のいく返答を組み立て、マイクに向かって制限時間内で話し、それを録音する。

　こうした作業を繰り返しながら、制限時間に合わせて返答の長さを調整していくとよい。具体的には、理由や具体例の言い回しを長くしたり短くしたりして調整を試みる。また、録音したものと模範解答を聴き比べ、話の速度やリズムについても学んでいく。さらに、初めに録音したものと、解説を読んで再考してから録音したものとを比べて、自己の力がどれくらい向上したのかを確認し、自信をつけていく。その際に、話す速度や流ちょうさ、聴きやすさも確認しておくとよい。

　「読む・聴く・話す」と「聴く・話す」という統合型問題では、模擬試験を受ける際に返答のアウトラインを考えながら、メモを取る練習をしておくとよい。また、解説を読んでから、必要であればトランスクリプトを見たり訳例を読んだりもできる。いずれにしても、次の設問に取り組む前に、模範解答を何回か聴いて、短時間で英語を話すときのリズムも身につけておこう。また、「読むテキスト」と「聴くテキスト」のトランスクリプトを読んで、言い換え表現についても学んでおこう。

その他の重要事項▶ 独立型問題は、誰もが考え得る一般的な身の回りのトピックについて、個人の経験や意見、好みを問う問題である。したがって、本書でもそのようなトピックを採用した。ちなみに、比較的平易で、設問を聴きながら読むだけで何が問われているのかを理解しやすい独立型問題では、必ず何かを話して点数を稼いでおきたい。

　模範解答の音声は、英語を母語とする話者が流ちょうに話すことを想定したものなので、多少スピードが速いと感じるかもしれないが、そのリズムに慣れておくとよい。また、試験では、あまりくだけた会話表現は使わず、模範解答にあるような標準的な言い回しを使おう。

　なお、本書では、便宜上「話の組み立て方」の項目で重要なポイントだけを取り出して説明しているが、本来であれば、談話の流れのなかでそれらについて考えていかなくてはならない。

【目標点に達するために】

　独立型問題に関しては、まず設問をよく読み、自分の意見を決め、それをサポートする理由や具体例を加えていくという話の展開を身につけておく。また、それと同時に 15 秒でアウトラインを考え 45 秒話すという練習も繰り返す。

　総合型問題では、北米の高校で使われている教科書（p.12 で調べたサイトを参照）を用いて、そこにある問題に口頭で答える練習をする。ここでも、まず設問に答えてから、理由や具体例をつけることで話を膨らませていく。また、新聞や雑誌などの短い記事を読み、口頭でそれらを要約したり言い換えたり（パラフレーズ）する練習も役に立つ。読んで、口頭で答えることに慣れてきたら、短いニュースや講義などを聴いて（インターネットを使って見つけるとよい）、話すときのアウトラインを考えながらノートを取り、それをもとに口頭で答える練習をする。そして最後に、それらのトピックについて 1 分間で話す練習をし、制限時間内に話せる長さと速度を身につけておく。

　全体としては、英語を話す機会を増やし、自然に会話ができるようになることや、語彙力を高めたり、慣用表現を使えるようにしたりすることが大切である。また、話す前の準備時間が短いので、15 〜 20 秒でアウトラインを作成する練習も大切だ。さらに、聴きやすい返答をするために、英語のイントネーションや強勢、息継ぎについて研究しておく必要もある。最後に、日本語でカタカナ表記をしている言葉は、英語に直すとまったく違う語彙になったり（例：レンジ、ウインカー、ゲレンデ）、強勢の位置が変わってきたりするので気をつけよう。

ライティング・セクション

【試験を受けるにあたって】

① まず、ETS が提供している練習問題（TOEFL iBT Writing Section (ets.org) をやり、問題の傾向について学ぶ。

② 試験ではまず設問を読み、何が問われているのかを明確にする。"lecture" というのは、聴くもので、読むものは、"reading passage" である。

③ 統合型問題では 20 分で 150 〜 225 語を、オンライン投稿文問題では読むの

も含めて 10 分で 100 語以上を目安に書く。

④ 統合型問題では、まず、講義（聴いたこと）の本旨を要約し、講義が読んだ箇所のポイントにどのように対応しているかを説明する。

　ここで、大切なのは、講義は一回しか聞けないので、最初にくる講義の本旨を聞き逃さないようにしておくことである。

　最後に、書く際のアウトラインは、まず、講義の要点、それを裏付けるポイントを読んだ部分にも貢献できるように 2 つか 3 つ考え、最初の 3 分で作成する。

⑤ 統合型問題は、「読むテクスト」とリスニングのメモをもとに設問に答えることを念頭に、言い換えをしながら必要な情報を押さえていく。要求されている語数で書けば、設問に答えるのに必要な情報はすべて網羅できるので、それ以上多く書く必要はない。

⑥ オンライン投稿文問題では、10 分間で、問題提起と設問を読んで自分の意見を考えて、他の学生の意見も読み、自分の意見を述べ、その裏付けを書く。つまり、読んで、考えて書くのを 10 分間でやらなくてはならない。実際には 130 〜 150 語書いてもいいが、初心者は一つのパラグラフを 100 語以上書くことを目標にしよう。また、オンライン投稿文問題には、「二者択一式」、「yes/no 形式」と「自由形式」があり、それぞれに対応の仕方が異なる（詳細は以下の【オンライン投稿文問題】参照）。

【統合型問題】

　統合型問題は、同じトピックに対して 2 つの異なる視点から見ているので、「読むテクスト」と「聴くテクスト」の内容は対立関係にある。

【オンライン投稿文問題】

　以下の①は、基本パターンなので、問題に臨機応変に対応する必要がある。

　ここで覚えておかなくてはならないのは、10 分で読んで考えて書き上げるという全てをこなさなくてはならないということだ。そのためには、まず聞かれていることを明確にし、自分の意見を考え、他の学生の意見をさらっと読みポイン

トをつかみ、他の学生の意見も踏まえて、解答をすぐに書き始めることだ。

① -1 二者択一問題【トピックに対しての二者択一で、どちらがいいかを考える】

① -2 どちらがいいか聞かれる時は、"which is better 提案 A、提案 B?" という ような形できかれるので【まず自分の意見を述べる because 根拠となる 理由をつける】。その際に、他の学生の考えに言及するときは、賛成なら、 副詞を用いて誇張して賛成し（I certainly agree with ...）、その理由も述べ る。反対ならまず【前置き】(I can understand 他学生 A's viewpoint とか I think 他学生 A makes a good point) をしてから【自分の反対意見を述べる】 ＋【意見の根拠を述べて裏付けをする（その際に、理由と共に他学生の弱 いポイントにふれてもいい】という形をとる。

① -3 yes/no は、根拠と共に【自分の意見を述べる】と議論に貢献しやすい。 "Do you think ...?" というような形で聞かれることが多い。答える時は【I believe that ... というような形で自分の意見を述べる because ... とし根拠 となる理由をつける】つまり、【自分の意見の根拠を述べて裏付けをする】 という形をとる。

② 自由に解答できる形式の問題に答える時【自分の考えを述べるのだがその前 に他学生たちの意見にも言及しながら、それを自分の論点へと発展させても いい（他学生 -A makes a good point, but 自分の考えを書く because ...)】➡ [そうすることによってディスカッション（議論）に貢献することもできるし 話の流れも自然になり、自分の意見を言いやすくなる。]

③ まとめ➡上記①や②を基本的な流れとして習得し、臨機応変に対応できるく らいの力をつけるため、YouTube も含めて様々な練習問題を通して、パター ンを自由自在に使いこなせるようにしておくとよい。また、他の生徒の意見 を読む時に時間をかけ過ぎないように時間の使い方に工夫をすることも大切 だ。そして、準備ができたら本書を使用して最後の仕上げをするといい。

④ 自分が知らないようなトピックが試験に出た時の対処方法としては、まず教 授による講義内容の説明（ほとんどの場合は詳しく説明してあるのでさらっ と読めば内容が把握できる）とそれに続く設問をしっかり読んでポイントを

つかむ。どんな問題が出ても文脈を理解すれば、わからないことはない。従って、教授の講義の内容がよくわからなくてもパニックにならずに落ち着いて、他の学生たちの意見を参考にしてどういうことになっているのかを分析できるような力をつけておこう。それには、数多くの問題をこなして自己分析をする訓練をしておこう。つまり問題の傾向を自分で研究してみる必要もあるということだ。

【ライテイングで大切なこと】

1. 文章に一貫性を持たせるために「転換語」とよばれるつなぎことば（注）を効果的に使おう。

2. パラグラフ内での理論の展開は、まず、大きな概念を書いてそれを裏付ける根拠（具体例など）を書くという形を作る。

3. スペルミスなどを、極力避けるため書き終えたら、見直しをするようにしよう。

注：「転換語」の詳細は以下を参考のこと。

川手-ミヤジェイエフスカ　恩（2009）『新装版 海外の大学・大学院で授業を受ける技術』：アルク刊 (pp. 236-238)

【目標点に達するために】

　総合型問題では、history、geology、literature、physics、psychology など本書に掲載されたトピックを使い、言い換えをしながら要約する練習をする。また、新聞や雑誌などの短い記事を読み、それらを要約してコンピュータに打ち込む練習もしてみよう。また、要約をする時は、言い換え（同意語を使ったり、文の構成を変えたりする）をする練習も大切である。

　オンライン投稿文問題では、新聞や雑誌などの短い記事を読みそれに賛成か反対かを考え、論破できるくらいの理由も考える練習をしておくと役立つ。また、インターネットで ibt TOEFL academic discussion topics を検索し、さまざまな問題を読んで書く練習をし、10 分で全てをまとめられるような練習をしておくことが大切である。10 分というのは、読んで考えて書きあげる全体の時間である。従って普段から練習を繰り返し、答え方に慣れておくといい。

音声の内容と使い方

　本書の学習に使用する音声は、スマートフォンやパソコンに無料でダウンロードできます。

スマートフォンでダウンロードする場合

　学習用アプリ「booco」をインストールの上、ホーム画面下「さがす」の検索窓に本書の商品コード「7024020」を入力して検索し、音声をダウンロードしてください。

▶「英語学習アプリ booco」について
https://booco.page.link/4zHd

パソコンでダウンロードする場合

　下記のウェブサイトにアクセスの上、商品コード「7024020」で検索し、音声ファイル（MP3 形式。zip 圧縮済み）をダウンロードしてください。

▶アルク「ダウンロードセンター」
https://portal-dlc.alc.co.jp/

※アプリ「booco」および「ダウンロードセンター」のサービス内容は、予告なく変更する場合があります。
　あらかじめご了承ください。

★リスニング・セクションでは、すべての設問で音声を使います。各設問文が読み上げられた後で、「ピー」というビープ音が鳴るので、ここでポーズボタンを押し、音声を止めて問題を解いてください。1問につき 40 秒以下のペースで解くとよいでしょう。解答したらポーズを解除し、次の設問に進みます。

★スピーキング・セクションでは、すべての設問で音声を使います。途中、準備時間（Preparation time）と返答時間（Response time）の開始と終了のタイミングをビープ音でお知らせします。模範解答例は、各テストの最後に収録されています。

★ライティング・セクションでは、統合型問題（設問 1）で音声を使います。設問の冒頭で該当するトラックを再生してください。指示文（Read the following passage.）が流れた後、ビープ音があり、3 分間の無音状態が続きます。制限時間の 3 分が経過すると、再びビープ音が鳴ります。そのままリスニングを始めてください。リスニング後、設問が流れビープ音が鳴ったら音声を止めてライティングに取りかかりましょう。

Test

1

Reading Section

Listening Section

Speaking Section

Writing Section

解答・解説

Reading Section

Ulysses S. Grant

If it were not for the outbreak of the Civil War, Ulysses S. Grant would probably have lived out his life working as a clerk in his father's store. Tired of a military career that had sent him to live and work in a remote area of the western United States, Grant felt that it was in his best interest to leave the military and focus his energies elsewhere. In his case, he believed his best opportunities lay in the business world. Business, however, proved not as easy to conquer as he had hoped, and he failed at several **ventures**, eventually winding up with the only job he could get: that of clerk in his father's store.

But the Civil War encouraged Grant to reenter the military. It was **here** that his life turned around, for he displayed all the abilities of a great general. His military career reached its peak when he forced the Southern general, Robert E. Lee, to surrender in 1865, thus ending the Civil War.

With his new widespread fame, he was nominated for president and subsequently won the election. However, he had little understanding of politics and what was required of a president. Though often criticized as being ineffective as the 18th president, he had become president at a time that would have proved challenging for any man.

④→ The country had just finished the Civil War, still the bloodiest war in United States history, and was in a deplorable state. The South was in ruins and major reconstruction efforts were underway. The economy had been devastated. The many lives that had been lost or disrupted led to animosity among various sectors of the population. Freed black slaves had nowhere to go and no real way to make a living. And just when a strong government was needed, corruption within the government was becoming commonplace. It was, in fact, this last problem that was to cause Grant's reputation the greatest harm.

⑤→ At a time when any president would have needed the best advisers possible, Grant selected poorly and found himself the easy victim of those who were more **adept** at using corruption to benefit themselves. His vice president, Schuyler Colfax, and others in his administration were accused of taking bribes, his private secretary tried to conspire with whiskey distillers to defraud the government of taxes, and his secretary of war, William W. Belknap, was impeached. All of this reflected negatively on Grant's abilities as a leader.

⑥→ It was also during his presidency that Jay Gould and James Fisk tried to corner the gold market, which would have meant that they could have controlled the price of gold to their own advantage. (A) ■ Although Grant had been warned of the consequences of this affair, he was slow to react and nearly waited until it was too late. He did, however, eventually order the U.S. Treasury to release a large amount of its gold reserves onto the market which dramatically lowered its price but, at the same time, caused the collapse of the stock market. (B) ■ The resulting panic on September 24, 1869, known as **Black Friday**, financially destroyed thousands of investors. (C) ■ Later in his administration another market collapse, known as the Panic of 1873, took place and resulted in widespread unemployment and a similar loss in economic confidence. (D) ■ These financial disasters coupled with the problems of corruption and social unrest were beyond Grant's ability to deal with and few were sad to see his second term as president come to an end.

After leaving the presidency, Grant took a long trip around the world. He returned to the U.S. and tried to run for president again, possibly because he had no idea of what else to do, but failed to win support. Disappointed, he went to New York where he opened a firm on Wall Street. But in 1884, the company collapsed and Grant nearly became bankrupt. In order to get money for his family, he wrote his autobiography while fighting cancer. He died the following year.

1. Why did Grant first leave the military?

    (A) He wanted to become a businessman.
    (B) He wanted to work for his father.
    (C) He saw no future in the military.
    (D) He wanted to fight in the Civil War.

2. The word **ventures** in the passage is closest in meaning to

    (A) battles
    (B) attempts
    (C) possibilities
    (D) companies

3. According to paragraph 4, what problem lowered the people's opinion of Grant the most?

    (A) His failure to solve economic problems.
    (B) Corruption within his administration.
    (C) The problem of recently freed black slaves.
    (D) His lack of strong leadership.

Paragraph 4 is marked with an arrow [→].

4. According to paragraph 4, why was there animosity among different sectors of the population?

    (A) Because freed black slaves had nowhere to go and couldn't find jobs.
    (B) Because there were economic problems.
    (C) Because people's lives had been dramatically changed by the war.
    (D) Because people were tired of corruption.

Paragraph 4 is marked with an arrow [→].

5. In paragraph 5, why does the author mention Grant's vice president and personal secretary?

(A) To describe what bad advisers did to Grant.
(B) To give examples of corruption that affected Grant's presidency.
(C) To contrast the different types of people who worked for Grant.
(D) To imply that Grant was corrupt.

Paragraph 5 is marked with an arrow [→].

6. What can be inferred from paragraph 5 about Grant?

(A) He was naive.
(B) He was honest.
(C) He was dishonest.
(D) He was not very intelligent.

Paragraph 5 is marked with an arrow [→].

7. Why does the author mention **Black Friday**?

(A) To show the results of Grant's economic policies.
(B) To give an example of the influence of corruption.
(C) To compare it to the Panic of 1873.
(D) To suggest that the stock market was being controlled by the U.S. Treasury.

8. According to paragraph 6, why were few people sad to see Grant's presidency come to an end?

(A) Because many people felt sorry for Grant.

(B) They were tired of bad economic conditions.

(C) There were few positive developments during Grant's administration.

(D) He was too slow to react to the attempt to corner the gold market.

Paragraph 6 is marked with an arrow [→].

9. Look at the four squares [■] that indicate where the following sentence could be added to the passage.

Unfortunately, this was not the last economic downturn to affect his presidency.

Where would this sentence best fit?

10. *Directions:* An introductory sentence for a brief summary of the passage is provided below. Complete the summary by selecting the THREE answer choices that express the most important ideas in the passage. Some sentences do not belong in the summary because they express ideas that are not presented in the passage or are minor ideas in the passage. **This question is worth 2 points.**

Although Ulysses S. Grant was a brilliant general, he failed to bring his military success to his presidency.

- _____
- _____
- _____

Answer Choices

(A) Grant tried and failed to be a successful businessman after his years in the military.

(B) One such example of corruption influenced the stock market causing it to collapse and further undermined Grant's standing with the voters.

(C) Grant's autobiography sold well but since this occurred after his death he was not able to benefit from it.

(D) The large number of serious problems that existed after the Civil War would have made it difficult for any man to have a successful presidency at this time in U.S. history.

(E) However, it was corruption, especially within his own administration, that most ruined Grant's reputation.

(F) Grant tried to run for the presidency for a third time but failed and was forced to try his hand at business again.

Marketing

In its simplest form, marketing is the bringing of a product or service to the attention of potential customers. This is especially true in the case where a company or individual has a new product, service or idea that people have never seen before. However, most situations are not of this type. In fact, most new businesses are simply copies of other, preexisting businesses selling products or services that customers have had long associations with. In such cases, marketing presents a whole different problem.

The problem, in its most basic form, is that customers have already formed an opinion about the product or service being offered. Once an impression already exists in customers' mind, it is very difficult to change it. Once they have worked with or used a product from a previous company, it is only dissatisfaction with that product or company that would make them ever consider changing. The question such customers have when presented with a new option is why they should choose this new company over some previous company. If the customer already knows and has good associations with the No. 1 company for a particular product, what would **induce** them to choose another company?

③→ The **market share strategy** is the more traditional of the approaches to **luring away** customers from the number one competitor in a field. The idea behind it is simple. The company needs to capture a certain number of interested people in order to make a profit. The basic tool of this strategy is advertising. **Current thinking says that if you outspend your competitors in advertising, you can get your market share, even if your product or service has no appreciable differences from others.** It basically captures the market by a sort of brute force.

④→ This strategy may work well enough for large companies with plenty of capital to spend on advertising, but what can small companies do when they are trying to sell the same product as a big, rich company? They clearly do not have the money to out-advertise them, so what is the alternative? In such a situation, it would prove hopeless to challenge the leader directly and, in truth, it might prove better not to challenge the leader at all. One marketing theory suggests that it is better for a small company to admit that it is not as powerful as "X" company but that they can do something more for the customer. In this way, they can use the associations with the more powerful company that are already in the customers' minds. These associations may have taken the more powerful company many years and much money to build but now these same associations can be used by the new company to their own advantage.

⑤→　　Here is where the idea of the **market niche** is most effective. In this strategy you try to find a quality that your product has but your competitor's does not. But it is more than that. Customers seem always to remember which company was first with an idea. So strong is this association that some marketing experts believe that to be first is the most important **attribute** a product can have. (A) ■ However, if a small company cannot be first with the product itself, it could still be first in some other area related to the product. This could be a lower price, better quality, better service or any number of other factors. In this way the smaller company can use the No. 1 company to position its product in the market while offering a certain feature that customers may be looking for. (B) ■ If they have not been looking for this feature, it is the role of advertising to convince them that they should have been looking for it. (C) ■ In short, you must convince customers that this quality is essential for them to enjoy complete satisfaction with a product. If your **market research** has been done effectively, you should be able to survive in this niche you are creating. (D) ■

11. Based on the information in paragraph 3, which of the following best explains **market share strategy**?

    (A) If a company spends enough on advertising, they will get customers and make a profit.

    (B) If you use simple ideas, you will attract customers.

    (C) If your product is different from that of the competitors, you will attract customers.

    (D) If your advertising is strong enough, it will force customers to try your product.

Paragraph 3 is marked with an arrow [→].

12. Which of the sentences below best expresses the essential information in the highlighted sentence in the passage? *Incorrect choices change the meaning in important ways or leave out essential information.*

Current thinking says that if you outspend your competitors in advertising you can get your market share, even if your product or service has no appreciable differences from others.

    (A) Spending more money on advertising than your competitors will always lead to a product's success.

    (B) If your product is different from your competitors, you do not need to spend money on advertising.

    (C) Spending a lot of money on advertising can lead to success if your product is similar to a competitor's.

    (D) The more different your product is from your competitors', the less you need to spend on advertising.

13. According to information in paragraphs 3 and 4, what can small companies try to do to capture market share from larger, wealthier companies?

(A) They can try to advertise more than the larger companies.
(B) They should do nothing because in this situation, it is hopeless to try to compete with larger companies.
(C) They can try to find a unique difference in their product and advertise it.
(D) They can try to mention their competitors as much as possible when they advertise.

Paragraph 3 and paragraph 4 are marked with arrows [→].

14. According to paragraph 5, which of the following is true about **market niche** strategy?

(A) You can best use this strategy when you are the first one to present a new product.
(B) You can use this strategy when you want to advertise how similar your product is to the product of the No. 1 competitor.
(C) This strategy is best used by companies that do not have enough money to advertise.
(D) This strategy is good for companies whose product differs in some way from the No. 1 competitor.

Paragraph 5 is marked with an arrow [→].

15. In paragraph 5, the author states that effective **marketing**

(A) can help you be first with a new product.
(B) can help you find what a competitor's customers are looking for.
(C) can convince customers that they need certain features in a product.
(D) can remind customers that you were the first with a particular product.

Paragraph 5 is marked with an arrow [→].

16. In paragraph 5, what can be inferred about customers?

   (A) They are easily manipulated by advertising.

   (B) Customers are mostly attracted to smaller companies with new ideas.

   (C) They always remember the company that was first with an idea and nothing can really be done to change this association.

   (D) If you are the first company with a new idea, you will likely attract customers for a long time.

Paragraph 5 is marked with an arrow [→].

17. In paragraph 5, why does the author mention **market research**?

   (A) To show how important it is in determining what type of advertising to use.

   (B) To show that it is an important tool for understanding customers' needs.

   (C) To show how important it is in understanding your competition.

   (D) To show how important it is in understanding how to survive in your market niche.

Paragraph 5 is marked with an arrow [→].

18. Which of the following most accurately reflects the author's opinion about market niche strategy?

   (A) It is a useful strategy for small companies with new products.

   (B) It is not a useful strategy for large companies which had the first example of a product on the market.

   (C) It is a useful strategy for a company that can outspend its competitor on advertising.

   (D) It is a useful strategy for those companies willing to do market research.

19. Look at the four squares [■] that indicate where the following sentence could be added to the passage.

In this way, advertising is a sort of customer education, giving them information on particular features of a product that they may never have considered before.

Where would this sentence best fit?

20. *Directions:* An introductory sentence for a brief summary of the passage is provided below. Complete the summary by selecting the THREE answer choices that express the most important ideas in the passage. Some sentences do not belong in the summary because they express ideas that are not presented in the passage or are minor ideas in the passage. **This question is worth 2 points.**

Market share strategy and market niche strategy are two methods a company can use to market a product.

- _____
- _____
- _____

Answer Choices

(A) Large companies do not have to worry about customers because customers already know their product.

(B) Market niche strategy is the most effective strategy for companies with new products.

(C) A small company can use market niche strategy to advertise differences between its product and a similar product of the major competitor.

(D) A large company with large amounts of capital can simply outspend its competition in advertising to capture its necessary market share whether its product is similar to a competitor's or not.

(E) The strategy used is dependent on the size of the company and the similarities between its product and a competitor's product.

(F) Small companies should always mention their competitors when they advertise to get a market share.

Listening Section

Questions 1-5

mp3
01

1. Why is the man talking to the woman?

(A) He wants her to give him a job.

(B) He wants information about finding a job.

(C) He is having problems with too much homework.

(D) He is worried because he has no money left.

2. What is the work-study program?

(A) A program that allows foreign students to work in the U.S.

(B) A program that allows students to work part time in fast-food restaurants

(C) A program that allows any student to work on campus

(D) A program that gives students free meals for working on campus

3. What can be an additional benefit of the work-study program?

    (A) Foreign students may be able to meet more Americans.
    (B) A student may be able to work in the library.
    (C) The pay is great.
    (D) A student can work more than 12 hours a week.

4. Listen again to part of the conversation. Then answer the question. 🎧

Why does the woman say this? 🎧

    (A) She's really saying it's OK to work off campus for more than 12 hours a week.
    (B) She's making him aware that she knows how many foreign students break the law.
    (C) She's warning him about the possible consequences of working more than 12 hours a week.
    (D) She's really telling him not to risk working off campus.

5. Listen again to part of the conversation. Then answer the question. 🎧

What is the woman implying by this question? 🎧

    (A) She thinks he is lying about not having enough money.
    (B) She doubts that he really needs any extra money.
    (C) She's confused about what he has been saying.
    (D) She thinks he may be just panicking and really may have enough money.

Biology

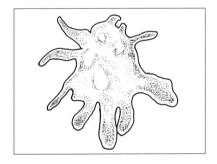

6. What is the main topic of this lecture?

    (A) The similarities between plants and animals
    (B) The difficulty of distinguishing plants from animals
    (C) The Kingdom Protista
    (D) Technology and biological classification

7. Listen again to part of the lecture. Then answer the question. 🎧

Why does the professor say this? 🎧

    (A) She wants to show the students how little they really know.
    (B) She feels bad that she must explain something difficult to them.
    (C) She is going to show how difficult biological classification can be.
    (D) She is disappointed that the students don't understand much about biological classification.

8. Why was the amoeba once classified as an animal?

Choose 2 answers.

    (A) It could move.
    (B) It contained chlorophyll.
    (C) It had a brain and could breathe.
    (D) It captured food.

9. Listen again to part of the lecture. Then answer the question. 🎧

What does the professor imply when she says this? 🎧

(A) She expects some students to answer this question.
(B) She wants to show how confused she is herself.
(C) She doesn't want an answer and only uses this question to show how difficult the problem is.
(D) She doesn't expect an answer but expects the students to ask her some questions.

10. What made some unicellular organisms difficult to classify?

(A) They had no nucleus.
(B) They moved but used photosynthesis.
(C) They could not be easily seen under a microscope.
(D) They could not reproduce by dividing into two parts.

11. The professor describes the history of classifying the amoeba. Summarize this history by putting the events in order.

• Kingdom Protista was created.
• Amoebas were classified as animal.
• Unicellular organisms could no longer classified as animals.
• Unicellular organisms were classified according to type of nucleus they possessed.

1.	
2.	
3.	
4.	

12. Why does the man go to visit the professor?

(A) He wants to apologize.

(B) He wants to get a better grade.

(C) He does not understand why he received a low grade on his paper.

(D) He wants help writing his paper.

13. What did the man do that was wrong?

(A) He received a failing grade on his paper.

(B) He went to an American university.

(C) He forgot the professors' office hours.

(D) He copied reference material into his paper.

14. Why did the man plagiarize reference material?

(A) He didn't know it was wrong.
(B) He was busy.
(C) He did not know the professor's office hours and couldn't get help.
(D) He forgot to write references.

15. Listen again to part of the conversation. Then answer the question. 🎧

Why does the professor say this? 🎧

(A) The professor is sure the student knew he did something wrong.
(B) The professor is checking to see if the student understood that what he did was wrong.
(C) The professor is giving the student advice about copying, so he will not do it in the future.
(D) The professor is surprised that the student did something wrong.

16. Listen again to part of the conversation. Then answer the question. 🎧

What is the professor implying when she says this? 🎧

(A) She is complimenting the student on being very good at writing.
(B) She's surprised that his grammar changes so much from one paragraph to another.
(C) She is telling the student that she knows he copied from reference material.
(D) She is confused at why the student's grammar and vocabulary are sometimes good and at other times bad.

Sociology
(Chinese immigrants)

17. What is the talk mainly about?

(A) Chinese immigration
(B) Discrimination against immigrants in the U.S.
(C) Laws against immigration
(D) The importance of immigrant education

18. In the discussion, the professor gives reasons why Chinese immigrants had problems integrating into U.S. society. Indicate whether each of the following is or is not one of these reasons.

	True	*False*
They were non-European.		
New immigrants lived in their own communities.		
They were prevented from receiving education.		
They were not allowed to become citizens.		
They took jobs that Americans wanted.		

19. What were three features of the Chinese Exclusion Act?

Choose 3 answers.

(A) It prevented all Chinese from immigrating to the U.S.
(B) It prevented Chinese from becoming U.S. citizens.
(C) It forced Chinese to have their own schools.
(D) It prevented the Chinese from owning land.
(E) It restricted the Chinese to their own communities.

20. According to the professor, what is the importance of education for immigrant children?

    (A) It lets them learn about the U.S.
    (B) It helps them gain citizenship.
    (C) It breaks up the immigrant communities.
    (D) It helps them become Americanized.

21. What does the professor say about immigrant communities?

    (A) They prevented Americanization.
    (B) They were natural for all immigrants.
    (C) They always disappeared after a couple of generations.
    (D) They are an important part of American culture.

22. Listen again to part of the lecture. Then answer the question. ∩

Why does the professor say this? ∩

    (A) He wants to politely disagree with the student.
    (B) He plans to define "Americanized."
    (C) He really doesn't know how to describe "Americanized."
    (D) He wants to emphasize what was just mentioned.

Questions 23-28

mp3
05

Astronomy
(The formation of
the Moon)

23. What is this discussion mainly about?

(A) The mysteries of the solar system

(B) The moon

(C) The formation of the moon

(D) The lack of hydrogen on the moon

24. The professor describes the possibility of the moon forming after a large body struck the Earth. Summarize the idea by putting the events in order.

• Hydrogen is driven away
• Light material circling the Earth forms a new object
• Earth's crust forms
• A collision occurs

1.	
2.	
3.	
4.	

25. What are two mysteries of the moon's formation mentioned in the discussion?

Choose 2 answers.

(A) Why it has no hydrogen

(B) How it was formed

(C) How material circling the sun came together to form the moon

(D) How the collision of the Earth with a large planet formed the moon

26. According to the discussion, what are some theories about the formation of the moon?

Choose 3 answers.

(A) It was formed from meteors.

(B) It was formed from a collision.

(C) It was formed with the Earth.

(D) It was formed from rocks with no hydrogen.

(E) It was formed near the sun.

27. Listen again to part of the lecture. Then answer the question. ♫

What does the professor mean when she says this? ♫

(A) She does not accept this theory.

(B) She thinks it possibly explains the formation of the moon but not very well.

(C) She thinks that of the two theories she's mentioned, this is the weakest.

(D) She thinks that no theory can explain the formation of the moon.

28. Listen again to part of the lecture. Then answer the question. ♫

What can be inferred about the professor from this interaction? ♫

(A) The professor's plan was to talk about the formation of the moon.

(B) The professor just thought of a good example.

(C) The professor is upset that the student interrupted her.

(D) The professor is happy that the student asked this question.

Speaking Section

1. Independent Speaking [Paired Choice]

Listen to the following question.

Some people like to live in places that have the same weather all year round while others prefer a place where the weather changes several times a year. Which do you prefer? Give examples to support your opinion.

Prepare your response after the beep. | Preparation time 15 seconds |

Start your response after the beep. | Response time 45 seconds |

2. Integrated Reading / Listening / Speaking Situational
—— Portion of a Notice Posted on a Bulletin Board

Standards of Conduct

No matter what the reason, any student conduct that is academically dishonest or shows a lack of academic integrity or trustworthiness, or unfairly attempts to use the intellectual rights of others is prohibited. Such conduct includes:

Now, read the passage about Standards of Conduct. You have 45 seconds to read the passage. Begin reading, now.

Reading (45 seconds):

A. Cheating on Exams and Other Assignments

Cheating is the unauthorized use or attempted use of materials, information, study aids or collaboration in order to pass an examination or other academic exercise. It is the responsibility of the student to consult with the professor if in doubt about what may constitute unethical behavior. It is very important to emphasize that if there is any doubt in a student's mind about what constitutes proper or improper conduct, the student must be certain to clarify this with the professor prior to taking any exam. Cheating or assisting another student in cheating in connection with an examination or assignment is academically unacceptable. Punishment for such offenses is generally at the discretion of the professor and may include automatic failure of the examination or expulsion from the course.

Listening:

Now listen to a conversation between two students.

mp3
08

Question:

The man gives information about Peter's behavior during the exam. Does the man think that the professor's actions were justified? Why does he think Peter did this?

Prepare your response after the beep. | Preparation time 30 seconds |

Start your response after the beep. | Response time 60 seconds |

3. Integrated Reading / Listening / Speaking Academic

—— History (Levittown)

mp3 **09**

Now, read the passage about Levittown. You have 45 seconds to read the passage. Begin reading now.

Reading (45 seconds):

Levittown was the first successful suburban housing development in the United States. It was successful because it enabled ordinary, working class people to own homes in the suburbs.

After the Second World War, many young people wanted to start a new life. Most were tired of living in small apartments in crowded cities. They wanted a better quality of life in which to raise their new families. At that time, however, few young families could afford the limited number of such housing available. William Levitt understood the problem and developed a plan to build affordable housing for these people. By 1951, he had built over 15,000 houses using an assembly-line style of production to keep the prices down.

Listening:

Now listen to part of a lecture on this topic in a history class.

mp3 **10**

Question:

Explain how the social conditions of the time encouraged the development of Levittown. Discuss how Levitt managed to meet the needs of his customers.

Prepare your response after the beep. | Preparation time 30 seconds |

Start your response after the beep. | Response time 60 seconds |

4. Integrated Listening / Speaking [Summary] —
Psychology (Intelligence)

Now listen to part of a lecture in a psychology class.

Question:

Using points and examples from the talk, discuss the problems of measuring intelligence and possible limitations of the IQ test.

Prepare your response after the beep. | Preparation time 20 seconds |

Start your response after the beep. | Response time 60 seconds |

Writing Section

1. Integrated Writing — Biology Lecture (Symbiosis)

Directions:

For this integrated task, you have 3 minutes to read the passage. Then you will listen to part of a lecture on the topic you have just read about. Following the lecture, you have 20 minutes to plan and write your response. An ideal response will be 150 to 225 words.

Read the following passage.

Reading:

Symbiosis in biology can, in general terms, be described as the interdependence of two different species, whether they be plants and plants, animals and plants, or animals and animals. It should be noted that few symbiotic relationships are equally beneficial to both species, as often one of the members in the relationship receives greater benefits from the other. A detrimental relationship, in which one member is actually injured by the other, is more commonly known as parasitism. Thus, symbiosis can encompass any point on the spectrum from parasitism to perfectly equal sharing.

The equal sharing end of the spectrum can be best exemplified by lichens and their relationships with algae. In fact, lichens are composite organisms consisting of a fungus and an alga. The fungus generally forms the base and roots, or hyphae, while the alga grows upon it. In most lichens, the fungus supplies a base upon which the alga can grow. It is thought by most scientists that the fungus supplies necessary growing conditions such as moisture, the absence of which would prevent the alga from growing on its own. In its turn, the alga supplies carbohydrates which can be used as food by the fungus. Such well balanced examples of symbiosis are often referred to as mutualism.

Another type of symbiosis, called commensalism, is often found among marine invertebrates. Certain species of simple animals such as polyps may grow on the shells of other animals such as crabs, thus providing them with protection and camouflage. On the other hand, the colonizing animal receives more food when the animal which they colonized feeds. The first animal, in this case, the polyp, would be considered a parasite if it eventually harmed the colonized animal, but this is not usually the case. In fact, some hermit crabs actually seek out sea anemones which they then place on their bodies.

Listening:

Now, listen to part of a lecture on symbiosis, which you have just read about. You may take notes while listening to the lecture.

Now, get ready to answer the question. You may use your notes to help you answer.

Question:

Explain the variations of symbiosis from mutualism to parasitism. How does the ant use symbiosis to improve its life? Discuss how the professor's view of mutualism differs from that of the reading.

2. Writing for an Academic Discussion

Your professor is teaching a class on small business management. Write a response to the professor's question.

Please contribute your own ideas to this discussion, and support them with some details.

Your response should be at least 100 words in length.

Doctor Thompson

This week we will be discussing the qualities necessary for people contemplating starting their own small businesses. Of course, there are practical concerns such as the amount of capital available for investment and the importance of a good location, but many entrepreneurs simply don't realize that they have to have a personality that is suitable for such a challenge. A good businessperson needs to be well-organized, knowledgeable, and budget-conscious. However, they must also be passionate, personable, and persistent. I would like to know what qualities you think are necessary to become a successful small business owner and explain why you think so.

Anna

In my country, it would be important for a person opening a small business to have patience. This is because there are a lot of problems they will face when working with the government. There are many regulations on businesses and if a person doesn't have patience, they will probably give up the idea of opening a business before they even get started.

Peter

I think Anna makes a good point. A person who wants to start a business should not be frustrated too easily because they are certain to find many obstacles to overcome. For this reason, I think that someone who wants to start a business must be persistent and passionate about their ideas. Being passionate will make you goal-oriented. It will stop you from giving up on your plans so easily.

解答・解説

Reading Section

Listening Section

Speaking Section

Writing Section

Reading

1 C		**2** B		**3** B		**4** C		**5** B		**6** A	
7 B		**8** C		**9** C		**10** D, E, B		**11** A		**12** C	
13 D		**14** D		**15** B		**16** D		**17** B		**18** B	
19 C		**20** E, D, C									

Listening

1 B	**2** C	**3** A	**4** C	**5** D	**6** B
7 C	**8** A, D	**9** C	**10** B		

11 1. Amoeba classified as animal.

2. Kingdom Protista was created.

3. Unicellular organisms could not be animals.

4. Unicellular organisms classified according to type of nucleus they possessed.

12 C	**13** D	**14** B	**15** A	**16** C	**17** A

18 They were non-European. (True)

New immigrants lived in their own communities. (False)

They were prevented from receiving education. (False)

They were not allowed to become citizens. (True)

They took jobs that Americans wanted. (False)

19 B, C, D	**20** D	**21** B	**22** D	**23** C

24 1. Earth's crust forms

2. A collision occurs

3. Hydrogen driven away

4. Light material circling the earth forms new object

25 A, B	**26** B, C, E	**27** B	**28** A

Reading Section　解答・解説

Questions 1-10

ユリシーズ・S・グラント

　もし南北戦争が起こっていなかったら、ユリシーズ・S・グラントはたぶん彼の父の店で店員として人生を送っていただろう。合衆国西部の人里離れた地域に住みつき、仕事をしていた軍隊生活にうんざりし、グラントは軍隊を離れてどこかほかの場所で彼のエネルギーを使うことが自分にとって最善であると感じていた。彼の場合、絶好のチャンスはビジネスの世界にあると思った。しかし、ビジネスは彼が望んだように簡単に征服できるものではなく、彼はいくつかのビジネスの試みに失敗した。そして、ついには彼の父の店での店員という、彼が唯一得られた仕事をする羽目になった。

　しかし、南北戦争が勃発しグラントは再び軍隊に入隊することになった。この南北戦争が彼の人生を転換し、彼は偉大な将軍としてのあらゆる能力をあらわし始めた。彼が南軍のロバート・E・リー将軍を1865年に降伏させ、南北戦争が終結したとき、彼の軍人としてのキャリアは最高点に達した。

　新たに得た全国的な名声のおかげで、彼は大統領候補者として推薦され、その後その選挙で勝利を収めた。しかし、彼は政治問題やまた大統領として何が求められているかについてほとんど理解していなかった。18代大統領として無能であるとしばしば批判されたが、彼は誰にとっても困難だったと思われる時代に大統領となったのだ。

　合衆国の歴史でいまだに最も血なまぐさい戦争である（と考えられている）南北戦争がちょうど終わったときで、国はひどい状態にあった。南部は崩壊しており、主要な復興への取り組みは進行中であった。経済は荒廃していた。多くの人々の生活の喪失や崩壊は、さまざまな地域の異なるグループの住民たちの間での対立をもたらした。解放された黒人奴隷たちは行く所がなく、生活するための実質的な手段を持ち合わせていなかった。そして、強い政府が必要とされたちょうどそのとき、政府内での汚職が当たり前のことになりつつあった。実は、この汚職に関する問題が、グラントの評判を最もひどく傷つけることになったのである。

　大統領が最高のアドバイザーを必要とするであろうときに、グラントはお粗末にも汚職を自分自身の利益のために利用するのにたけているような人たちを選び、彼自身が彼らの格好の餌食になってしまったわけだ。副大統領、スカイラー・コルファクスとほかの内閣閣僚は収賄で起訴され、彼の私設秘書は政府から税金をだまし取るためウイスキー製造者と共謀しようとした。そして軍事長官ウイリアム・W・ベルクナップは弾劾された。これらすべてはグラントのリーダーとしての能力に暗い影を落とした。

　ジェイ・グールドとジェームズ・フィスクが、彼らの有利になるように金の価格を操作するために、金を買い占めようとしたのも彼の大統領任期中であった。グラントにもこの出来事の成り行きが通知されていたが、彼はそれに対処するのが遅く、ほとんど手遅れにな

で待っていた。彼は最終的には合衆国財務省に、政府の保有金の大部分を金の市場に放出することを命じ、金の価格が劇的に下げられたが、これは同時に株式市場の崩壊を引き起こしてしまった。これに起因すると考えられる、ブラック・フライデーとして知られている 1869年 9月 24日に起こった恐慌は、何千もの投資家を財政的破滅へと追いやった。不運にも、これが彼の大統領としての立場に影響を及ぼす最後の景気低迷ではなかった。彼の在任中に、後に 1873年の恐慌として知られるようになるもうひとつの市場崩壊が引き起こされ、結果として全国的な失業が起こったのと同時に経済的信頼も失われた。これらの財政上の惨事と汚職問題、そして社会不安は、グラントの能力を超えたものであり、彼の大統領としての 2期目が終わることを悲しむ人はほとんどいなかった。

　大統領としての任期を終了した後、グラントは世界中を回る長い旅へと出掛けた。彼は合衆国に戻り、おそらくほかには何をしたらよいのかわからなかったため、再び大統領選挙に出馬しようとしたが、支援を勝ち得るには至らなかった。失望した彼はニューヨークへ行きウォールストリートで会社を始めた。しかし 1884年に、その会社は倒産し、グラントはほとんど破産状態になった。彼はがんと戦いながら家族のためにお金を稼ごうとして自叙伝を書いた。そしてその翌年に亡くなった。

重要語句

- [ ] accuse（動詞）告発する、起訴する
- [ ] adept（形容詞）熟練した、熟達した
  ※ be adept at ... ～が上手だ、～の名人だ
- [ ] administration（名詞）政府、内閣
- [ ] affair（名詞）出来事、情勢
- [ ] animosity（名詞）悪意、敵意、恨み
- [ ] benefit（動詞）利益を与える
- [ ] bribe（名詞）わいろ
- [ ] challenging（形容詞）骨の折れる、簡単にいかない、興味をかき立てる
- [ ] Civil War（アメリカの）南北戦争
- [ ] clerk（名詞）店員、事務員
- [ ] collapse（名詞）崩壊、倒壊
- [ ] commonplace（形容詞）普通の、ありふれた、当たり前の
- [ ] confidence（名詞）信用、信頼
- [ ] conquer（動詞）打ち勝つ、征服する、獲得する、克服する
- [ ] consequence（名詞）結果、成り行き、重要性
- [ ] conspire（動詞）共謀する、陰謀を企てる
- [ ] corner（動詞）買い占める
- [ ] corruption（名詞）汚職、堕落、腐敗
- [ ] couple（動詞）結びつけて考える、結び合わせる
- [ ] defraud（動詞）だまし取る
- [ ] deplorable（形容詞）悲しむべき、ひどい
- [ ] devastate（動詞）荒らす、荒廃させる
- [ ] disaster（名詞）災難、惨事
- [ ] disrupt（動詞）混乱させる、崩壊させる、分離する、引き裂く
- [ ] distiller（名詞）蒸留酒製造者
- [ ] elsewhere（副詞）どこかよそで、ほかの所で
- [ ] encourage（動詞）勇気づける、自信（希望）を与える、その気にさせる、励ます

- [ ] fame（名詞）名声、評判
- [ ] financially（副詞）財政的に、財政上
- [ ] freed 動詞 free（解放する、自由にする）の過去・過去分詞
- [ ] general（名詞）将軍
- [ ] harm（名詞）害、損害、危害
- [ ] impeach（動詞）告発する、弾劾する
- [ ] ineffective（形容詞）役に立たない、無能な、効果のない
- [ ] nominate（動詞）候補者として推薦する、任命する
- [ ] outbreak（名詞）突発、突然の出現
- [ ] panic（名詞）恐慌、パニック
- [ ] politics（名詞）政治学、政治、政治問題
- [ ] presidency（名詞）大統領の任期（職務・地位）
- [ ] prove（動詞）判明する、証明する、示す
- [ ] reconstruction（名詞）再建、復興
- [ ] remote（形容詞）遠い、遠隔の、人里離れた
- [ ] ruin（名詞）破壊、倒壊、崩壊
- [ ] similar（形容詞）類似の
- [ ] subsequently（副詞）その後に、その次に
- [ ] surrender（動詞）降伏する、引き渡す
- [ ] tired（形容詞）飽きた、うんざりした、疲れた
- [ ] Treasury（名詞）財務省
- [ ] underway（形容詞）進行中で
- [ ] unemployment（名詞）失業
- [ ] unrest（名詞）不安、心配
- [ ] venture（名詞）投機的事業、ベンチャービジネス
- [ ] victim（名詞）犠牲者
- [ ] warn（動詞）警告する
- [ ] widespread（形容詞）広げた、広範囲に及ぶ
- [ ] wind up（～という）羽目になる、終わりになる

1. 解答 (C)

グラントはなぜ最初に除隊したのか。

(A) 実業家になりたかった。

(B) 父の下で働きたかった。

(C) 軍隊に将来性を感じていなかった。

(D) 南北戦争で戦いたかった。

解説 第 1 パラグラフの Tired of a military career that had sent him to live and work in a remote area of the western United States, ... から、グラントは軍隊生活にうんざりしていたことがわかる。そこで、事実を基に理由を考えてみると、(C) の He saw no future in the military. が最適である。(A) の「ビジネスマンになりたかった」は辞めた理由ではなく、辞めてから何をしようかと考えたときに思いついたことである。

2. 解答 (B)

本文にある ventures に最も近い語は

(A) 戦闘

(B) 試み

(C) 可能性

(D) 企業

解説 ventures が含まれる文から、「ビジネスにおいて何かを試みた結果、失敗した」ことがわかる。(B) の attempts が適切な選択肢である。

3. 解答 (B)

第 4 パラグラフによると、グラントの評価を最も下げた問題は何か。

(A) 経済問題を解決できなかったこと。

(B) 政府内での汚職。

(C) 解放されたばかりの黒人奴隷の問題。

(D) 彼の強いリーダーシップの欠如。

解説 第 4 パラグラフの最後に this last problem that was to cause Grant's reputation the greatest harm. とあり、この this last problem とは、その前に出てくる corruption within the government である。従って正解は、(B) の Corruption within his administration. となる。

4. 解答 (C)

第 4 パラグラフによると、さまざまな地域の異なるグループ間に敵対意識があったのはなぜか。

(A) 解放された奴隷には行き場がなく、仕事も見つからなかったから。

(B) 経済的な問題があったから。

(C) 戦争によって生活が劇的に変えられてしまったから。

(D) 人々が汚職にうんざりしていたから。

解説 第 4 パラグラフの半ばに、The many lives that had been <u>lost or disrupted</u> led to animosity among various sectors of the population. とあり、many lives は lost or disrupted と言っている。つまり、(C) の people's lives had been <u>dramatically changed</u> by the war（戦争により生活が劇的に変えられてしまった）という事実が、animosity（恨むという感情）を生み出したわけである。

5. 解答 (B)

第 5 パラグラフで著者はなぜグラントの副大統領と秘書について言及したのか。

(A) グラントに対して良からぬ助言をしたことを説明するために。

(B) グラントの大統領職に影響を与えた汚職の例を挙げるために。

(C) グラントの下で働いていたさまざまな種類の人々を対比するために。

(D) グラントが腐敗していたことを暗に伝えるために。

解説 第 5 パラグラフの冒頭にある Grant selected poorly and found himself the easy victim of those who were more adept at using corruption to benefit themselves. の後に、これをサポートする具体例が続いている。従って正解は (B) となる。英語の文章に見られる典型的な展開（general から specific へ）である。

6. 解答 (A)

第5パラグラフから、グラントについてどんなことが推測できるか。

(A) 彼は世間知らずだった。

(B) 彼は正直だった。

(C) 彼は不正直だった。

(D) 彼はそれほど知的ではなかった。

解説 まず、第5パラグラフの冒頭、... and found himself the easy victim of those who were more adept at using corruption to benefit themselves. から、グラントが自己利益のために汚職を利用するような人たちの犠牲になってしまったことがわかる。その理由として真っ先に考えられるのは、グラントが大統領として知らなくてはならないすべを知らなかったということである。つまり彼は naive（世間知らず）なのだ。選択肢の (B) と (C) はまったく関係がないことに最初に気づきたい。

7. 解答 (B)

なぜ著者はブラックフライデーに言及したのか。

(A) グラントの経済政策の成果を示すために。

(B) 汚職の影響の例を挙げるために。

(C) 1873 年の恐慌と比べるために。

(D) 米国財務省によって株式市場が操作されていたことを示唆するために。

解説 第6パラグラフの冒頭、Jay Gould and James Fisk tried to corner the gold market, which would have meant that they could have controlled the price of gold to their own advantage. をサポートする具体例として Black Friday の記述がある。従って正解は、(B) の To give an example of the influence of corruption. である。

8. 解答 (C)

第 6 パラグラフによると、グラントの大統領の任期終了に悲しむ人がほとんどいなかったのはなぜか。

(A) 多くの人がグラントを気の毒に思ったから。

(B) 経済状況が良くないことにうんざりしていた。

(C) グラント政権の期間中、好ましい進展がほとんどなかった。

(D) 金の市場を独占しようとする動きへの彼の対応が遅すぎた。

解説　消去法で考えてみる。「悲しむ人はほとんどいなかった」のだから、(A) は正解ではない。また、人々は特定の出来事だけを考えているわけではないので (D) も違う。話の流れから、人々は数多くの問題を解決しようとする前向きな姿勢を望んでいたのに、それがほとんど見られなかったため大統領に失望したといえる。

9. 解答 (C)

次のセンテンスの挿入箇所の候補として本文中に示された 4 つの■を見なさい。

あいにく、これが彼の大統領としての立場に影響を及ぼす最後の景気低迷ではなかった。

このセンテンスを挿入するのに最もふさわしい場所はどこか。

解説　挿入文を見ると、... this was not the last economic downturn ... とあり、Black Friday が最後の economic downturn ではなかったと言っているので、この文の後にも economic downturn に関する記述が続くことがわかる。従って、もうひとつの市場崩壊の the Panic of 1873 について述べている (C) に挿入するのが適当である。

10. 解答 （下の英文を参照）

(D) The large number of serious problems that existed after the Civil War would have made it difficult for any man to have a successful presidency at this time in U.S. history.

(E) However, it was corruption, especially within his own administration, that most ruined Grant's reputation.

(B) One such example of corruption influenced the stock market causing it to collapse and further undermined Grant's standing with the voters.

指示文：以下に提示された導入文は本文の要約である。本文の中で最も重要な考えを選択肢から 3 つ選び、要約を完成させなさい。いくつかの選択肢は本文中で示されていないことを提示しているか、または重要ではない内容であるため、要約には不適切である。**この設問の配点は 2 点である。**

ユリシーズ・S・グラントは優秀な将軍であったが、軍隊での成功を大統領職にもたらすことには失敗した。

選択肢

(A) グラントは従軍した後、実業家としての成功をもくろんだが、失敗した。

(B) そうした汚職の一例が、株式市場に影響を与え、市場の暴落を引き起こし、有権者のグラントに対する評価をさらに低下させた。

(C) グラントの自叙伝はよく売れたが、そうなったのは彼の死後であったため、彼がこの恩恵を受けることはなかった。

(D) 南北戦争後に数多くの深刻な問題が生じたために、米国の歴史におけるこの時期には、誰であろうと大統領として成功するのは難しかったであろう。

(E) しかし、グラントの名声を最も傷つけたのは汚職であり、特に彼自身の政権の内部で起きたものだった。

(F) グラントは 3 度目の大統領選出馬を試みたが失敗し、再び事業に身を投じることを余儀なくされた。

解説 与えられた文に選択肢から 3 つの文を選んで話をつなげ、パッセージの要約を完成させる問題である。本問は、ただ文を並べるだけではなく、順番も考えるといいだろう。接続詞にも十分注意したい。冒頭に与えられた ..., he failed to bring his military success to his presidency. に、失敗に至った経緯が続くとうまくつながる。また、ここでも英語の文章に見られる典型的な展開（general から specific へ）が使われていることを強調しておく。

Questions 11-20

マーケティング

　マーケティングとはその最も簡潔な形態として、製品やサービスに潜在顧客の注意を向けさせることである。企業や個人が、人々が今までに見たことがない新しい製品やサービス、アイデアを持っている場合は、このことが特に当てはまる。しかし、ほとんどの場合はこのタイプに当てはまらない。実際、ほとんどの新しいビジネスは、顧客が長い間つき合いを持つ製品やサービスを販売する既存のビジネスの単なるまねである。このような場合、マーケティングにはまったく違った問題が発生する。

　その問題の最も基本的な形とは、顧客が提供される製品やサービスについてすでになんらかの意見を持っているということである。ある印象がいったん顧客の心の中にすでに存在してしまうと、それを変えるのは非常に難しい。いったん彼らがほかの会社の製品で仕事をしたり、それを使っているのであれば、彼らが別の会社の製品を使ってみようかと考えるのはその製品やその会社に不満がある場合だけである。新しい選択肢を示されたときに、そのような顧客が持つ疑問は、なぜ既存の会社の代わりにこの新しい会社を選ばなければならないかである。もし顧客がある製品のナンバーワン企業を知っており、よい関係を持っているとしたら、何が彼らに別の会社を選ばせるのだろう。

　マーケットシェア戦略は、ある分野のナンバーワン企業から顧客を誘い出す、より伝統的なアプローチ方法である。その裏にある考え方は単純である。企業は利益を出すために、一定数の興味を持つ人々を集める必要がある。この戦略の基本的なツールが広告である。最近の考え方では、もし広告に競争相手より多くのお金を使えば、たとえその製品やサービスがほかに比べてこれという違いがなかったとしても、マーケットシェア（市場での取り分）を得ることができる。広告は、ある種野蛮な力によって市場を獲得するわけだ。

　この戦略は広告宣伝を行うための、豊富な資本を持つ大企業にとっては十分効果的かもしれない。しかし、大きな資金力のある会社と同じ製品を売ろうとしている小さな会社はどうすればよいのか。大企業をしのぐだけの広告を打つ資本を明らかに持っていない彼らにとっての代案はなんなのか。このような状況では、先駆者に直接勝負を挑んでも見込みはないだろう。実際のところ、まったく勝負を挑まないほうがましだとも言えるだろう。あるマーケティング理論は、小さい会社は自らが X 会社ほど力を持っていないことを認めたうえで顧客のためにもっと何かできることがあると考えたほうがよいと提唱する。この方法であれば、小さな会社はより強力な企業が顧客の心との間に築き上げたつながりを利用することができる。このつながりは強力な企業が長い時間と多くの資金を費やして築き上げたものであるかもしれないが、この同じつながりを今度は新規企業が自らの利益のために使うことができるのである。

　ここでは特定市場（マーケット・ニッチ）という考え方が最も効果的になる。この戦略において各自は、自己の製品が持っていて、競争相手が持っていない特性を見つけようとする。しかし、それだけではない。顧客はいつもどの会社があるアイデアをいちばん先に出したかを覚えているようである。その会社とそのアイデアのつながりは非常に強く、何人かのマーケティングの専門家はある製品が持ち得る最も重要な特質は最初に出ることだと考えているほどである。小さな会社は、製品それ自体で一番になることができないとしても、製品に関

係するほかのことにおいて一番になることはできるだろう。これは例えば低価格、よりよい品質、よりよいサービス、またはほかの数多くの要素などによってである。このように、小さな会社はナンバーワン企業を利用して自社製品をマーケットに位置づけることができる一方で、顧客が求めているかもしれない特徴を提供するのだ。もし顧客がその特徴を求めていないのであれば、彼らがそれを求めるべきであることを納得させるのが広告の仕事である。このように、広告とはある種の顧客教育であり、顧客がそれまで考えたこともなかった商品特性に関する情報を提供することなのだ。つまり各自は、製品に対して完全に満足するのにこの特性は必要不可欠なものであると顧客に納得させなければならない。もし自己の市場調査が効果的に行われたとしたら、各自は自分が作り上げたこの特定分野で生き残れるだろう。

重要語句

- □ advertising（名詞）広告
- □ alternative（名詞）代案、二者択一
- □ appreciable（形容詞）これという、容易に判断できる
- □ association（名詞）つながり、つき合い、関連
- □ attention（名詞）注意、注目
- □ attribute（名詞）特質、特性、属性
- □ brute（形容詞）理性のない、動物の、野獣的な、野蛮な
- □ capture（動詞）つかまえる、攻略する
- □ convince（動詞）納得させる
- □ current（形容詞）最新の、今の
- □ dissatisfaction（名詞）不満、不平
- □ induce（動詞）説いて～させる、～する気にさせる、引き起こす

- □ lure（動詞）誘惑する、誘い出す、おびき出す
- □ niche（名詞）特定分野、適所、壁などのくぼみ
- □ once（接続詞）いったん～すれば、～するやいなや
- □ outspend（動詞）～より多くの金を使う
- □ previous（形容詞）以前の、前の
- □ prove（動詞）～となる、わかる
- □ quality（名詞）特性、特質、品質
- □ remember（動詞）思い出す、覚えている
- □ share（名詞）分け前、取り分
- □ situation（名詞）状態、立場、事態
- □ suggest（動詞）提唱する、提案する、ほのめかす
- □ thinking（名詞）考え方、見解
- □ traditional（形容詞）伝統的な

11. 解答 (A)

第3パラグラフの情報に基づき、**market share strategy** を最もよく説明しているのはどれか。

(A) 企業が広告に十分な費用をかければ、顧客を獲得でき、利益が得られる。

(B) 単純なアイデアを使えば、顧客を引きつけることができる。

(C) 製品が競合他社のものと異なっていれば、顧客を引きつけることができる。

(D) 広告が十分に強力なものであれば、顧客は製品を使ってみようという気になる。

解説 第3パラグラフの中ほどに、The basic tool of this strategy is advertising. とあり、さらに、Current thinking says that if you outspend your competitors in advertising, you can get your market share, ... と続いているので、(A) が正解であるとわかる。

12. 解答 (C)

以下のセンテンスのうち、本文中でハイライトされたセンテンスの中の重要な情報について最もよく表しているのはどれか。不適切な選択肢は意味的に大きく違っているか、必要な情報を省いてしまっている。

最近の考え方によると、もし広告に競合他社よりも多くの費用を投じれば、たとえ自社の製品やサービスにほかとの明確な違いがなくても、マーケットシェアを獲得できるという。

(A) 競合他社よりも広告費を多く使えば、必ず製品の成功につながる。

(B) 競合他社とは異なる製品であれば、広告にお金をかける必要はない。

(C) 製品が類似していれば、広告費を多くかけることで成功へつなげられる。

(D) 競合他社の製品との違いが大きいほど、広告にかける費用は少なくてよい。

解説 消去法を用いるとよい。太字の部分の後半に ... even if your product or service has no appreciable differences from others. とあり、(B) と (D) は正解ではない。no appreciable differences from others は選択肢 (C) ... if your product is similar to... のことを言っている。

13. 解答 (D)

第3と第4パラグラフの内容によると、小企業は、資金が豊富な大手企業が占めるマーケットを獲得するために何ができるか。

(A) 大企業よりも多く広告を打ってみることができる。

(B) この状況で大手企業と張り合うことは無意味なので、何もすべきではない。

(C) 自社製品の独自の特徴を見つけようと努め、それを宣伝することができる。

(D) 広告を打つ場合には、できるだけ競合他社に言及しよう努めることができる。

解説 これも消去法を用いる。第4パラグラフ前半の ... do not have the money to out-advertise them から、(A) は正解ではないとわかる。続いて後半の ... they can do something more for the customer. から (B) も違うとわかる。続く ... they can use the associations with the more powerful company ... まで読み進めると (C) ではなくて (D) が正解であるとわかる。

14. 解答 (D)

第5パラグラフによると、特定市場戦略について正しいものはどれか。

(A) 他社に先駆けて新製品を投入する場合に、この戦略を最も効果的に活用できる。

(B) 自社製品がトップの競合他社の製品とどれほど似ているかを宣伝したいときに、この戦略が使える。

(C) 広告に十分に費用をかけられない企業に最適な戦略である。

(D) この戦略は、自社製品がトップの競合他社の製品と何らかの点で異なる場合に有効である。

解説 第5パラグラフの **market niche** に続く In this strategy you try to find a quality that your product has but your competitor's does not. から、正解 (D) にたどり着ける。

15. 解答 (B)

第 5 パラグラフで、著者はこう述べている。効果的なマーケティングは

(A) 新製品をもってトップに立つのに役立つ。

(B) 競合他社の顧客が求めているものを見つけ出すのに役立つ。

(C) 顧客を説得し、ある特性を製品に求めるよう促すことができる。

(D) 顧客に、自分が特定の製品の最初の利用者だったことを思い出させることができる。

解説 第 5 パラグラフの最後にヒントがある。effective **market research** は、... you must convince customers that this quality is essential for them to enjoy complete satisfaction with a product. のためになされると言っている。そこで下線部を可能にするものは何かと考えると、(B) が正解になる。 (C) は、you must convince customers ... を言い換えただけである。

16. 解答 (D)

第 5 パラグラフで、顧客についてどのようなことが推測できるか。

(A) 顧客は広告によって簡単に操作できる。

(B) 顧客はたいてい、新しいアイデアがある小規模な会社に引きつけられる。

(C) 顧客は常に、あるアイデアとそれを最初に提示した会社を覚えているので、どうやってもこの結び付きは変えられない。

(D) ある新しいアイデアを最初に提示した会社であれば、長期にわたって顧客を引きつける可能性が高い。

解説 第 5 パラグラフ前半の Customers seem always to remember which company was first with an idea. と、それに続く So strong is this association that ... から、(D) が正解だとわかる。ここで注意したいのは、(C) に惑わされないことである。 ... and nothing can really be done to change this association. とあるが、第 5 パラグラフ中ほどの However, ... 以下を読み取ろう。

17. 解答 (B)

第5パラグラフで、著者はなぜ市場調査に言及したのか。

(A) 市場調査が、どんな種類の広告を打つかを決めるうえでいかに重要かを示すために。

(B) 市場調査が、顧客のニーズを理解するための重要なツールであることを示すために。

(C) 市場調査が、競合他社を理解するうえでいかに重要かを示すために。

(D) 市場調査が、特定市場で生き残るすべを理解するうえでいかに重要かを示すために。

解説 market research が何のためにあるのかを読み取る。第5パラグラフ後半の ..., you must convince customers ... with a product. から、正解は (B) だとわかる。

18. 解答 (B)

特定市場戦略についての著書の意見を最も正確に反映しているのは、次のうちのどれか。

(A) 新製品を出す小企業にとって効果的な戦略だ。

(B) 当該市場に最初に新製品を投入した大企業にとっては効果的な戦略ではない。

(C) 競合他社よりも多く広告費を投じられる企業にとって効果的な戦略だ。

(D) 市場調査をいとわない企業にとって効果的な戦略だ。

解説 小さな会社（製品それ自体で一番になることができない）がいかにして生き延びていくかに関連して market niche というアイデアが出てきた経緯を考えれば、正解は (B) になる。

19. 解答 (C)

次のセンテンスの挿入箇所の候補として本文中に示された4つの■を見なさい。

このように、広告とはある種の顧客教育であり、顧客がそれまで考えたこともなかったかもしれない商品特性に関する情報を提供することなのだ。

このセンテンスを挿入するのに最もふさわしい場所はどこか。

解説 直前の文では the role of advertising について述べているので、In this way と直前の文とのつながりを示し、さらに、advertising についても述べている挿入文は、(C) の位置に入る。

20. 解答 （下の英文を参照）

(E) The strategy used is dependent on the size of the company and the similarities between its product and a competitor's product.

(D) A large company with large amounts of capital can simply outspend its competition in advertising to capture its necessary market share whether its product is similar to a competitor's or not.

(C) A small company can use market niche strategy to advertise differences between its product and a similar product of the major competitor.

指示文：以下に提示された導入文は本文の要約である。本文の中で最も重要な考えを選択肢から 3 つ選び、要約を完成させなさい。いくつかの選択肢は本文中で示されていないことを提示しているか、または重要ではない内容であるため、要約には不適切である。**この設問の配点は 2 点である。**

マーケットシェア戦略と特定市場（マーケット・ニッチ）戦略は、企業が製品を市場に投入するために使える 2 つの方法だ。

選択肢

(A) 大企業は、顧客が自社製品についてすでに知っているので、顧客のことを心配する必要がない。

(B) 特定市場戦略は、新製品を投入する企業には最も効果的な戦略である。

(C) 小企業は特定市場戦略を使って、競合する大企業の類似製品との違いを宣伝することができる。

(D) 資本力の大きい大企業は、単に広告費を競合他社よりも多く投じさえすれば、必要なマーケットシェアを獲得できる。これには、自社製品が競合他社の製品と似ているか否かは関係ない。

(E) 使われる戦略は、企業規模や、自社製品と競合他社の製品の類似性によって変わってくる。

(F) 小企業は、広告によってマーケットシェアを獲得しようとする場合、必ず競合他社に言及するべきである。

解説　与えられた文は strategy のことで始まるので、それを受けて The strategy ... の文が続く。さらにその内容から、the size of the company と product に関する事柄が次に続くことがわかる。最後に大きい会社と比較するものとして小さい会社についての記述が続く。

Listening Section 解答・解説

講義や会話を部分的に聴き直して答える問題のトランスクリプトには🎧マークを記してあります。このうち設問に直接対応する部分は太字で示しました（問題文ではこの部分の音声をもう一度聴くことができます）。なお、全体のトランスクリプトでは太字部分のみが示されています。

Questions 1-5

トランスクリプト

Woman: Hi. Can I help you?

Student: Yes, I'm a foreign student and I'd like to know if it's possible to work on a student visa (Q1).

Woman: Well, you can but there are some limitations. First of all, you are only allowed to work 12 hours a week.

Student: That's OK, I certainly can't work full time — not with all the homework I've got to do. Can I work anywhere?

Woman: Yes, but it may be difficult to find someone off campus who will hire you for only 12 hours a week. Sometimes fast-food restaurants may need workers at peak times or at times no one else wants to work. Also you might not qualify for other benefits like insurance if you're only a part-time employee. **I know many students, and you've probably talked to some, who work more than 12 hours a week off campus, but you should realize that it's illegal and you would be taking a risk** (Q4). **Are you sure you need the money?** (Q5)

Student: I thought I had enough, but I never expected so many expenses. I calculated tuition, food and housing, but there is much more than this. I mean, books are much more expensive than I ever thought. I'm really worried that I may have some problems. I'm not sure I'll make it through the semester.

Woman: Have you considered working on campus? (Q2)

Student: I'll take anything. What kind of work would that be?

Woman: It could be anything from helping in the cafeteria to working in the library. The pay's not great but it's OK. And you won't have to worry about breaking the law or having too far to go for a job.

Student: Would I be able to choose where I worked; I mean the kind of job I would have?

Woman: You may, but it probably depends on what's available. But can I make a suggestion?

Student: Sure.

Woman: A lot of students don't really want to work in the cafeteria, so you may be able to get some kind of job there. It's not glamorous work. You may have to wash dishes or do some other menial task but — and this could be important for you — if you work at the cafeteria, you will be able to get free meals during the time you work (Q1). This could save you quite a bit of money.

Student: Really? Yeah, that would be nice. I'm not really particular about the kind of work I do. I just need a job.

Woman: Then why don't I set you up for an interview with the work-study people. You know, I've learned there's more to the work-study program (Q1) than most foreign students think.

Student: What's that?

Woman: Well, I've noticed that work-study allows people, especially foreign students, to make friends with other students more easily than by just attending classes with them (Q3).

Student: Other foreign students or Americans? But I guess there aren't many Americans who need to work on campus (Q2).

Woman: Well, you'd be wrong there. A lot of American students (Q2) aren't as rich as you may think. A lot of them are trying to pay their own way through college and need work to help them out.

Student: But they could work full time off campus.

Woman: Sure, but they're the same as you. They need time to study, and save time by working on campus (Q2). Of course, many do work off campus, too, but not all of them.

Student: Well, to be honest I haven't had as much luck meeting Americans as I thought before I came here. Everything you've said makes this work-study idea sound even better.

女性：こんにちは。どういうご用件ですか。

学生：はい、私は留学生なのですが、学生ビザで働くことができるかどうか知りたいのですが。

女性：ええ、できますがいくつか制限があります。まず、週に 12 時間しか働けません。

学生：それは大丈夫です。宿題もやらなくてはいけないので、フルタイムでは絶対に働けませんから。どこで働いてもいいのですか。

女性：ええ、でも週に 12 時間しか働けない学生を雇ってくれる人をキャンパスの外で見つけるのは難しいかもしれませんね。ピーク時や誰も働きたがらない時間に、ファストフードのレストランが働き手を必要とすることもありますが。それに、パートタイムの従業員だと保険などの手当をもらう資格はないかもしれませんよ。キャンパスの外で 12 時間以上働いている学生を私はたくさん知っていますし、あなたも彼らと話したことがあるかもしれませんが、それは違法で危険を冒していることを知っておかなければいけませんよ。本当にお金が必要なのですか。

学生：十分あると思っていたんですが、こんなに物入りだとはまったく予想していませんでした。授業料、食費、住居費は計算していたのですが、それよりもずっと多く必要なのです。教科書代が考えていたのよりかなり高くつきます。なんらかの問題を抱えてしまうのではないかと本当に心配しているのです。今学期やっていけるかどうかも確かではありません。

女性：キャンパス内で働くことを考えてみましたか。

学生：何でもやります。どんな仕事がありますか。

女性：カフェテリアでの手伝いから図書館での仕事までなんでもありますよ。給料はあまりよくありませんが、まあまあですよ。それに、法律を破ったり、仕事のために遠くに行かなければならないことを心配しなくても済みますね。

学生：どこで働くか、つまり、仕事の種類を選ぶことはできますか。

女性：できるかもしれませんが、どこに空きがあるかによるでしょうね。とはいってもおすすめしたいことがあるのですが。

学生：お願いします。

女性：多くの学生はカフェテリアで働きたいとは思っていないのですよ。だから、カフェテリアでなら何か仕事が見つかるかもしれませんね。魅力的な仕事ではないのですね。皿を洗ったり、ほかの退屈な仕事をしたりしなければいけないでしょう。でも、これがあなたには重要だと思うのですが、つまり、カフェテリアで働けば、アルバイトをしている間はただで食事をすることができるのです。そうすればたくさんのお金が節約できますよね。

学生：本当ですか。いやあ、それはいいですね。職種については、それほど好みがあるわけではありません。ただ仕事が必要なだけなのです。

女性：では、ワークスタディの人との面接を設定しましょう。多くの留学生の皆さんが考えているよりも、ワークスタディ・プログラムには役に立つことがあるのですよ。

学生：それは何ですか。

女性：そうですね、ワークスタディに参加すれば、特に留学生は、ただ授業に出ているだけよりも簡単にほかの学生と友達になれるんですよ。

学生：ほかの留学生やアメリカ人学生とですか。でも、キャンパスで働かなければならないアメリカ人学生はそんなにたくさんはいないと思いますが。

女性：いえ、そんなことはないですよ。多くのアメリカ人学生はあなたが考えているほど恵まれているわけではないのです。彼らの多くは自分で大学の費用を払おうとしていて、そのためには働かなければいけないのです。

学生：でも、彼らはキャンパスの外でフルタイムで働けるのでは。

女性：ええ、でも彼らもあなたと同じですよ。勉強する時間が必要なので、キャンパスで働くことによって時間を節約するのです。もちろん、キャンパスの外で働いている学生もたくさんいますが、

すべての学生というわけではありませんよ。

学生：なるほど、正直に言うと、ここ（この大学）に来る前に考えていたほどアメリカ人と出会う機
会が今のところありません。今まで伺ったお話から察すると、ワークスタディはとてもいいもの
のようですね。

1. 解答 (B)

男性はなぜ女性と話しているのか。

(A) 彼は彼女が仕事をくれることを望んでいる。

(B) 彼は仕事を見つけるための情報を欲しがっている。

(C) 彼は宿題の量が多すぎて困っている。

(D) 彼はお金が残っていないので心配している。

解説 トランスクリプトの下線部参照。

- I'd like to know if it's possible to work on a student visa.
- if you work at the cafeteria, you will be able to get free meals during the time you work.
- the work-study program

2. 解答 (C)

ワークスタディ・プログラムとは何か。

(A) 外国人留学生がアメリカで働くことを許可するプログラム

(B) 外国人留学生がファストフード店でアルバイトすることを許可するプログラム

(C) 学生なら誰にでもキャンパス内で働くことを許可するプログラム

(D) キャンパス内で働く学生に無料の食事を提供するプログラム

解説 トランスクリプトの下線部参照。下線部の the work-study program (Q1) は、working on campus の話の一環として出てきている。また、キャンパスのカフェテリアで働けば、その時間は食事が付くということなので、選択肢 (D) は正解ではない。

- working on campus?
- ... there aren't many Americans who need to work on campus.
- They (American students) need time to study, and save time by working on campus.

3. 解答 (A)

ワークスタディ・プログラムのさらなる利点は何か。

(A) 外国人留学生がより多くのアメリカ人と出会えるかもしれない。

(B) 学生が図書館で働けるかもしれない。

(C) 給料がとてもよい。

(D) 学生が週に 12 時間を超えて働ける。

解説 トランスクリプトの下線部参照。

- work-study allows people, especially foreign students, to make friends with other students more easily than by just attending classes with them.

4. 解答 (C)

会話の一部をもう一度聞きなさい。それから、質問に答えなさい。

女性はなぜこのように言っているのか。

(A) 彼女は実際には、キャンパス外で週に 12 時間を超えて働いても構わないと言っている。

(B) 彼女は彼に、自分がどれほどの外国人留学生が規則を破っているかを知っていることを気づかせようとしている。

(C) 彼女は彼に、週に 12 時間を超えて働くことで起こり得る結果について警告している。

(D) 彼女は実際には、彼にあえてキャンパス外で働かないように伝えている。

解説 トランスクリプトの下線部参照。（学生ビザで）キャンパス外で週 12 時間以上働くのは違法なので、危険を冒すことになると警告している。

Woman: **I know many students, and you've probably talked to some, who work more than 12 hours a week off campus, but <u>you should realize that it's illegal and you would be taking a risk</u>.** Are you sure you need the money?

Man: I thought I had enough but I never expected so many expenses.

5. 解答 (D)

会話の一部をもう一度聞きなさい。それから、質問に答えなさい。

女性はこの質問で何をほのめかしているのか。

(A) 彼女は、彼がお金が足りないと嘘をついていると思っている。

(B) 彼女は、彼が本当にもっとお金を必要としているわけではないだろうと思っている。

(C) 彼女は、彼の話していることについて困惑している。

(D) 彼女は、彼が単にうろたえているだけかもしれず、本当は十分にお金があるのかもしれないと思っている。

解説 与えられた状況の中で選択肢を考えると、このような発言は、(D) She thinks he may be just panicking and really may have enough money. のように、相手が冷静さを失っているのではないかと疑問を抱いたときに使われる。また、下線部からも、なぜ「お金が必要なのか」と聞いたのかがわかる。

Woman: I know many students, and you've probably talked to some, who work more than 12 hours a week off campus, but you should realize that it's illegal and you would be taking a risk. **Are you sure you need the money?**

Man: I thought I had enough but I never expected so many expenses.

トランスクリプト

OK, last time I started to talk about biological classification, by which I mean how all living things are classified into various groups and subgroups. Now, you might think that, since we're in the 21st century and we have all sorts of sophisticated technology, that all biologists agree on the classifications of plants and animals. But if you think this, you'd be wrong. It sometimes seems the more we know, or the closer we look at something, the more complicated the picture becomes. **But, you'll probably think that at least we can tell, let's say, the difference between plants and animals. Well, I hate to disappoint you, but even something that seems as obvious as this on the surface is not so easy to do in practice** (下線 Q6: 太字 Q7). Of course some things are obvious. A dog and a tree are completely different. But if we begin to look at smaller organisms under the microscope, the line between plants and animals gets a little blurry (Q6).

So let's look at an organism we've all heard about, the amoeba, and decide whether we can call it an animal or not. It's a one-celled or unicellular organism. It has no real brain (Q8) but does have a nucleus, which seems to play some kind of role in organizing its behavior. It can move. It can capture and digest food. It absorbs oxygen from water and releases carbon dioxide. I guess you could call this a kind of breathing (Q8). It reproduces by dividing into two parts. It doesn't have any chlorophyll (Q8) like a plant, so it cannot produce food by photosynthesis. **So, is it an animal or a plant?** (Q9)

Well, the answer to this question isn't easy (Q9). In the past, biologists classified the amoeba as an animal (Q11-1). At that time, it seemed relatively easy to differentiate a plant from an animal. Plants stayed in one place and produced food through photosynthesis. But there were problems. There were some unicellular "animals" that moved but also used photosynthesis (Q10). What were they? There were other animals that didn't move, but captured their food. In fact, the closer biologists looked at these small organisms, the more the distinction between plant and animal became unclear.

This created a kind of crisis in biological classification, so much so that in the late 1800's a new classification, the Kingdom Protista, was created (Q11-2), which made it impossible for a unicellular organism to be classified as an animal (Q11-3). Animals had to be multicellular.

Unfortunately, this didn't solve the problem either. For it seems that some of these unicellular organisms like to live in colonies where they take on different roles in order to improve their chances for survival. In this manner they begin to resemble some primitive multicellular animals like the sponge or jellyfish. Again the distinction between plant and animal seemed impossible to delineate.

In fact, it wasn't until recently, when techniques for examining cells were improved, that it was decided that the true distinction was between those living things with no enclosed nucleus and those whose nucleus was enclosed by a nuclear membrane (Q11-4). This did not mean that plants had one type of nucleus and animals had another. It simply meant that this was the main distinction among unicellular organisms that they could find (Q11-4). So what are we really saying here? I guess that at this unicellular level, the words "plant" and "animal" have no real meaning. The real problem was that when biologists first began to classify all living things, they assumed that they all had to be either plants or animals, and they then tried to force every living thing into these classifications.

訳例

さて、前回は、どのようにすべての生物がさまざまなグループやサブグループに分類されるかという、生物学の分類についての話を始めました。皆さんは、私たちは 21 世紀にいて、さまざまな種類の極めて高度な技術を持っているので、すべての生物学者が植物や動物の分類に関して同意していると考えているかもしれませんが、もしそう考えているのなら、それは間違っています。私たちがよく知れば知るほど、またはより近くで何かを見るようになればなるほど、その実態は複雑になるように、ときどき感じます。けれども、皆さんは少なくとも、例えば植物と動物の差は見分けられると考えていることでしょう。失望させたくはありませんが、表面上は明らかなような何かでさえ、実際はそんなに簡単ではないのです。もちろん、明らかなものもあります。犬と木は完全に別個のものです。しかし、顕微鏡でより小さな生物を見始めると、植物と動物の間の線引きは少しあいまいになります。

では、私たち皆が聞いたことのある生物、アメーバを取り上げ、それが動物といえるかどうかを判断しましょう。アメーバはひとつの細胞、つまり単細胞の生物です。本物の脳は持っていませんが、行動を制御するある種の役割のようなものを演じる核を持っています。動くことができます。食物を捕獲して消化することができます。水から酸素を吸収し、二酸化炭素を出します。ある種の呼吸といえるかもしれませんね。2 つに分かれることによって、繁殖します。植物のように葉緑素を持っていないので、光合成によって食物を作り出すことは

できません。さて、これは動物ですか、それとも植物ですか。

　実は、この質問に答えるのは容易ではありません。過去には、生物学者たちはアメーバを動物として分類していました。そのころは、植物と動物を区別するのは比較的容易だったようです。植物はひとつの場所にとどまり、光合成によって食物を作り出すものでした。しかし問題はありました。動くのですが、光合成を使う単細胞の「動物」がいたのです。それらは何なのでしょうか。動かないのに食物を捕獲するほかの動物もいました。実際、生物学者がこれらの小さな生物を近くで見れば見るほど、植物と動物の区別は不明瞭になっていったのです。

　これは、生物学上の分類にある種の危機となりました。そこで、1800年代後半に原生生物界という新たな分類が作られました。これにより、単細胞の生物が動物に分類されることが不可能になったのです。動物は多細胞でなければなりませんでした。

　不幸なことに、これによっても問題は解決されませんでした。これらの単細胞生物のいくつかは、コロニーとして存在することを好んでいるように見えたからです。コロニーでは、生存の可能性を高めるためにそれぞれが異なる役割を果たすのです。この意味で、これらは海綿動物やクラゲのような、原始的な多細胞生物に似始めたのです。植物と動物の区別をはっきりつけるのは再び不可能になりました。

　実際、細胞を調べる技術が改良された最近まで、本当の違いは、核膜に包まれている核を持たない生物と持っている生物との間にあるということがはっきりしなかったのです。これは、植物がある種類の核を持っており、動物がまた別の種類の核を持っていることを意味しているわけではありません。このこと（核膜に包まれている核を持っているか否かということと）が、発見されている単細胞生物の中での主な区別であることを単に意味しているだけなのです。ここで、私たちが本当に言おうとしていることは何でしょうか。単細胞のレベルでは、「植物」とか「動物」という言葉は何の意味も持たないということです。本当の問題は、生物学者たちが最初にすべての生物を分類し始めたときに、すべての生物は植物か動物のどちらかであると仮定し、それぞれの生物をこれらの分類の中に無理やり押し込めようとしたことだったのです。

6. 解答 (B)

この講義の主題は何か。

(A) 植物と動物の類似点

(B) 植物と動物を区別する難しさ

(C) 原生生物界

(D) テクノロジーと生物学的分類

解説 トランスクリプトの下線部参照。

- Well, I hate to disappoint you, but even something that seems as obvious as this on the surface is not so easy to do in practice.
- the line between plants and animals gets a little blurry.

7. 解答 (C)

講義の一部をもう一度聞きなさい。それから、質問に答えなさい。

教授はなぜこのように発言するのか。

(A) 彼女は学生たちに、いかに彼らの知識が乏しいかを示したがっている。

(B) 彼女は、自分が彼らに難解なことを説明しなくてはならないことを不愉快に感じている。

(C) 彼女は、生物学的な分類がどれほど困難なものになり得るかを示そうとしている。

(D) 彼女は、学生たちが生物学的な分類についてあまり理解していないことにがっかりしている。

解説 太字中にある ... I hate to disappoint you, but ... から、その前にある文章を否定しているものであることがわかり、生物学的分類（biological classification）がいかに難しいかをわかってもらおうとしている。

🎧 It sometimes seems the more we know, or the closer we look at something, the more complicated the picture becomes. **But, you'll probably think that at least we can tell, let's say, the difference between plants and animals. Well, I hate to disappoint you, but even something that seems as obvious as this on the surface is not so easy to do in practice.**

8. 解答 (A)、(D)

アメーバはなぜ、かつて動物に分類されていたのか。

解答を 2 つ選びなさい。

(A) 動けた。

(B) 葉緑素を含んでいた。

(C) 脳があり、呼吸することができた。

(D) 食物を捕獲した。

解説 トランスクリプトの下線部参照。

- It has no real brain
- It can move. It can capture and digest food. It absorbs oxygen from water and releases carbon dioxide. I guess you could call this a kind of breathing.
- It doesn't have any chlorophyll.

9. 解答 (C)

講義の一部をもう一度聞きなさい。それから、質問に答えなさい。

教授はこのように発言することで、何をほのめかしているのか。

(A) 彼女は、何人かの学生がこの質問に答えるだろうと予想している。

(B) 彼女は、自分自身が混乱していることを示したがっている。

(C) 彼女は答えを求めておらず、ただこの問題がいかに難しいかを示すためにこの質問を使っている。

(D) 彼女は答えを期待してはいないが、学生たちが彼女にいくつか質問するだろうと予想している。

解説 トランスクリプトの下線部参照。So, is it an animal or a plant? のすぐ後に、Well, the answer to this question isn't easy. と続き、さらに「この質問に答えるのがいかに難しいか」という具体例を挙げてサポートしていることから、この発言は単に植物と動物を区別することの難しさを伝えるためのレトリカル・クエスチョン（答えを要求しない質問）であることがわかる。

- Well, the answer to this question isn't easy.
- 🎧 It doesn't have any chlorophyll like a plant so it cannot produce food by photosynthesis. **So, is it an animal or a plant?**

10. 解答 (B)

何が一部の単細胞生物の分類を難しくしていたのか。

(A) それらには細胞核がなかった。

(B) それらは動くのに、光合成を行っていた。

(C) それらは簡単に顕微鏡で観察できなかった。

(D) それらは2つに分裂して増殖することができなかった。

解説 トランスクリプトの下線部参照。

- There were some unicellular "animals" that moved but also used photosynthesis.

11. 解答 （下の表を参照）

1. Amoebas were classified as animal.
2. Kingdom Protista was created.
3. Unicellular organisms could no longer be classified as animals.
4. Unicellular organisms classified according to type of nucleus they possessed.

教授はアメーバの分類の歴史について説明している。その歴史を、出来事を時系列に並べて要約しなさい。

- 原生生物界が作られた。
- アメーバが動物に分類された。
- 単細胞生物はもはや動物に分類できなくなった。
- 単細胞生物が持っている核の種類によって分類された。

解説

- In the past, biologists classified the amoeba as an animal. (1)
- the Kingdom Protista, was created, ... (2)
- which made it impossible for a unicellular organism to be classified as an animal. (3)
- it was decided that the true distinction was between those living things with no enclosed nucleus and those whose nucleus was enclosed by a nuclear membrane. (4)
- It simply meant that this was the main distinction among unicellular organisms that they could find. (4)

トランスクリプト

Professor: Well, Mr. Kim, I expected you might come in to see me.

Student: Yes, I have a question about the grade you gave me on my paper (Q12).

Professor: You mean you want to know why you failed? (Q12)

Student: That's right (Q12).

Professor: Did you read my comments?

Student: Yes, you wrote the same comment, "Your words?", several times. I'm not sure what you mean by that.

Professor: It means that I was wondering if the words you wrote were yours or if they were copied from the reference material (Q13).

Student: But you said we could use reference material.

Professor: Yes, of course. **But you can't simply copy that material into your paper and put your name on it. Surely you must know that by now** (Q15). I mean, you didn't even put the material in quotations or list the reference in your paper. Are you saying you didn't realize you can't copy from a source without giving a reference to it?

Student: But a lot of it is my own words.

Professor: Yes, I'm sure it is. Here, let me show you something in your paper. **See, in this paragraph you make several grammar mistakes and misuse some vocabulary, yet, in the very next paragraph your vocabulary and grammar suddenly show miraculous improvement. How do you explain that?**(Q16)

Student: I'm sorry. Writing papers is very difficult for me, and this week I had to write three major papers. I was just trying to finish all of them (Q14). I guess if I had had more time, I wouldn't have needed to copy so much (Q13).

Professor: Well, I understand that it's difficult to do so much work in a language that is not your native language. Even many American students have problems doing all the work required. But, to be honest with you, we cannot have two standards — one for international students and one for American students — and then give them both the same degrees. I think you must have realized this when you decided to go to an American university, right?

Student: Yes, but maybe I didn't really understand how hard it would be.

Professor: OK, look, if you rewrite this paper in your own words and give it to me on Monday, I'll consider giving you a passing grade on it. I'm not promising anything, but I'll give you a chance. But remember, if you use information from a book and don't put it into your own words, you must either quote it or make a reference to it at the end of your paper. If you don't do this, it's called plagiarism. And plagiarism is a crime. Look at it this way. It's like stealing; in this case you steal someone else's words or ideas and present them as if they were your own. Do you understand why that is wrong?

Student: Yes, I understand, and I promise to be more careful next time.

Professor: Good, because next time I can't give you another chance. If you are having problems with writing your paper please come and see me. Do you know my office hours? Remember I told you all the first day of class?

Student: I know you told us but I didn't write them down. I just took a chance that you might be here today. I never thought I would need to talk to you. To be honest I'm kind of nervous about talking to teachers.

Professor: Well, my office hours are Monday and Wednesday from four to five. Come in and I can help you organize your paper or answer any other questions. That's why I have office hours. Anyway, try to finish your paper by Monday, OK?

Student: Yes, I will. Thanks a lot. I promise I'll have the paper done by Monday.

訳例

教授：ああ、キムさん。会いに来ると思っていましたよ。
学生：はい、私のレポートに対する評価について質問があるのです。
教授：なぜ落第したか知りたいということですね。
学生：そうです。
教授：私のコメントは読みましたか。
学生：はい。「あなたの言葉ですか」と何度か書かれていましたが、どういう意味かわかりません。

教授：あなたが書いていた言葉があなた自身のものか、それとも参考文献から写したものかという意味です。

学生：でも、参考文献を使ってもいいとおっしゃいました。

教授：ええ、もちろん。でも、参考文献をあなたのレポートにただ写して、あなたの名前を書くことはできませんよ。そんなことはこれまでに知っていなければならないことです。あなたはレポートの中で引用した参考文献をきちんと示していないし、参考文献の一覧表もつけていませんね。出典を明らかにすることなく文献から引き写してはいけないことを知らなかったとでも言うのですか。

学生：でも、多くは私自身の言葉です。

教授：ええ、そうでしょうね。これはあなたのレポートの一部分です。あなたはこの段落ではいくつかの文法の間違いをし、語彙も誤って使っています。けれども次の段落では、あなたの語彙と文法は突如、奇跡的に改善されています。これをどのように説明しますか。

学生：すみません。レポートを書くのは私にとってとても難しいことで、今週私は３つもの大きなレポートを書かなければいけなかったのです。ただ全部を終わらせようとしただけなのです。もしもっと時間があったら、こんなに写す必要はなかったと思います。

教授：ええ、母語ではない言語でそんなに多くの課題をこなすのが難しいことは理解できます。多くのアメリカ人学生でさえ求められている課題のすべてをするのに苦労しているのですから。でも、正直に言って、留学生のためとアメリカ人学生のための二重の基準を設けたうえで、同じ学位を与えることはできないのです。アメリカの大学に来ようと決めたときにそのことは理解していたはずでしょう。

学生：はい、でもそれがどんなに大変なことかを本当にはわかっていなかったのかもしれません。

教授：いいでしょう、このレポートをあなた自身の言葉で書き直して月曜日に提出すれば、合格点を与えることを考えてみましょう。何も約束はしませんが、チャンスは与えます。でも、本からの情報を使用して自分の言葉で書き直さない場合は、その情報に引用符をつけるか、レポートの最後に出典を明らかにしなければいけないことを覚えておいてください。そうしなければ、剽窃行為*と呼ばれます。剽窃行為は犯罪です。こういうふうに考えてください。これは泥棒のようなものです。この場合に当てはめると、あなたは誰かの言葉やアイデアを盗み、あたかも自分のもののようにして発表しているのです。なぜそれが悪いことなのかわかりますか。

学生：はい、わかります。次はもっと注意することを約束します。

教授：いいでしょう。次は、もう一度チャンスを与えることはできませんからね。レポートを書くときに問題があったら、私に会いに来てください。私のオフィスアワー**を知っていますか。クラスの最初の日に話しましたよね。

学生：先生が話されたことは覚えていますが、書き取りませんでした。今日も先生がいらっしゃればいいなと思って来てみただけなのです。先生とお話しする必要があるかもしれないなんてまったく思っていませんでしたから。正直言って、先生方とお話しすると少し緊張してしまうのです。

教授：そうですか。私のオフィスアワーは月曜日と水曜日の４時から５時ですよ。来てくれればレポートをまとめる手助けをしますし、どんな質問にも答えます。そのためにオフィスアワーがあるのです。とにかく、月曜日までにレポートを書き終えてください、いいですね。

学生：はい、そうします。ありがとうございました。月曜日までにレポートを書くことをお約束します。

注：＊　剽窃（ひょうせつ）行為：plagiarism と呼ばれ絶対に許されない行為とされている。この会話にもあるように、参考文献として書籍、雑誌、ウェブサイトなどから、第三者の考えや文献を引用したり参考にしたりするときは出典を明らかにしなくてはならない。詳しくは『海外の大学・大学院で授業を受ける技術』（川手‐ミヤジェイエフスカ恩著／アルク刊）を参照のこと。

　　＊＊オフィスアワー：大学教師が訪ねてくる学生たちのために研究室にいる時間。学生は、教授に質問

や相談があるときは、このオフィスアワーに教師を訪ねる。ちなみに、オフィスアワー以外の時間には、教師とアポイントメント（教師を訪ねるための予約）を取らなくてはならない。

12. 解答 (C)

男性はなぜ教授を訪ねているのか。

(A) 彼は謝りたがっている。

(B) 彼はもっといい成績を取りたがっている。

(C) 彼はなぜ自分のレポートに低い成績が付けられたのかわからない。

(D) 彼はレポートの執筆を手伝ってほしがっている。

解説 トランスクリプトの下線部参照。

- I have a question about the grade you gave me on my paper.
- You mean you want to know why you failed?
- That's right.

13. 解答 (D)

男性はどんな間違いを犯したのか。

(A) 彼はレポートで不合格点を取った。

(B) 彼はアメリカの大学へ行った。

(C) 彼は教授のオフィスアワーを忘れた。

(D) 彼は参考文献をレポートに丸写しした。

解説 トランスクリプトの下線部参照。

- I was wondering if the words you wrote were yours or if they were copied from the reference material.
- I guess if I had had more time, I wouldn't have needed to copy so much.

14. 解答 (B)

男性はなぜ参考文献を盗用したのか。

(A) 彼はそれが悪いことだとは知らなかった。

(B) 彼は忙しかった。

(C) 彼は教授のオフィスアワーを知らなかったので、助けてもらえなかった。

(D) 彼は参考文献を書き忘れた。

解説 トランスクリプトの下線部参照。

- Writing papers is very difficult for me, and this week I had to write three major papers. I was just trying to finish all of them.

15. 解答 (A)

会話の一部をもう一度聞きなさい。それから質問に答えなさい。

教授はなぜこのようなことを言うのか。

(A) 教授は、この学生が不正を働いたことを自覚していると確信している。

(B) 教授は、この学生が自分のしたことを悪いとわかっているかどうか確認しようとしている。

(C) 教授は、この学生に丸写しについて助言を与え、将来同じことをやらないようにしている。

(D) 教授は、この学生が不正を働いたことに驚いている。

解説 トランスクリプトの下線部参照。

Student: But you said we could use reference material.

Professor: Yes, of course. **But you can't simply copy that material into your paper and put your name on it. Surely you must know that by now.** I mean, you didn't even put the material in quotations or list the reference in your paper.

16. 解答 (C)

会話の一部をもう一度聞きなさい。それから質問に答えなさい。

教授はこのように発言することで、何をほのめかしているのか。

(A) 彼女は、書くことがとてもうまい、とこの学生を褒めている。

(B) 彼女は、段落ごとに彼の使う文法が大きく変わることに驚いている。

(C) 彼女はこの学生に、彼が参考文献から丸写しをしたことはわかっている、と伝えている。

(D) 彼女は、この学生の文法や語彙の使い方がときによって正しかったり間違っていたりすることに混乱している。

解説 トランスクリプトの下線部参照。How do you explain that? という発言の含意と、そこに至るまでの事実の説明から、「あなたが文献を書き写したという事実は明白ですよ」と言っていることがわかる。

Student: But a lot of it is my own words.

Professor: Yes, I'm sure it is. Here, let me show you something in your paper. **See, in this paragraph you make several grammar mistakes and misuse some vocabulary, yet, in the very next paragraph your vocabulary and grammar suddenly show miraculous improvement. How do you explain that?**

トランスクリプト

Professor: OK, let's get started. And I'd like to begin by asking a question. When I talk about immigration to the U.S., what nationalities generally come to mind?

Student A: The Irish, Italians ...

Student B: Poles, Germans, Swedes.

Professor: Right, right. We think of the immigration of Europeans to the U.S. usually beginning in the mid-to-late 19th century and continuing into the 20th century. We almost always forget about the immigration of the Chinese (Q17) to the West Coast of America at the same time. Why? Well, maybe it's because the West wasn't really as developed. Maybe it's because we are mainly descendants of Europeans so we have a bias in that direction (Q18-a).

Student A: But I think our society was mainly European to begin with so it was easier for European immigrants to blend into it. I mean, they may have all been from different European countries, but they shared a lot of the same ideas...like, like, Christianity, for example.

Student B: Yeah, and, I mean, let's be honest here. They looked more like us, so maybe they were just more accepted.

Student A: No, that's not really true. Almost all new immigrants faced some form of discrimination. Isn't that right?

Professor: Well, I think you both make some good points. Certainly all immigrants faced discrimination, but it seems the Chinese faced far more of it than our European ancestors (Q17). Part of that may have been caused by the fact that it was harder for them to integrate into mainstream society (Q18), and this caused them to stay much longer in isolated communities for support. Then, of course, they were probably blamed for isolating themselves so much and became even more discriminated against, which made them isolate themselves even more and so on and so on. Just one sort of endless circle.

Student A: Yeah, but all immigrant groups had their communities (Q18-b : Q21). Many of them still do.

Professor: True. It's normal, I suppose, to gather with others who share your language and customs (Q21). Life is certainly easier, and you can make it similar to what you remember back in your home country. But many of the immigrant communities died out after only a couple of generations (Q18-b). Once the kids became Americanized, they really had little interest in maintaining the ways of a country that was essentially foreign to them.

Student B: So what happened to Chinese kids? (Q17) Didn't they feel the same when they became Americanized?

Professor: **Well, that's just it. They** (Q17) **couldn't become Americanized in the real sense of the word** (Q22). I mean, as early as 1882 the U.S. government passed something called the Chinese Exclusion Act, which prohibited all but the most educated Chinese from immigrating for 10 years. It also prohibited all Chinese then living in the U.S. from being naturalized (Q18-d : Q19).

Student B: I know this may seem like a stupid question, but what exactly do you mean by "naturalized"?

Professor: Well, it's basically the process of being granted citizenship and all that comes with citizenship, like the right to own land (Q19) and things such as education. And if you think about it, education may be the most important part of becoming Americanized (Q20). Really, it was the intermixing of immigrant children with American children in schools that caused, and is still causing, Americanization. But the Chinese (Q17) were not allowed to send their children to regular American schools (Q18-c : Q19). In fact, in 1906, California passed a law which prevented Asian children from going to the same schools as white children. And I should add that the Chinese Exclusion Act wasn't repealed until 1943. No other group of immigrants seemed so intentionally isolated from mainstream American society.

Student A: I'm not sure I understand. Why was there so much animosity? What was it that the Chinese did to be so discriminated against? I guess I mean, was it just the Chinese or all Asians that were in this position?

Professor: Good question. Yeah, it was all Asians that were discriminated against but the Chinese (Q17) seemed to bear the brunt of discrimination. Why? Well, it's the same story that you see with Mexicans coming to the U.S. today. People in California began to worry about losing their jobs to Chinese, who were willing to work for a fraction of the pay that Americans doing the same job would get. Then, as always, there were people stirring up emotions against them, and even though this fear was unjustified, I mean, not many Americans wanted to do the heavy labor that the Chinese did (Q18-e). Still, it became a good excuse for discrimination.

訳例

教　授：では、始めましょう。質問から始めたいと思います。アメリカへの移民といえば、一般的にどの民族を思い浮かべますか。

学生Ａ：アイルランド人、イタリア人……。

学生Ｂ：ポーランド人、ドイツ人、スウェーデン人。

教　授：そう、いいですね。私たちは通常 19 世紀の半ばから後半に始まり 20 世紀まで続いたヨーロッパからアメリカへの移民を思い浮かべます。そしてほとんどの場合、同時期のアメリカ西海岸への中国人移民のことは忘れてしまいます。なぜでしょうか。もしかしたら、西部があまり開発されなかったからかもしれません。もしかしたら、私たちが主にヨーロッパ人の子孫であるために、そちらに偏ってしまうのかもしれません。

学生Ａ：でも、私たちの社会はそもそも主にヨーロッパ人だったのですから、ヨーロッパからの移民にとって社会に溶け込むのはより簡単だったと思います。つまり、彼らはすべて異なるヨーロッパの国々から来たのかもしれませんが、多くの同じ考え方を分かち合っていました……。例えばキリスト教信仰のような。

学生Ｂ：そうですよ、正直にいきましょう。彼らはより私たちに似ていたから、より受け入れられやすかったのです。

学生Ａ：いや、そんなことはないよ。新しくやって来た移民のほとんどすべては、なんらかの差別を受けましたよね。そうではないですか。

教　授：君たちは 2 人ともいい点を突いていると思いますよ。すべての移民が差別を受けたのは確かでしょうが、中国人たちは私たちの祖先であるヨーロッパ人よりもずっと多くの差別を受けたように思います。その差別のある部分は、社会の主流に溶け込むことが彼らにとってより難しかったという事実によって引き起こされたのかもしれませんし、そのせいで彼らは互いを助け合うために非常に長い間、孤立したコミュニティーにとどまることになりました。そうなるともちろん、彼らは自分たちをそれほどに孤立させたことで非難され、より多くの差別を受け、そのことによって彼らはより自分たちを孤立させ、というようなことなのです。まるで、ある意味終わりのない循環です。

学生Ａ：はい、でもすべての移民のグループは自分たちのコミュニティーを持っていました。多くは

今でも持っています。

教　授：そうですね。同じ言語と習慣を共有する人々と集まるのは当然だと思います。生活が容易になるのは確かですし、母国について覚えているのと似たような状況をつくることができます。しかし、多くの移民コミュニティーは、たった何世代かのうちに廃れてしまいました。子どもたちがいったんアメリカナイズされると、彼らは自分たちにとっては本質的に外国でしかない（先祖や父母の）国の様式を維持することにほとんど興味を持たなかったのです。

学生Ｂ：それで、中国人の子どもたちには何が起こったのですか。彼らがアメリカナイズされたとき、同じように（中国も彼らにとって外国でしかないと）感じなかったのでしょうか。

教　授：ええ、まさにそこです。彼らは本当の意味でアメリカナイズされなかったのです。つまり、早くも1882年にはアメリカ政府は中国人排斥法と呼ばれるものを可決しました。それは10年にわたり、知識階級を除いたすべての中国人の移住を禁止しました。また、そのときアメリカに住んでいたすべての中国人は帰化することも禁止されたのです。

学生Ｂ：ばかげた質問かもしれませんが、「帰化」とは正確に何を意味しているのですか。

教　授：基本的には、市民権や、市民権とともに与えられるすべてのもの、土地を所有し、教育を受ける権利などが与えられる過程のことです。そのことについて考えてみれば、アメリカナイズされるためには教育が最も重要だとわかるでしょう。実際、アメリカナイズの要因となり、今でも要因であり続けているのは、学校で移民の子どもたちがアメリカ人の子どもたちと一緒になることなのです。しかし、中国人には子どもを通常のアメリカの学校に送ることが許されていませんでした。実際、1906年には、カリフォルニアはアジアの子どもたちが白人の子どもたちと同じ学校に行くことを阻止する法律を可決したのです。それに、中国人排斥法が1943年まで廃止されなかったこともつけ加えておくべきでしょうね。これほど意図的にアメリカ社会の主流から分離された移民のグループはほかにありません。

学生Ａ：よく理解できないのですが。なぜそんなに強い敵意があったのでしょうか。それほど差別される何を中国人がしたのですか。同じ状態にあったのは中国人だけですか、それともすべてのアジア人ですか。

教　授：いい質問ですね。ええ、すべてのアジア人が差別されましたが、中国人は特にひどい差別を受けたようです。なぜでしょうか。今日、アメリカにやって来るメキシコ人に関してあなたたちが知っているのと同じことなのです。カリフォルニアの人々は、アメリカ人が同じ仕事をして得る賃金のほんの一部のお金で働くことをいとわない中国人たちに、自分たちの仕事が奪われるのではないかと心配し始めました。そしていつものことですが、中国人に対する感情をあおる人々がいたために、この恐れが不当なものであったにもかかわらず、つまり、多くのアメリカ人は中国人がやっていたような重労働はやりたくなかったのに、それでもこのことが差別を行うのに都合のよい口実になってしまったのです。

17. 解答 (A)

この話は主に何に関するものか。

(A) 中国人移民

(B) アメリカでの移民に対する差別

(C) 移民に反対する法律

(D) 移民教育の重要性

解説 トランスクリプトの下線部からもわかるように、講義全体を通して中国人移民のことを話題にしている。

- the immigration of the Chinese
- Chinese faced far more of it than our European ancestors.
- what happened to Chinese kids?
- They (Chinese kids)
- the Chinese

18. 解答 (下の表を参照)

		True	*False*
a	They were non-European.	○	
b	New immigrants lived in their own communities.		○
c	They were prevented from receiving education.		○
d	They were not allowed to become citizens.	○	
e	They took jobs that Americans wanted.		○

この講義の中で、教授は中国人移民がアメリカ社会に溶け込めなかった理由について話している。次のそれぞれが、その理由に当たるか否かを指摘しなさい。

彼らはヨーロッパ人ではなかった。

新たな移民は独自のコミュニティーに暮らしていた。

彼らは教育を受けることを妨げられていた。

彼らは国民になることを許可されなかった。

彼らはアメリカ人が求める職を奪った。

解説 「なぜ中国人移民たちはアメリカ社会に溶け込むのが困難であったか」の答え（理由）として、まず1番目の「彼らがヨーロッパ人ではなかった」が挙げられる。次に、ヨーロッパからの移民たちは自分たちのコミュニティーに住んでいたにもかかわらず、アメリカ社会に溶け込むことができたので、これは、なぜ中国人移民がそこに

溶け込めなかったのかという理由にはならない。従って、2 番目は False となる。教育に関しては、教育は受けられたが白人の子どもたちが通う学校には行けなかったのだから、3 番目も正しい理由ではない。ほかに、市民権の取得が許されていなかったことや、アメリカ人が「やりたがらない仕事」をしていたという理由もある。

トランスクリプトの下線部参照。

- Part of that may have been caused by the fact that it was harder for them to integrate into mainstream society.

《**True の根拠**》

- we are mainly descendants of Europeans so we have a bias in that direction. (a)
- It also prohibited all Chinese then living in the U.S. from being naturalized. (d)

《**False の根拠**》

- all immigrant groups had their communities. But many of the immigrant communities died out after only a couple of generations. (b)
- the Chinese were not allowed to send their children to regular American schools. (c)
- not many Americans wanted to do the heavy labor that the Chinese did. (e)

19. 解答 (B)、(C)、(D)

中国人排斥法の3つの特徴は何か。

解答を3つ選びなさい。

(A) あらゆる中国人のアメリカへの移住を阻止した。

(B) 中国人がアメリカ国民になることを阻んだ。

(C) 中国人に自分たちの学校を持つことを強制した。

(D) 中国人が自分たちの土地を所有することを阻止した。

(E) 中国人を自分たちのコミュニティーだけに制限した。

解説 トランスクリプトの下線部参照。中国人移民はアメリカの市民権を取得できなくなり、その結果、自国の学校を持つことを強要され、土地を所有することもできなくなった。

- It also prohibited all Chinese then living in the U.S. from being naturalized.
- all that comes with citizenship like the right to own land
- the Chinese were not allowed to send their children to regular American schools.

20. 解答 (D)

教授によると、移民の子どもたちにとって教育の重要性とは何か。

(A) アメリカについて学べるようにする。

(B) 市民権を得る手助けになる。

(C) 移民のコミュニティーを解体する。

(D) アメリカナイズされる手助けになる。

解説 トランスクリプトの下線部参照。

- education may be the most important part of becoming Americanized.

21. 解答 (B)

教授は移民のコミュニティーについてどう述べているか。

(A) アメリカナイズを阻んだ。

(B) 全ての移民にとって自然なものだった。

(C) 数世代後には必ず消滅した。

(D) アメリカ文化の重要な一部分である。

解説 トランスクリプトの下線部参照。

- all immigrant groups had their communities.
- It's normal, I suppose, to gather with others who share your language and customs.

22. 解答 (D)

講義の一部をもう一度聞きなさい。それから質問に答えなさい。

教授はなぜこのようなことを言うのか。

(A) 彼はこの学生に対して丁重に反対意見を述べたがっている。

(B) 彼は「アメリカナイズされる」ことを定義するつもりである。

(C) 彼は「アメリカナイズされる」ことをどう説明すればいいのか、実はわからない。

(D) 彼は直前に述べたことを強調したがっている。

解説 トランスクリプトの太字部参照。"that's just it" という表現は、相手の発言を受け、それを強調するときに使われる。そして、後には普通、その内容をさらにはっきりさせるような具体的な発話が続く。

Student B: So what happened to Chinese kids? Didn't they feel the same when they became Americanized?

Professor: **Well, that's just it. They couldn't become Americanized in the real sense of the word.**

トランスクリプト

Professor: So before we talk about the planets of our solar system and I tell you what facts we know and all that, I'd like you to remain a little skeptical about what you might hear me say.

Student A: Skeptical? You mean we shouldn't believe what you say?

Professor: Well, yes, I suppose you should be a little careful about what some people consider as facts, even about objects that are as relatively close to the Earth as the other planets.

Student A: But surely some things are known for certain. I mean, there have to be some facts that we can say are true, right?

Professor: Of course. I don't mean measurable data like, say, the time it takes to orbit the sun or something, but so-called facts that are based on interpreting data, because these kind of facts have been seen to fall apart on closer investigation.

Student B: **Can you give us an example?** (Q28)

Professor: **Actually, I'm about to do just that. I want to look at the object in space that we probably know most about, and one, in fact, that we have even visited. I'm talking about the moon** (下線 Q23：太字 Q28). Now you might think, because it's so close and because we've sent probes and people and come back with rocks from its surface and all, that we know just about all there is to know about the moon. But the fact is that the moon is still a big mystery to astronomers (Q23).

Student B: I don't know. How mysterious can it be? We know what it's made of and how the craters were formed, and as far as I can see, there's really not that much to know about it, is there?

Professor: Well, to some extent you're right. I suppose, at least in composition, it's a rather simple object. But it is still mysterious, especially in one significant aspect. We really have no idea of how it was formed (Q23：Q25).

Student A: I think I heard that it somehow came from the Earth.

Professor: Yeah, one theory has it that it formed with the Earth (Q26) but somehow became separated from it during formation and ended up being a satellite. Another is that it formed from smaller objects near the sun (Q26) and was later moved to its present location.

Student B: Sorry, but I'm not sure why a theory has to begin with the moon forming near the sun. Why not simply forming near the Earth? That seems more logical to me.

Professor: Well, it would seem more logical, except for one thing: there doesn't seem to be any hydrogen in the composition of the moon's rocks. This is strange because hydrogen is the most common element in the universe (Q25). So any theory has to somehow account for this fact. If the moon formed near the sun, then the heat of the sun may have "burned off" all the hydrogen. You're right. It seems strange that it would somehow move to the Earth, though.

Student A: But doesn't this fact that there's no hydrogen in the moon's composition make it unlikely that it formed from the Earth or along with the Earth? I mean, the Earth has plenty of hydrogen, right?

Professor: That's right. Every time you see water you are seeing some hydrogen. **So some scientists think that if the moon formed from, or with, the Earth then maybe somehow the hydrogen was driven away, say, by meteor impacts. But to be honest, this theory seems about as weak as the first one** (Q27).

Student B: So we don't have any theory that's perfect. Which theory do most scientists accept?

Professor: A variation on the second one — that the moon came from the Earth, but that it was formed when some huge object, something about the size of Mars, crashed into the Earth (Q24-2 : Q26). Now, this would have to have happened after the Earth's crust had formed (Q24-1) because the moon is similar in composition to the mantle of the Earth — that is, the top layer of the Earth. The iron cores of the two colliding objects would have melted together (Q24-3) and the lighter rocks of the mantle would have been blasted into space (Q24-4). Later they would have combined to form the moon as we now know it.

Student B: But how does this solve the problem of the lack of hydrogen (Q24-3) that you told us about?

Professor: Well, people who support this theory say that it was burned off during the massive explosion that occurred during the collision (Q24-3).

訳例

教　授：それで太陽系の惑星について話したり、それについて私たちが知っている事実などについて伝える前に、私が言うことについて少し懐疑的でいてほしいと思っています。

学生Ａ：懐疑的？　つまり、先生のおっしゃることを信じるべきではないという意味ですか。

教　授：ええ、そうです。皆さんは誰かが真実だと考えていること、ほかの惑星のように比較的地球に近い物体に関することについてでさえ、少し注意深くしたほうがいいと思います。

学生Ａ：でも、確かなものと思われている事柄もあります。つまり、真実だといえる事実もあるのではないでしょうか。

教　授：もちろんです。私は測定可能なデータ、例えば太陽や何かの周りを回るのにかかる時間などについて言っているわけではなく、データを解釈することによって導き出された、いわゆる事実について話しているのです。なぜかというと、これらの種類の事実はより周到な調査がなされたことにより崩壊してしまうことがあったからです。

学生Ｂ：例を挙げていただけませんか。

教　授：実は、そうしようと（例を挙げようと）していたところです。私たちがそのほとんどについて知っていると思われる宇宙の物体についてお話ししたいと思います。実際、訪れたことさえある物体です。月についてお話ししましょう。皆さんは、月はとても近いし、私たちは宇宙探査機や人を送り、その表面から岩石を持って帰ってきたりもしたので、月について知っておくべきことはすべて網羅していると考えているかもしれませんね。でも、実際には、月はいまだに天文学者にとって大きな謎なのです。

学生Ｂ：そうでしょうか。月がどれほど謎めいたものになれるのでしょうか。私たちは、それが何でできているか、そしてクレーターがどのように形成されたかは知っています。私が知っている限りにおいては、月にはそれほど多くの知っておくべきことはないのではないでしょうか。

教　授：そうですね。君の言うことは、ある程度は正しいですね。少なくともその構成においては、月は非常に単純な物体だと思います。しかし月は、特にひとつの重要な側面において、いまだに謎めいているのです。私たちは月がどのように形成されたかまったくわかっていないのです。

学生Ａ：なんらかの方法で地球からできたと聞いたように思いますが。

教　授：ええ、ある学説は、月は地球とともに形成されましたが、その形成過程においてどういうわけか地球から離れ、結局衛星になったとしています。もうひとつの学説は、月は太陽の近くの小さな物体から形成され、その後現在の位置に動かされたとしています。

学生Ｂ：すみません、その学説は、なぜ太陽の近くで月が形成されたというところから始めなければいけないのかわからないのですが。なぜ、単純に地球のそばで形成されたとしないのですか。そのほうがより論理にかなっているように思えるのですが。

教　授：そうですね、ひとつのことを除けば、そのほうがより論理にかなっているように思えますね。でも、月の岩石の構成物には水素がまったく含まれていないようなのです。水素は宇宙で

最も一般的な成分ですから、これはおかしなことですね。ですから、どんな学説でもなんらかの方法でこの事実を説明しなければならないのです。もし月が太陽のそばで形成されたのであれば、太陽の熱がすべての水素を「焼き払って」しまったのかもしれません。君の言い分は正しいですね。月がなぜか地球のほうへ動いたというのは奇妙に思えますから。

学生Ａ：でも、月の構成物の中に水素がないという事実があるということは、月が地球から形成されたとか地球とともに形成された可能性が低いということになりませんか。地球には多くの水素がありますよね。

教　授：そうですね。水を見るたびに水素を見ているわけです。ですから、ある科学者たちは、もし月が地球から形成されたか、地球とともに形成されたのであれば、なんらかの方法で、例えばいん石の衝撃によって、水素が取り除かれたのではないかと考えています。しかし、正直言ってこの学説は最初の学説と同じように弱いようです。

学生Ｂ：すると、完全な学説はないのですね。ほとんどの科学者はどの説を受け入れているのですか。

教　授：第2の学説を変化させたものです。月は地球からできたのですが、何か大きな物体が、火星ぐらいの大きさの何かが地球に衝突したときに形成されたという説です。でも、これは、地殻が形成された後に起こったのでなければいけません。なぜならば、月の構成は地球の最上層にあるマントルの構成に似ているからです。2つの衝突している物体の鉄心が互いに溶け合い、マントルの軽い岩石が宇宙へと飛ばされたのです。その後、岩石は合体して私たちが現在知っている月を形成したのです。

学生Ｂ：でも、それは、先生が話された水素の欠如の問題をどのように解決するのですか。

教　授：ええ、この説を支持する人たちは、衝突の間に起こったすさまじい爆発の間にそれが焼き払われたのだと言っています。

23. 解答 (C)

この話は主に何に関するものか。

(A) 太陽系の謎

(B) 月

(C) 月の形成

(D) 月の水素不足

解説　トランスクリプトの下線部参照。

- I want to look at the object in space that we probably know most about, and one, in fact, that we have even visited. I'm talking about the moon.
- But the fact is that the moon is still a big mystery to astronomers.
- But it is still mysterious, especially in one significant aspect. We really have no idea of how it was formed.

以上のような流れで、月の形成に関する問題を提起し、それについての講義を行っている。

24. 解答 （下の表を参照）

1. Earth's crust forms
2. A collision occurs
3. Hydrogen is driven away
4. Light material circling the Earth forms a new object

教授は、地球に大きな物体が衝突して月が形成された可能性について説明している。その出来事を時系列に並べ、考えを要約しなさい。

- 水素が取り除かれる
- 地球を周回する軽い物体は新たな物体を形成する
- 地殻が形成される
- 衝突が起こる

解説 トランスクリプトの下線部参照。

- this would have to have happened after the Earth's crust had formed (1)
- it was formed when some huge object, something about the size of Mars, crashed into the earth. (2)
- The iron cores of the two colliding objects would have melted together (3)
- how does this solve the problem of the lack of hydrogen (3)
- it was burned off during the massive explosion that occurred during the collision. (3)
- the lighter rocks of the mantle would have been blasted into space. (4)

25. 解答 (A)、(B)

講義の中で述べられた月の形成に関する 2 つの謎は何か。

解答を 2 つ選びなさい。

(A) なぜ月に水素がないのか

(B) 月がどのように形成されたか

(C) 太陽を周回していた物体がどのように集まって、月を形成したか

(D) 地球と大きな惑星の衝突がどのように月を形成したか

解説 トランスクリプトの下線部参照。

- But it is still mysterious, especially in one significant aspect. We really have no idea of how it was formed.
- there doesn't seem to be any hydrogen in the composition of the moon's rocks. This is strange because hydrogen is the most common element in the universe.

26. 解答 (B)、(C)、(E)

講義によると、月の形成に関するいくつかの理論とは何か。

解答を 3 つ選びなさい。

(A) 月はいん石によって形成された。

(B) 月は衝突によって形成された。

(C) 月は地球から形成された。

(D) 月は水素を含まない岩石から形成された。

(E) 月は太陽の近くで形成された。

解説 トランスクリプトの下線部参照。

- it formed with the Earth
- it formed from smaller objects near the sun
- it was formed when some huge object, something about the size of Mars, crashed into the Earth.

27. 解答 (B)

講義の一部をもう一度聞きなさい。それから質問に答えなさい。

教授はこのように発言することで、何を言おうとしているのか。

(A) 彼女はこの説を受け入れていない。

(B) 彼女は、それで月の形成に説明がつくかもしれないが、あまりうまい説明とは言えないと考えている。

(C) 彼女は、自分が取り上げた2つの説のうち、これが最も弱いと考えている。

(D) 彼女は、どの説も月の形成について説明できないと考えている。

解説 太字のトランスクリプトの下線部参照。

🎧 That's right. Every time you see water you are seeing some hydrogen. **So some scientists think that if the moon formed from, or with, the earth then maybe somehow the hydrogen was driven away, say, by meteor impacts. But to be honest, <u>this theory seems about as weak as the first one.</u>**

28. 解答 (A)

講義の一部をもう一度聞きなさい。それから質問に答えなさい。

このやり取りから教授について何が推測できるか。

(A) 教授は月の形成について話すつもりだった。

(B) 教授は良い例を思いついたところだ。

(C) 教授は、この学生が彼女の話に割って入ってきたことを腹立たしく思っている。

(D) 教授は、この学生がこの質問をしたことを喜んでいる。

解説 トランスクリプトの太字部分参照。あとに続く教授と学生とのやりとりを聞けば、ここでの教授の発言の意図がいっそうはっきりする。また、下線部からも、教授の計画性が伺える。

🎧
- Student B: **Can you give us an example?**
- Professor: **<u>Actually, I'm about to do just that.</u> I want to look at the object in space that we probably know most about, and one, in fact, that we have even visited. I'm talking about the moon.**

Speaking Section　解答・解説

1. 比較選択に関する問題

［15 秒で準備して、45 秒話す］

質問の訳

1 年中、気候が同じ場所に住むことを好む人と、年に数回気候が変わる場所に住む
ほうがいいと思う人がいる。あなたはどちらをより好むか。自分の考えを裏付ける例
を挙げなさい。

模範解答 （一例）

mp3
13

　　Well, I don't know why anyone would want the same climate or weather all
year round. Maybe it's because I come from a place that has four seasons and
that's what I'm used to. But I've been to tropical countries where the weather
is generally the same no matter what the season is. Yeah, it's nice for a while.
But I think that somewhere around Christmas time I would probably be
wondering where the snow was and I would get kind of tired of the hot sun. It's
true that life is easier in such countries. I mean, for one thing you don't need
such a wide variety of clothes to go with all the seasons. You could probably
save a lot of money on clothes. But I like the winter and winter sports like
skiing and skating and, anyway, I think a tough climate can make you tougher
as a person.

訳例

　　そうですね、なぜ 1 年を通じて同じ気候や天候を望む人がいるのかわかりません。もしや
私が四季のある場所の出身で、それに慣れているからかもしれません。とはいえ、私は熱帯
の国々に行ったこともあります。そこでは季節が何であれ、おおむね気候が同じです。まあ、
短期間ならそれも快適です。でも、クリスマスの前後になると、雪はどこに降っているのか
と思ったり、暑い日差しにいささかうんざりしたり、ということになるでしょう。確かに、
そうした国のほうが生活は楽です。つまり、例えば、あらゆる季節に備えてさまざまな衣類
をそろえる必要はありません。おそらく衣服にかかるお金をかなり節約できるでしょう。で
も、私は冬が好きですし、スキーやスケートといった冬のスポーツも好きです。それに、い
ずれにせよ、厳しい気候の中にいると人はより強くなるものだと思います。

　本問は「一年中変わらない同じ気候の地に住むのと、何回か季節が変わる地に住むのと、どちらが好きか」いう問題である。時間がごく短いので、聞かれていることに忠実に解答を組み立てること。まず設問に答える形で自分の考えを述べ、それをサポートする理由をつけていくとよい。具体例を挙げるときは、解答例にあるように熱帯（tropical）地域の長所を挙げ、それに反駁していく方法で「四季があったほうがいい」という自分の見解をサポートするとよい。時間が許せば、最後に結論を述べて締めくくる。また、短いスピーチに簡潔に内容を盛り込むためにも、つなぎ言葉は大切である。解答例ではその目的に合わせて、Well、it's because、But、Yeah、It's true that、I mean、anyway、I think などが使われている。

45 秒の構成

設問に対する解答
　　※解答例では「1 年中同じ季節がいいなんていう人がいるのだろうか」、つまり話し手は「季節が変わったほうがいい」と言っている。
自分の意見をサポートする理由
具体例
 ・ 長所
 ・ 反駁
結論

話の組み立て方

① いちばん大きな概念（設問に対する解答　季節が変わったほうがいいかどうか）

Well, I don't know why anyone would want the same climate or weather all year round.

② 自己の見解をサポートする理由：

Maybe it's because I come from a place that has four seasons and that's what I'm used to.

③ 自分の見解をサポートする理由と経験を使った具体例：

But I've been to tropical countries where the weather is generally the same no matter what the season is.

長所　Yeah, it's nice for a while.

反駁　But I think that somewhere around Christmas time I would probably be wondering where the snow was and I would get kind of tired of the hot sun.

長所　It's true that life is easier in such countries. I mean, for one thing you don't need such a wide variety of clothes to go with all the seasons. You could probably save a lot of money on clothes.

反駁　But I like the winter and winter sports like skiing and skating and, anyway,

④ 結論：

I think a tough climate can make you tougher as a person.

2. 読む・聴く・話す問題
——掲示板に貼られた通知の一部分
［30秒で準備して、60秒話す］

質問の訳

質問：

男性が試験中のピーターの行動について説明している。男性は教授の行動が正当なものだったと思っているか。彼はなぜピーターがこのようなことを行ったと考えているか。

模範解答（一例）

mp3
14

　　The man doesn't think that the teacher was wrong to tear up the exam because the university policy is clear that cheating will not be tolerated and that the teacher can do what he or she wants when they catch someone cheating. Moreover, the man believes that Peter was cheating on the exam. In fact, he was sitting near Peter and he saw the other student trying to copy from Peter's paper. In addition, the other student seemed to expect that Peter would let him copy from his paper. As for the reasons, the man thinks that Peter needed money so he allowed the other student to copy from him. Besides, he probably never expected that he would get caught and thought that there was little risk.

訳例

　　男性は、教員が試験用紙を破ったことを間違いだとは考えていません。というのも、大学の方針は明確で、不正行為が許されることはなく、誰かの不正行為を見つけた教員は自分の思うとおりの対応を取れるからです。しかも、男性はピーターが試験で不正を行ったと思っています。実際のところ、彼はピーターの近くに座っており、別の学生がピーターの答案用紙を写そうとしているところを目撃しました。さらに、その学生はピーターが答案用紙を写させてくれることを期待しているように見えました。その理由について男性が考えているのは、ピーターはお金を必要としていたので、その学生に自分の答案を写させた、ということです。そのうえ、おそらく彼は、よもや捕まるとは思っておらず、ほとんどリスクがないと思い込んでいたのでしょう。

ポイント

　　リーディング、リスニングを終えた後、設問に対して30秒で解（返答）をまとめ、60秒（1分）で話す問題。まず、設問に対する解答を述べ、それをサポートする理

由をつけていくという英語式の答え方がよい。答えるときは、読んだことや聴いたことをそのままの文章で言うのではなく、自分なりの言葉に置き換えて話すことが大切だ。具体的には、最初の質問、Does the man think that the professor's actions were justified? に答えてから、それをサポートしている次の質問、Why does he think Peter did this? の答えとなる理由を述べていく（下線部参照）。

Does the man think that the professor's actions were justified?

The man doesn't think that the teacher was wrong to tear up the exam because the university policy is clear that cheating will not be tolerated and that the teacher can do what he or she wants when they catch someone cheating.

　以下の3文は、不正行為の事実を挙げ、なぜ教師の行為は正当であるかを具体的に説明している。

Moreover, the man believes that Peter was cheating on the exam. In fact, he was sitting near Peter and he saw the other student trying to copy from Peter's paper. In addition, the other student seemed to expect that Peter would let him copy from his paper.

Why does he think Peter did this?

As for the reasons, the man thinks that Peter needed money so he allowed the other student to copy from him. Besides, he probably never expected that he would get caught and thought that there was little risk.

読むテクスト

Standards of Conduct

　No matter what the reason, any student conduct that is academically dishonest or shows a lack of academic integrity or trustworthiness, or unfairly attempts to use the intellectual rights of others is prohibited （解答では the university policy is clear that cheating will not be tolerated）. Such conduct includes:

A. Cheating on Exams and Other Assignments

　Cheating is the unauthorized use or attempted use of materials, information, study aids or collaboration in order to pass an examination or other academic exercise. It is the responsibility of the student to consult with

111

the professor if in doubt about what may constitute unethical behavior. It is very important to emphasize that if there is any doubt in a student's mind about what constitutes proper or improper conduct, the student must be certain to clarify this with the professor prior to taking any exam. Cheating or assisting another student in cheating in connection with an examination or assignment is academically unacceptable（本問で問題となっている行為）. Punishment for such offenses is generally at the discretion of the professor（解答では *the teacher can do what he or she wants when they catch someone cheating.*）and may include automatic failure of the examination or expulsion from the course.

訳例

行動規範

　どのような理由があろうとも、学生による、学究的に不誠実な、または学究的な品位や信用性を欠く行い、または他人の知的所有権を利用した不公正な企ては禁止されている。このような行いとは以下を含む：

A.　試験またはそのほかの課題における不正行為

　不正行為とは、試験やそのほかの学究的課題に合格するために、許可なく教材、情報、参考書を使用したり、使用しようと計画したり、ほかの学生と協力したりすることである。何が反倫理的行動を構成するか確かでない場合は、学生は教授に相談する義務を負う。何が適切で何が不適切な行いを構成するか確かでない場合は、学生は試験を受ける前に教授に確認しなければならないことを強調しておく。試験や課題において不正を行ったり、ほかの学生の不正行為を助けたりすることは学究的に許されない。このような違反行為に対する処罰は通常教授の判断に委ねられるが、試験の自動的不合格またはコースからの除籍をも包括している可能性がある。

mp3 08

聴くテクスト

Student A: Hey, did you hear what happened to Peter at the geology midterm yesterday?

Student B: Peter? No, what?

Student A: The professor tore up his exam for cheating!

Student B: What! Impossible. Peter's a good student and he certainly has no trouble with geology.

Student A: Maybe, but the professor thought he was letting another student copy from his paper. In any event, it's still cheating and you know how strict they are about that here.

Student B: Yes, I know but doesn't the professor have to prove this before he just tears up the exam? I mean, Peter could have simply been unaware that the other student was trying to look at his paper.

Student A: Well, maybe, but I really don't think so.

Student B: Why not?

Student A: Well, I was sitting near Peter at the exam when all this happened. All through the exam the other student, who was sitting behind him, kept telling him to move the paper or move his arm so he could see the answers better. You know, like it had all been arranged before the exam （解答では *Moreover, the man believes that Peter was cheating on the exam. In fact, he was sitting near Peter and he saw the other student trying to copy from Peter's paper. In addition, the other student seemed to expect that Peter would let him copy from his paper*）.

Student B: Really? But I don't understand. Why would he agree to do something so stupid and risk getting caught?

Student A: Well, I'm not sure he thought there was much risk first of all. But he could have done it for the money （解答では *Besides, he probably never expected that he would get caught and thought that there was little risk*）. I'm sure the other student would have paid at least fifty dollars to look at his paper. I know for a fact that Peter is a little low on cash right now and may have thought this would be a pretty good way to earn some money （解答では *the man thinks that Peter needed money so he allowed the other student to copy from him*）. I doubt if he ever thought he would get caught （解答では *Besides, he probably never expected that he would get caught and thought that there was little risk*）.

Student B: Man, that's too bad. So what's going to happen to him now?

Student A: Well, he's already got a zero on the midterm so he's in danger of failing the whole course unless he works awfully hard.

Student B: Well, it's a hard way to learn a lesson.

訳例

学生A： やあ、昨日、地質学の中間試験でピーターに何があったか聞いた？

学生B： ピーター？　ううん、どうしたの？

学生A： 教授が不正行為としてピーターの試験（答案用紙）を破ったんだ！

学生B：何ですって！　信じられない。ピーターはきちんとした学生だし、地質学ではまったく問題なかったはずよ。

学生A：たぶんね。でも教授はピーターがほかの学生に自分の答案用紙を写させていたと思ったんだ。とにかく、それは結局不正行為だし、ここでは不正行為に関してどんなに厳しいか知っているだろう。

学生B：ええ、知っているわ。でも、教授はただ試験（答案用紙）を破るのではなく、その前に、不正行為があったと証明しなければいけないんじゃない？　つまり、ピーターはほかの学生が彼の答案用紙を見ようとしていることに気づかなかっただけかもしれないでしょう。

学生A：ううん、たぶんね。でも、僕にはちょっとそうは思えないんだ。

学生B：どうして？

学生A：ううん、試験でこのことが起こったとき、僕はピーターの近くに座っていたんだよ。それで、試験中ずっと、ピーターの後ろに座っていた学生が、答えがもっとよく見えるように、ピーターの答案用紙をずらせとか腕を動かせと言い続けていたんだ。まるで試験の前に全部計画されていたみたいにね。

学生B：本当？　でも、わからないわ。どうして彼は捕まる危険を冒してそんなばかなことをするのに同意したの？

学生A：さあ、そもそも彼が、その行為が、それほど危険なことだと思っていたかどうかわからないよ。でも、お金のためにやったのかもしれないね。その学生はピーターの答案用紙を見せてもらうのに少なくとも50ドル払ったのは確かだと思うよ。ピーターが今お金に困っているのは確かだから、いくらかのお金を稼ぐのにはいい方法だと思ったのかもしれないし。自分がまさか捕まるとは思わなかったんじゃないかな。

学生B：ひどいわね。これから彼はどうなるの？

学生A：いやあ、すでに中間試験で0点を取ってしまったんだから、猛烈に勉強しない限りこのコースそのものに落第するかもしれないね。

学生B：まあ、苦い思いをして教訓を学ぶってことね。

重要語句

- □ academic 学究的な、学問的な
- □ academically 学究的に、学問的に
- □ aid 援助、補助（教材）
- □ arrange 用意する
- □ assignment 宿題
- □ attempted 未遂の、計画された
- □ awfully とても、ひどく、恐ろしく
- □ bulletin board 掲示板、連絡板
- □ cheating カンニング、不正行為
- □ clarify 明確にする
- □ collaboration 協力、共同制作
- □ constitute 構成する
- □ discretion 思慮、判断力
- □ dishonest 不誠実な、不正の
- □ exercise 課題
- □ expulsion 追放、除籍
- □ first of all 第一に、何よりも
- □ for a fact 確かに、事実として
- □ geology 地質学
- □ in any event いずれにしても、とにかく
- □ in connection with ... ～に関連して
- □ integrity 誠実、高潔、品位
- □ intellectual 知的な、知力の
- □ material 資料、教材
- □ notice 通知
- □ offense 違反、違法
- □ portion 一部分
- □ prohibit 禁ずる、禁止する
- □ punishment 処罰、刑罰
- □ Standards of Conduct 行動規範
- □ tear up ... ～を引き裂く、ビリビリ裂く
- □ trustworthiness 信用性、信頼性
- □ unacceptable 受け入れられない、許されない
- □ unauthorized 権限のない、未許可の、無断の
- □ unaware 気づかない、知らない
- □ unethical behavior 反倫理的な行動
- □ unfairly 不当に

114

3. 読む・聴く・話す問題
——歴史学（レビットタウンについて）
[30秒で準備して、60秒話す]

質問の訳

質問：
当時の社会情勢がレビットタウンの発展をどのように促したかを説明しなさい。レビットが顧客の要望にどう応えたか説明しなさい。

模範解答 （一例）

mp3
15

When the war was over, many people returned home with the goal of starting families. But they did not want to live in conditions similar to those in which they had grown up. Since many of these people were the sons and daughters of immigrants, they had mainly grown up in cities. Now, they wanted to live in houses away from the city. The problem was that there were not many affordable houses available away from the city.

William Levitt recognized this need and figured out a way to meet it. He was able to build low-cost housing for these new families. He was able to keep the prices low by using production methods similar to Henry Ford's automobile assembly line. Each team of workers was required to do only one specific job. By doing this, he kept prices down. Even though this technique made all the houses look the same, it did not stop many of these new families from buying them and moving to Levittown.

訳例

　戦争が終わると、多くの人が故郷に戻り、ゆくゆくは家庭を持とうと考えました。しかし、彼らは自分が育ったのと同様の環境で暮らすことを望みませんでした。そうした人々の多くは移民の子女だったので、主に都市部で育ちましたが、今や彼らは都会から離れた家に住むことを望んだのです。問題は、都会から離れると、手頃な価格の住宅があまり多くないことでした。
　ウィリアム・レビットはこの需要に気づき、それを満たす方法を考え出しました。彼は、こうした新しい家庭のために低価格の住宅を建てることを可能にしたのです。彼は、ヘンリー・フォードの自動車組み立てラインを模した生産方法によって、価格を低く抑えることができました。労働者の各チームが特定の作業を一つだけ行いました。こうすることで、彼は低価格を維持したのです。この手法によってあらゆる住宅の外観は同じになりましたが、それでもこうした新しい世帯の多くが家を購入し、レビットタウンに移住しました。

　同じく、リーディング、リスニングに続いて設問を読み、解（返答）を30秒でまとめ、60秒で話す問題だ。本問では、当時の人々の要望や背景、社会状況なども含め、当時の社会の抱えていた問題（social conditions）を提起することにより、最初の設問である how the social conditions of the time encouraged the development of Levittown に答えることができる。ここでは、歴史的出来事の流れに沿って生じた結果が、当時の社会が抱えていた問題となるので、前半の質問に答えるときは時間の流れに沿って話していくとよい。問題提起が終わったら、いかにして Levitt が彼の顧客の要望に応えたのか（how Levitt managed to meet the needs of his customers）を述べる。結論からそれぞれの詳細へ（general → specific）という話の枠組みを作り、いちばん先に言いたいことを持ってくる。後半部分は大きな概念から詳細へと展開されている。

話の組み立て方

※ 前半は how the social conditions of the time encouraged the development of Levittown に対する解。

① トピックの提起（歴史的経過）：
When the war was over, many people returned home with the goal of starting families.

② 当時の人々の要望や背景：
But they did not want to live in conditions similar to those in which they had grown up. Since many of these people were the sons and daughters of immigrants, they had mainly grown up in cities. Now, they wanted to live in houses away from the city.

③ 当時の社会の抱えていた問題：
The problem was that there were not many affordable houses available away from the city.

※ 後半は how Levitt managed to meet the needs of his customers に対する解。

④ トピックの提起（結論）：
William Levitt recognized this need and figured out a way to meet it. He was

able to build low-cost housing for these new families.

⑤ いかにして顧客の要望に応えたのか（下線部は⑥に関連する内容）：

He was able to keep the prices low by using production methods similar to Henry Ford's automobile assembly line.

⑥ 具体例：

Each team of workers was required to do only one specific job.

⑦ まとめ：

By doing this, he kept prices down. Even though this technique made all the houses look the same, it did not stop many of these new families from buying them and moving to Levittown.

読むテクスト

　Levittown was the first successful suburban housing development in the United States. It was successful because it enabled ordinary, working class people to own homes in the suburbs （解答では *William Levitt recognized this need and figured out a way to meet it. He was able to build low-cost housing for these new families*）.

　After the Second World War, many young people wanted to start a new life. Most were tired of living in small apartments in crowded cities. They wanted a better quality of life in which to raise their new families. At that time, however, few young families could afford the limited number of such housing available （after から available をまとめると解答前半のパラグラフとなる）. William Levitt understood the problem and developed a plan to build affordable housing for these people. By 1951, he had built over 15,000 houses using an assembly-line style of production to keep the prices down （解答では *William Levitt recognized this need and figured out a way to meet it. He was able to build low-cost housing for these new families*）.

訳例

　レビットタウンはアメリカ合衆国で初めて成功した郊外型住宅開発であった。これが成功したのは、普通の労働者階級の人々が郊外に自分の家を持つことを可能にしたからである。

　第二次世界大戦後、多くの若者が新しい生活を始めたがっていた。彼らの多くは、込み合った都市の小さなアパートに住むことにうんざりしていた。彼らは、新たな家族をつくるためにより質の高い生活を求めていた。しかし、当時、限られた数しか存在しないそのような住

117

居を手に入れられる若い家族はほとんどいなかった。ウィリアム・レビットはその問題を理解しており、このような人々のために手ごろな価格の住居を建設する計画を立てた。1951年までに、彼は価格を抑えるための組み立てライン形式の製造法を使用し、1万5000戸以上の住居を建てた。

聴くテクスト

So we had all these people coming back from the war and a lot of them were getting married and having kids（解答では *When the war was over, many people returned home with the goal of starting families*). This, in fact, was the origin of the Baby Boom generation. Now, a lot of these people had been raised in cities. They were mainly the sons and daughters of immigrants and, generally, that's where new immigrants lived. But they wanted something different for their families（解答では *But they did not want to live in conditions similar to those in which they had grown up. Since many of these people were the sons and daughters of immigrants, they had mainly grown up in cities*). Ideally, they wanted a place in the country or at least somewhere away from the city（解答では*Now, they wanted to live in houses away from the city*). But, at this time there simply weren't enough houses available to meet the demand（解答では*The problem was that there were not many affordable houses available away from the city*).

Well, as usual, whenever there is a demand in business, someone will figure out a way to supply it, and that man was William Levitt（解答では*William Levitt recognized this need and figured out a way to meet it*). He bought an old potato farm on Long Island, not too far from New York City, and began to build houses; lots of houses. And he built them cheaply（解答では *He was able to build low-cost housing for these new families*).

And how did he manage this? Well, he looked at how Henry Ford had built automobiles on the assembly line. You know, one guy would work all day doing one job. Anyway, he applied this idea to building houses. One team would put in the foundation, another the frame, the third the plumbing and so on. The main point is he kept the prices down（解答では *He was able to keep the prices low by using production methods similar to Henry Ford's automobile assembly line. Each team of workers was required to do only one specific job. By doing this, he kept prices down*). True, he made them all look the same, but they were affordable. And what's more important, the people bought them as fast as he could build them（解答では*Even though this technique made all the houses look the same, it did not stop many of these new families from buying them and moving to Levittown*）.

訳例

　このように戦争から多くの人々が帰って来て、彼らの多くは結婚し、子どもを持ちました。実際これがベビーブーム世代の原点となったのです。これらの人々の多くは都市で育てられました。彼らは主に移民の息子や娘で、通常、新たな移民が住んだのは都市だったのです。しかし彼らは、自分たちの家族のために何か違うものを求めていました。理想的には、彼らは田舎に、もしくは少なくとも都市から離れたどこかに場所を求めていました。しかし、当時この要求に見合った住居は十分になかったのです。

　まあ、事業の需要があるとき、常に誰かがそれを満たす方法を見つけるものです。この場合は、それがウィリアム・レビットでした。彼はニューヨーク市からそう遠くないロングアイランドにある古いジャガイモの農地を買い、そこに家をたくさん建て始めました。しかも、安く建てたのです。

　彼はどのようにこれを成し遂げたのでしょうか。そうです、彼はヘンリー・フォードが組み立てラインで自動車を造ったのを見習ったのです。ご存じのように、組み立てラインを使えば、ひとりの人は一日中同じことをして働いていればいいのです。とにかく、彼はこのアイデアを家の建設に応用しました。ひとつのチームが土台を、もうひとつは骨組みを、3つ目は、配管工事などを請け負ったのです。重要な点は、彼が価格を抑えたということです。これらの家は、見た目はすべて同じだったのですが、手ごろな価格でした。そしてもっと重要なことは、レビットがこのような家を造るやいなや、人々がそれを買ったということです。

重要語句

□ afford 〜を持つだけの余裕がある、〜を買うことができる	□ immigrant 移民、移住者
	□ ordinary 普通の、並の
□ affordable 手ごろな価格の	□ origin 原点、源
□ apply 応用する、利用する	□ plumbing 配管（工事）
□ assembly 組み立て	□ suburban 郊外の
□ demand 需要	□ supply 供給する、（需要を）満たす
□ generation 世代	□ working class 労働者階級
□ ideally 理想的に	

4. 聴く・話す問題
——心理学（インテリジェンス）
［20秒で準備して、60秒話す］

質問の訳

質問：

講義の中のポイントと例を用いて、知能を測定する上での問題点とIQテストの限界について説明しなさい。

模範解答（一例）

The professor begins by stating how difficult intelligence is to define. This is because intelligence is a concept we understand intuitively but have problems putting into words.

An IQ test tries to define intelligence by means of a test score, but this may only measure part of a person's intelligence. Some people say that the test focuses on logical and mathematical intelligence and not on other types of intelligence. The professor gives an example of a person with great musical ability. This person may not do well on an IQ test, but most people would still agree that he or she is intelligent, just in a different way.

The professor also says that this may be because Western culture values logical and mathematical intelligence. There may be other cultures that value other parts of intelligence more. If this is true, then the IQ test could be biased against any culture that doesn't share the value of mathematical or logical intelligence.

訳例

　教授はまず、知性を定義することがいかに難しいかを述べることから始めました。これは、知性が直感的に理解できる概念ではあるものの、言葉で表現するのが難しいからです。

　IQテストでは試験のスコアによって知性を定義しようとしますが、これでは人の知性の一部しか測定できない可能性があります。人によっては、このテストは論理や数学的な知能に的を絞っており、他の種類の知性には焦点を当てていないと言います。教授は、優れた音楽的能力を持つ人の例を挙げました。この人物はIQテストの成績では振るわないかもしれません。しかし、大半の人が、別の点においては依然として知性的であることに賛同するでしょう。

　教授は、こうも述べています。これは西洋文化が論理や数学的な知性に価値を置いているからかもしれないのだと。他の部分の知性をより重視する別の文化もあるかもしれません。

もし、それが事実なら、IQ テストは、数学的あるいは論理的な知性に価値を置かない文化を、低く見積もっている可能性があるのです。

ポイント

　本問は要約をすることにより、解答を組み立てていく問題。聴いた内容を自分の言葉に置き換えながら、設問に対する答えを述べ、続けてそれをサポートする理由を伝える。このセクションで何度も登場するように、それが英語式の話の展開のさせ方である。講義の構成を考えると、まず講義のテーマと問題提起を行い、それをサポートする理由を述べるという順になる。そして intelligence を測定するものとして、サブ・トピックである IQ テストが出てくる。その後、IQ テストの持つ問題点を提起し、具体例などを用いてそれをサポートしていく。

60 秒の構成

講義のテーマ（メイン・トピック）
それをサポートする理由
IQ テストの役目とその欠陥（サブ・トピック）
それをサポートする一般例 (1)
具体例
一般例 (2)
欠陥の発展と締めくくり

話の組み立て方

① 講義のテーマ（メイン・トピック）：

The professor begins by stating how difficult intelligence is to define.

② それをサポートする理由：

This is because intelligence is a concept we understand intuitively but have problems putting into words.

③ IQ テスト（サブ・トピック）の役目：

An IQ test tries to define intelligence by means of a test score,

④ IQ テスト（サブ・トピック）の欠陥：

but this may only measure part of a person's intelligence.

⑤ IQ テストの欠陥をサポートする一般例（1）：

Some people say that the test focuses on logical and mathematical intelligence and not on other types of intelligence.

⑥ IQ テストの欠陥をサポートする具体例：

The professor gives an example of a person with great musical ability. This person may not do well on an IQ test, but most people would still agree that he or she is intelligent, just in a different way.

⑦ 一般例（2）：

The professor also says that this may be because Western culture values logical and mathematical intelligence. There may be other cultures that value other parts of intelligence more.

⑧ 締めくくり：

If this is true, then the IQ test could be biased against any culture that doesn't share the value of mathematical or logical intelligence.

聴くテクスト

mp3
11

Now, if I asked all of you to write down your own definition of intelligence, we would probably find that each of you wrote something a little different. This is normal when we try to define something that we intuitively understand. We know what it is, but putting it in words can be a problem. And not only for you. Scientists have been working on this same definition for many years.

（ここまでを要約すると、*The professor begins by stating how difficult intelligence is to define. This is because intelligence is a concept we understand intuitively but have problems putting into words.* となる）

Well, you've all heard of the IQ test. And although the IQ test is the standard accepted measure of intelligence, it has often come under attack by critics who say that it paints an incomplete picture. These critics point to the fact that even though it may measure, with some accuracy, a form of intelligence related to logic and mathematical skills, the test ignores skills that lead to creativity, which may also be a part of intelligent behavior. Why should a person of great musical ability, for example, be considered any less intelligent than a person of great mathematical ability? Yet, this could happen on an IQ test because the test is sort of weighted to favor the skills of logical thinking and mathematical ability.

（ここまでを要約すると、*An IQ test tries to define intelligence by means of a test score, but this may only measure part of a person's intelligence. Some people say that the test focuses on logical and mathematical intelligence and not on other types of intelligence. The professor gives an example of a person with great musical ability. This person may not do well on an IQ test, but most people would still agree that he or she is intelligent, just in a different way.* となる）

These critics say, this weighting of intelligence towards the mathematical perspective is a result of cultural values. I mean, if a culture values mathematical skills, then having them seems to be a mark of intelligence in that culture. But mathematical skills may be of less importance in some cultures and would not be necessarily considered as having the greatest intellectual value. The IQ test, they argue, could favor certain cultures over others and, because of this, may give only a limited idea of true intelligence. （最後の部分を要約すると、*The professor also says that this may be because Western culture values logical and mathematical intelligence. There may be other cultures that value other parts of intelligence more. If this is true, then the IQ test could be biased against any culture that doesn't share the value of mathematical or logical intelligence.* となる）

訳例

　さて、皆さんに知性についての自分の定義を書くようにと頼んだら、たぶんそれぞれが少しずつ異なったことを書くと思います。これは、私たちが直観的に理解している何かを定義しようとするときによくあることです。私たちはそれが何であるか知っているのですが、それを言葉にすると問題が生じることがあるのです。このようなケースは、皆さんだけではありません。科学者たちも知性の定義について長い間研究し続けているのです。

　皆さんはIQテストについて聞いたことがありますね。IQテストは知性を測る標準的な方法として受け入れられていますが、不完全なものとしてしばしば批評家たちに批判されてきました。これらの批評家たちは、IQテストは論理や数学的技能に関する知性についてはある程度正確に測定するかもしれないが、同じように知的な行為の一部であるかもしれない創造性につながる力を無視しているという事実を指摘します。例えば、なぜ素晴らしい音楽的能力を持つ人が、素晴らしい数学的能力を持つ人より知性が劣ると考えられなければいけないのでしょうか。ところが、IQテストではこのようなことが起こり得るのです。このテストは論理的思考力や数学的能力に関する力を幾分重視しているからです。

　批評家たちは、知性に数学的能力を重視することは、文化価値観の影響であると言っています。つまり、ある文化が数学的技能に価値を置いているとすれば、それを持っていることはその文化においては知性の象徴となるかもしれません。しかし、別の文化においては、数学的技能はそれほど重要ではないかもしれませんし、数学的技能がそれほど大きな知的価値を持っていると考えられる必要もないかもしれないのです。批評家たちは、IQテストは、ほかの文化よりもある文化に有利に働く可能性があり、このため、本当の知性を限定的に測

123

定してしまうのではないかと主張しています。

重要語句

□ argue 議論する、論じる	□ incomplete 不完全な
□ behavior 行動、行為	□ intelligence 知能、知性
□ come under attack 非難の的になる、攻撃の的	□ intuitively 直観的に、本能的に
になる	□ logical thinking 論理的思考
□ critics 批評家、評論家	□ mathematical 数学的、数学の
□ cultural values 文化的価値観	□ normal 通常の、普通の
□ definition 定義	□ perspective 考え方、観点

Writing Section　解答・解説

1. 読む・聴く・書く問題（20分で書き上げるエッセイ）
──生物学の講義（生物学における共生）

指示文・質問の訳

指示文：

このタスクでは、3分間でパッセージを読みます。その後、読み終えた文章の話題に関する講義の一部を聞きます。講義の後、20分間で解答を考え、作成します。理想的な解答は150から225語です。

次のパッセージを読みなさい。

リスニング：

では、読み終えた共生という話題に関する講義の一部を聞きなさい。講義を聞きながらメモを取ることができます。

では、質問に答えなさい。メモを使って解答できます。

質問：

相利共生から寄生まで、共生の種類について説明しなさい。アリはどのように共生を利用し、生活を改善しているのか。教授の相利共生の定義が読んだ内容とどう異なるのか説明しなさい。

模範解答（一例）

　　Symbiosis is a relationship between plants and plants, animals and plants, or animals and animals in which both members in the relationship receive some benefit. Often one member of the relationship receives more benefit than the other. However, in cases where such a relationship is perfectly balanced, it is called mutualism. The opposite of mutualism is parasitism. In such a relationship, one member actually injures or eventually even kills the other member. Most symbiotic relationships are on a spectrum somewhere between these two extremes.

There are many examples of symbiosis in nature, but one of the best is the relationship that exists between ants and aphids. Ants have found that aphids produce a substance called honeydew, which can be used as food by the ants. The ants, therefore, take care of the aphids as if they were herd animals. Many insects would like to eat the aphids but they are stopped by the ants. Therefore, the aphids receive safety while the ants get a source of food. This symbiosis is so well balanced that it could be called mutualism.

Although the reading claims that pure mutualism is rare, the professor disagrees. He discusses the ant which seems to display at least two mutual relationships. He says the concept of mutualism may be open to interpretation.

訳例

　共生とは、植物同士、動物と植物、または動物同士の関係のことで、その関係において両者が利益を享受する。往々にして、この関係にある種のうちの一方が、他方よりも多くの利益を得る。しかし、このような関係のバランスが完璧に取れている場合、それは相利共生と呼ばれる。相利共生の反対は寄生である。そのような関係においては、一方が他方を傷つけるか、最終的には殺してしまうこともある。共生関係のほとんどは、この両極の間のどこかに位置づけられる。

　自然界には共生の例がたくさんあるが、最良の例の一つはアリとアブラムシの間に見られる関係だ。アリには、アブラムシが蜜と呼ばれる物質を分泌し、それが自分の食料になり得ることがわかっている。だから、アリはアブラムシを、まるで家畜であるかのように世話する。多くの昆虫がアブラムシを捕食したがるが、アリによって阻止されてしまう。その結果、アブラムシは安全を手に入れ、一方でアリは食料源を得るのだ。この共生関係は実にバランスが取れているので、相利共生と呼べる。

　リーディングパッセージには、純粋な相利共生はまれだと書かれているが、教授は同意していない。彼は、少なくとも2つの相互関係を示していると思われるアリについて論じている。彼によると、相利共生にはさまざまな解釈が可能だという。

ポイント

　本セクションは、まず3分で与えられたトピックについて読み、次に読んだことについての講義を聴く。その後双方に基づいた設問に対し、20分で構想をまとめて書き上げるというものである。要求される単語数は150～225語と少ないので、質問に答える形で内容を簡潔に組み立てることだ。また、読んだり聞いたりしたことを自分の言葉で書き換えることはもとより、アカデミック・ライティングの基本を踏まえて書くことも大切である。つまり解答を書く際、最初のパラグラフでは一般的概念を書いてから、トピック・センテンスを書き、それをサポートする具体例などを書くという順

番で設問に答えていくことだ。具体的な書き方としては、まず最初の設問、Explain the variations of symbiosis from mutualism to parasitism. に答えてから、例として使われているアリについて書くことにより、How does the ant use symbiosis to improve its life? に答える。そして最後に、Discuss how the professor's view of mutualism differs from that of the reading. に答える。

エッセイの組み立て方　※🅠は設問からの引用です。

🅠 **Explain the variations of symbiosis from mutualism to parasitism.**

① 大きな概念である "symbiosis" の定義（一般的概念）：

Symbiosis is a relationship between plants and plants, animals and plants, or animals and animals in which both members in the relationship receive some benefit.

② 解答に関するトピック提起（mutualism と parasitism の相違を話すときに必要な一般概念）：

Often one member of the relationship receives more benefit than the other.

mutualism：However, in cases where such a relationship is perfectly balanced, it is called mutualism.

parasitism：The opposite of mutualism is parasitism.

③ parasitism をさらに詳しく説明：

In such a relationship, one member actually injures or eventually even kills the other member.

④ 簡単なまとめ：

Most symbiotic relationships are on a spectrum somewhere between these two extremes.

🅠 **How does the ant use symbiosis to improve its life?**

⑤ 解答に関するトピック提起：

There are many examples of symbiosis in nature, but one of the best is the relationship that exists between ants and aphids.

⑥ アリについて（アリがどのように symbiosis を使うかを書くことにより設問に答えている）：

Ants have found that aphids produce a substance called honeydew, which can be used as food by the ants. The ants, therefore, take care of the aphids as if they were herd animals. Many insects would like to eat the aphids but they are stopped by the ants. Therefore, the aphids receive safety while the ants get a source of food.

⑦ 簡単なまとめ：

This symbiosis is so well balanced that it could be called mutualism.

❶ Discuss how the professor's view of mutualism differs from that of the reading.

⑧ 設問の答え：

Although the reading claims that pure mutualism is rare, the professor disagrees.

⑨ 教授の見解を支える理由：

He discusses the ant which seems to display at least two mutual relationships. He says the concept of mutualism may be open to interpretation.

読むテクスト

質問文 Explain the variations of symbiosis from mutualism to parasitism. に、最初の2パラグラフより答える。第1パラグラフからは大きな概念と parasitism を理解し、要約する

　　Symbiosis in biology can, in general terms, be described as the interdependence of two different species, whether they be plants and plants, animals and plants, or animals and animals. It should be noted that few symbiotic relationships are equally beneficial to both species, as often one of the members in the relationship receives greater benefits from the other. A detrimental relationship, in which one member is actually injured by the other, is more commonly known as parasitism. Thus, symbiosis can encompass any point on the spectrum from parasitism to perfectly equal sharing.

第2パラグラフからは mutualism を理解し、要約する

　　The equal sharing end of the spectrum can be best exemplified by lichens and their relationships with algae. In fact, lichens are composite organisms consisting of a fungus and an alga. The fungus generally forms the base and roots or hyphae while the alga grows upon it. In most lichens, the fungus supplies a base upon which the alga can grow. It is thought by most scientists that the fungus supplies necessary growing conditions such as moisture, the absence of which would prevent the alga from growing on its own in harsh conditions. In its turn, the alga supplies carbohydrates which can be used as food by the fungus. Such well balanced examples of symbiosis are often referred to as mutualism.

Another type of symbiosis, called commensalism, is often found among marine invertebrates. Certain species of simple animals such as polyps may grow on the shells of other animals such as crabs, thus providing them with protection and camouflage. On the other hand, the colonizing animal receives more food when the animal which they colonized feeds. The first animal, in this case, the polyp, would be considered a parasite if it eventually harmed the colonized animal, but this is not usually the case. In fact, some hermit crabs actually seek out sea anemones which they then place on their bodies.

訳例

生物学における共生とは一般に、それが植物同士であれ、動物と植物であれ、または動物同士であれ、ふたつの異なる種の相互依存であると説明できる。共生関係にある種のうちのひとつが、もうひとつの種より多くの利益を享受することが頻繁であるため、両方の種に等しく有益である共生関係はほとんど存在しないことを覚えておくべきである。ひとつの種が実際にはもうひとつの種によって損害を与えられる有害な共生関係は、寄生として、よりよく知られている。つまり共生とは、寄生から完全に平等な共有までを結ぶ領域（スペクトル）上のすべての概念を含んでいる。

その領域の一方の端にある平等な共有の最もよい例は、地衣類と藻類との関係である。事実、地衣類は菌と藻から成る混成の生物なのである。一般に菌は土台と根っこ、または菌糸を形成し、藻はその上に育つ。多くの地衣類において、菌は藻が育つことのできる土台を提供する。菌は、それがないと藻が厳しい条件の下で育たなくなるような、水分など菌が生育するために必要な条件を提供すると、多くの科学者は考えている。その代わりに藻は菌の食物となる炭水化物を提供する。このようにうまくバランスの取れた共生の例は、しばしば相利共生と呼ばれる。

片利共生と呼ばれるもうひとつの種類の共生は、海洋無せきつい動物に頻繁に見られる。ポリプのような単純動物の一部の種は、カニなどのほかの動物の甲羅で成長することによってそれを保護したり、カムフラージュしたりする。一方で、寄宿している動物は、寄宿されている動物が食物を摂取するとき、より多くの食物を得る。この場合のポリプのような動物は、もしそれが最終的に寄宿される動物を傷つけるのであれば寄生動物と考えられるが、そういうことはめったにない。実際、ヤドカリは自らの体に住み着くイソギンチャクを探し求めるのである。

聴くテクスト

For homework, I had you read about parasitism and symbiosis in nature, and I would like to begin here by stating that these relationships are not unusual. All of you have symbiosis going on in your bodies right now. It means you are benefiting from another organism living on, or in this case, inside you. In fact, you would not be able to digest your food if it were not for the bacteria that live in your intestine. Perfect symbiosis. You give them a nice place to live and they give you the ability to digest food.

設問 How does the ant use symbiosis to improve its life? の答えとして、次のパラグラフを要約する

But I can think of no better example of symbiosis than the relationship between ants and aphids. First of all, you should know that aphids are parasites. Whenever you see a leaf on one of your garden plants begin to curl up or wrinkle, you can be pretty sure there are aphids there, sucking out the juices of the plant. So gardeners are not very fond of them. Not so the ant. Ants are always on the lookout for aphids because they can be used as a continuous source of food. Sort of in the same way we use chickens to get eggs.

設問 How does the ant use symbiosis to improve its life? の答えとして次のパラグラフを要約する

Aphids extrude a substance called honeydew which ants use as a food supply. So important is this source of food to the ants that they will do all they can to protect their aphid "herds" from harm. They must do this because the aphids themselves are sought after as food by many other insects like the ladybird beetle. They are also a favorite food of spiders and birds. So the ants set up guards all around the aphid colony to stop predators from feeding on them. Unfortunately for them, but fortunately for gardeners, one species of insect has found a way to fool these guards. The larva of the lacewing, sometimes referred to as aphid lions, will scrape off the waxy coating that covers an aphid's body, and smear it on their own bodies, thereby fooling the ant into thinking it is just another aphid. In effect, the guard ant then protects

設問 Discuss how the professor's view of mutualism differs from that of the reading. の答えとして以下のパラグラフからアイデアを取ってくる

Ants also have a symbiotic relationship with some fungi. The ants will actually cultivate the fungus in their underground nests for food. Some of these ants are called leaf-cutters because they cut pieces of leaves, which they use to make compost, in order to keep the fungus growing well. So, although they do use the fungus as a source of food, they spend a lot of time caring for it and, in general, giving it a good place to live. Although some biologists believe that perfect symbiosis, or mutualism, is rare in nature, the fact is that it is found quite commonly and is not as rare as some tend to imply. Often, when defining mutualism, it is more a matter of interpretation as to whether or not the relationship is perfectly balanced.

訳例

　宿題として皆さんに自然における共生と寄生について読んでもらいましたが、ここではこのような関係は珍しいものではないということからお話ししたいと思います。皆さんの体の中でも現在、共生が進行しているのです。皆さんは、この場合、皆さんの体の中にですが、そこに住んでいるほかの生物から利益を得ているのです。実際、もし皆さんの腸に細菌が住んでいなければ、皆さんは食べ物を消化することはできないでしょう。完全な共生です。皆さんは細菌が住むのに快適な場所を与え、細菌は皆さんに食べ物を消化する能力を与えているのです。

　しかし、共生の例としてアリとアブラムシの関係ほどよいものはないと思います。まず、アブラムシは寄生虫だということを知っておかなければいけません。皆さんの庭の植物の葉が巻き上がったり、しわが寄ったりし始めたら、アブラムシがいて植物の分泌液を吸い上げているのです。ですから、植木職人はアブラムシがあまり好きではありません。しかし、アリは違います。アブラムシは常にアリの食物の源となるので、アリはいつもアブラムシを待っています。私たちが卵を得るために鶏を利用するのと同じことです。

　アブラムシは、アリが備蓄食物とする蜜と呼ばれる物質を分泌します。アリにとってこの食料源は非常に重要なので、アリはアブラムシの「群れ」を危害から守るためには何でもします。アブラムシ自体はテントウムシなどほかの多くの昆虫に、食物として追われるので、守ってやらなければならないのです。アブラムシはまた、クモや鳥の好物でもあります。従って、アリは捕食昆虫の餌にされないようアブラムシの集落の周りを保護します。彼らにとって不運なことに、植木職人には幸運なことなのですが、ある昆虫はこの保護をごまかす方法を見つけたのです。アブラムシライオンと呼ばれるクサカゲロウの幼虫は、ときどきアブラムシの体を覆っているワックスのコーティングをこすり取り、それを自らの体に塗りつけることによって、アリがクサカゲロウの幼虫をほかのアブラムシだと思うように仕向けます。結果として、アブラムシを保護しているアリは、アブラムシを食べているクサカゲロウの幼

131

虫を守ることになるのです。

　アリはまたいくつかの菌類と共生関係を持っています。アリは実際のところ、食物として地中の自分たちの巣の中で菌を養っているのです。これらのアリの一部は、菌がよく育つための堆肥（たいひ）として使用するために葉を切り刻むので、リーフカッターと呼ばれています。従ってアリは菌を食料源として利用しますが、一般的には住むのによい場所を提供するために、菌のために、多くの時間を費やしています。一部の生物学者は、完全な共生または相利共生は自然においては珍しいと考えていますが、実際にはかなり頻繁に見受けられ、彼らがほのめかしているほどまれなものではありません。多くの場合、相利共生の定義は、その関係が完全にバランスの取れたものかどうかという解釈の問題なのです。

重要語句

- □ alga 藻
- □ algae 藻（類）の複数形
- □ aphid アブラムシ
- □ as to ... ～に関しては
- □ bacteria 細菌、バクテリア
- □ be fond of ... ～が好き
- □ beneficial 有益な、ためになる
- □ biology 生物学
- □ camouflage 擬装
- □ carbohydrate 炭水化物、糖質
- □ colonize 植民する、入植する
- □ composite 合成の、混合の
- □ compost たい肥、配合土
- □ cultivate 耕す、養う
- □ curl up 巻き上がる
- □ describe 述べる、記述する
- □ detrimental beneficial 有害な、不利な
- □ digest 消化する、要約する
- □ encompass 包み込む、包含する
- □ exemplify 実証する、～の良い例となる
- □ extrude 押し出す
- □ fool だます、ごまかす、けむに巻く
- □ fungi fungus 菌の複数
- □ fungus 菌類、キノコ
- □ harm 害、危害
- □ harsh 厳しい
- □ herd 群れ
- □ hermit crab ヤドカリ
- □ honeydew 甘い汁、甘露、蜜
- □ hyphae hypha（菌糸）の複数形
- □ if it were not for ... もし～がなかったら
- □ imply 暗示する、ほのめかす
- □ in general terms 一般論として、大まかに言えば
- □ interdependence 相互依存
- □ interpretation 解釈、説明、解説
- □ intestine 腸
- □ invertebrate 無せきつい動物
- □ lacewing クサカゲロウ
- □ ladybird beetle テントウムシ
- □ larva 幼虫
- □ leaf 葉
- □ lichen 地衣類、苔蘚、藻類と共生する子嚢菌類で、木の幹などにかさぶたのように生える。
- □ moisture 湿気、水分
- □ nest 巣
- □ organism 有機体、生命体
- □ parasite 寄生動物
- □ parasitism 寄生
- □ polyp ポリプ
- □ prodator 捕食者
- □ prevent 防ぐ、防止する、避ける
- □ scrape こする
- □ sea anemone イソギンチャク
- □ seek out 探し出す、追求する
- □ smear ～ on ～を…にこすりつける
- □ species 種
- □ spectrum 範囲、領域、多種多様
- □ suck 吸う
- □ symbiosis 共生
- □ symbiotic 共生の
- □ underground 地下
- □ wrinkle しわが寄る

2. オンライン投稿文

この課題では、オンラインのディスカッションを読みます。教授が質問を投稿しており、クラスメートがディスカッション掲示板に回答を寄せています。あなたは自分自身の回答を書き、ディスカッションに貢献することが求められています。読むのも含めて 10 分間で自分の意見を書いてください。

指示文と質問・議論の訳

教授が中小企業経営についての授業をしています。教授の質問に答える投稿文を書いてください。

解答では、自分の言葉で意見を述べ、その裏付けをしておきます。

効果的な解答は、最低でも 100 語が必要です。

トンプソン博士

　今週は、みずから中小企業を起業することを考えている人に必要な資質について話し合います。もちろん、投資に使える資本金の額や好立地の重要性といった現実的な懸案事項はありますが、起業家たちの多くはこのような挑戦に適した性格があることに気づいていません。優れたビジネスパーソンは、計画性があり、知識が豊富で、予算に注意を払う必要があります。しかしまた、情熱的で、人格者でもあり、粘り強くなければなりません。中小企業の経営者として成功するにはどのような資質が必要だと思うか、また、そう考える理由を説明してください。

アンナ

　私の国では、中小企業を立ち上げる人は忍耐力を持つことが重要です。それは、政府機関と仕事をするときに多くの問題に直面することになるからです。事業者に多くの規制があり、忍耐力がないと、おそらくまだ起業する前に諦めてしまうことになるでしょう。

ピーター

　アンナさんは良い指摘をしていると思います。起業したいと考える人はそんなに簡単に挫折すべきではありません、なぜなら乗り越えるべきたくさんの障害が必ず見つかるからです。このような理由で、起業したい人は粘り強く、自らのアイデアに情熱を

持って取り組む必要があると思います。情熱があれば目標がはっきりしてくるので、計画をたやすく諦めることはなくなるでしょう。

模範解答 (一例)

I certainly agree with both Anna and Peter that patience, persistence, and being goal-oriented are all necessary traits for those considering opening a small business. However, I think all of these are underpinned by one particular characteristic which I believe we would find in any successful business person; confidence. A person starting a business must truly believe in their ideas and have the necessary confidence to bring their dreams to fruition. I suggest that if you interviewed many small business owners you would find that most of them had to overcome frustration at some point. Keep in mind that even Steve Jobs was fired from Apple for some bad ideas, but he never lost confidence in his ability to innovate. I feel that the most successful businesspeople are people who are confident in their ideas and will let nothing stop them from being realized.

訳例

　私はアンナさんとピーターさんの両方の意見に同意します。忍耐力、粘り強さ、目標を明確に持つことはすべて、小規模での起業を考えている人たちに必要な特性です。しかし、これらはどれも、成功しているビジネスパーソンなら誰もが持っているはずの、ある一つの特質に後押しされていると思います。それは自信です。事業を始める人は、自分の考えを心から信じ、夢を実現するために必要な自信を持っていなければなりません。多くの中小企業経営者に話を聞いてみれば、その大半がどこかの時点で挫折を克服しなければならなかったことがわかるでしょう。覚えておくべきは、スティーブ・ジョブス氏ですら、いくつかの考えが評価されずアップルを解雇されましたが、彼は自らの革新能力への自信を失うことは一度もなかったのです。最も成功している経営者とは、自分のアイデアに自信を持ち、その実現を何物にも邪魔させない人だと思います。

ポイント

　この場合は、議論の参加者2人の理由のつけ方が異なるので、書き手はそれぞれの意見の要点をまとめて、自分が、まず、それぞれの理由をどう思うかを述べる。ここでは、2人の理由も踏まえて、自分は彼らの考えに同意し "I certainly agree with both Anna and Peter that patience, persistence, and being goal-oriented are all necessary traits for those considering opening a small business." と述べている。賛成のときには、"certainly" のような副詞を使い表現にメリハリをつけるとい

い。2人の意見も踏まえて自分の意見を大きな概念(2人の意見に対する自分の意見)で話してから、自分の意見を裏付けるために、独自の具体例 "However, I think all of these are underpinned by one particular characteristic which I believe we would find in any successful business person; confidence." をつける。ここで、アンナさんの意見を発展させて、書き手は「自信」という自分の具体例を加えている。そして、それを補足するために、ピーターさんの意見も発展させて、客観的な意見 "A person starting a business must truly believe in their ideas and have the necessary confidence to bring their dreams to fruition. I suggest that if you interviewed many small business owners you would find that most of them had to overcome frustration at some point" を述べている。そして、さらにその発言を裏付けるために、具体例 "Keep in mind that even Steve Jobs was fired from Apple for some bad ideas, but he never lost confidence in his ability to innovate." を挙げて、最後に自分の意見 "I feel that the most successful businesspeople are people who are confident in their ideas and will let nothing stop them from being realized." をまとめて、おちとしている。

大きな枠

1. まず、議論の参加者2人の意見を要約して自分の考えを述べる(これは、課題にとりかかりやすくするため)。
2. 自分の意見を裏付けする。
3. 最初は参加者 A の話を発展させる。
4. 次に、話の流れをつないで、参加者 B の意見も発展させる。
5. 自分の結論につなげていく。

Test
2

Reading Section

Listening Section

Speaking Section

Writing Section

解答・解説

Reading Section

The Hudson River School

The question could be asked as to who was the first truly American painter. To this question many art historians would probably respond that it was Thomas Cole. Though born in England, he became inspired with the American landscape, and for many years he became its finest **exponent**. But it was not just any landscape that interested him, he seemed especially influenced by the dramatic natural scenes he found in northern New York near Catskill on the Hudson River, and concentrated his efforts on producing landscapes of that region. Unlike many artists, his efforts did not go unrewarded and he rather quickly gained recognition for his paintings.

②→ The paintings themselves reflected the ideas of the Romantic Movement in art that was currently sweeping through Europe, but his subject matter was particularly American. All Romantic painters looked to nature as a source of inspiration and then used it to express scenes that depended largely on an emotional rather than analytical interpretation. Cole was no different except that he used American landscapes to **this end**. As his fame grew, so did interest in the part of the country represented in his landscapes. This influence was especially strong among other artists, many of whom began to **flock** to the Catskill area. Together they formed what is referred to as the Hudson River School. Generally speaking, they were a group of artists who produced detailed and romanticized landscapes of the Hudson River region.

③→ As time passed and their influence grew, other artists outside this region began to paint in a similar style. So it was that artists like the German-born Albert Bierstadt were referred to as belonging to the Hudson River School, even though his subject matter was generally scenes of the American West. In fact, nearly any American artist between about 1830 and 1880 who painted detailed landscapes which portrayed their love of nature was referred to as being from the Hudson River School.

④→ To some degree the Hudson River School artists were making an attempt to discover exactly what it meant to be an American rather than, say, a European artist. (A) ■ This attempt was mainly formed around the idea that the American landscape itself was unique, and that it represented a sort of wild beauty that had all but disappeared from Europe. (B) ■ The wilderness, in fact, formed a major theme in these artists' paintings. (C) ■ The paintings often show the frightening power of the **wilderness** while at the same time displaying a certain optimism in the face of this power, a sort of belief that America and the new Americans would prevail over all that nature could produce. (D) ■ The attention to detail tended to enhance the idea of the ability to control nature's power. It was as if painting the details was a way of controlling nature's random forces. But, although almost scientific in its concern for exact representation, the overall effect tended to be emotional.

⑤→ Despite its optimistic ideals, the movement lost its appeal when American artists began looking back to Europe for a source of inspiration. The Impressionist Movement that was beginning was offering another alternative to painters. The Impressionists had grown tired of what they considered to be the overly sentimental paintings of the Romantics. Though they maintained much of the subject matter of the Romantics, they believed that technical detail added nothing to a painting and that it was the ability to paint light that was important.

But the influence of the Hudson River School lived on despite such criticisms. From the Symbolist movement to the Expressionists, Surrealists, and Photorealists, the idea that emotion can and should be portrayed through art lived on.

1. The word **flock** in the passage is closest in meaning to

    (A) paint

    (B) meet

    (C) be attracted

    (D) go

2. According to paragraph 2, why were painters interested in the Catskill area?

    (A) Because it was beautiful.

    (B) Because Thomas Cole lived there.

    (C) Because they had seen Cole's paintings of the area.

    (D) Because they wanted to join the Hudson River School.

Paragraph 2 is marked with an arrow [→].

3. Why is Thomas Cole considered the first American painter?

    (A) He formed the Hudson River School for American artists.

    (B) He wanted to break from the tradition of European Romanticism.

    (C) He was able to understand the American landscape better as he was not from Europe.

    (D) He expressed Romanticism by painting American landscapes.

4. In paragraph 2, why does the author mention the Romantic Movement?

    (A) To define Romanticism

    (B) To show its influence on European painters

    (C) To contrast American and European history

    (D) To show similarities in all Romantic painting

Paragraph 2 is marked with an arrow [→].

5. What can be inferred from paragraph 3 about Albert Bierstadt?

(A) He was considered part of the Hudson River School although he painted in Germany.

(B) He expressed a love of nature in his paintings of the American West.

(C) Although German, he was not influenced by European Romanticism.

(D) The Hudson River School was popular even in Germany.

Paragraph 3 is marked with an arrow [→].

6. Why does the author mention the **wilderness** in paragraph 4?

(A) To contrast the influence of nature on American and European art

(B) To show that nature had a similar influence on artists both in America and Europe

(C) To suggest that Europeans could never truly understand American art

(D) To suggest that Americans were more controlled by nature

Paragraph 4 is marked with an arrow [→].

7. According to paragraph 4, why was the painting of detail important in American painting?

(A) It helped express the idea of the wilderness.

(B) It was a way to control nature.

(C) It showed a difference between American and European painting.

(D) It showed the American painters' interest in science.

Paragraph 4 is marked with an arrow [→].

8. According to paragraph 4, what contrast did American paintings try to show?

    (A) Nature could be beautiful but dangerous.

    (B) Nature was both scientific and artistic.

    (C) The wilderness was both pessimistic and optimistic.

    (D) American landscape was unique while European landscape was not.

9. Look at the four squares [■] that indicate where the following sentence could be added to the passage.

Though it certainly had its beautiful natural areas, it lacked the untamed beauty of the American wilderness.

Where would this sentence best fit?

10. *Directions:* An introductory sentence for a brief summary of the passage is provided below. Complete the summary by selecting the THREE answer choices that express the most important ideas in the passage. Some sentences do not belong in the summary because they express ideas that are not presented in the passage or are minor ideas in the passage. **This question is worth 2 points.**

Thomas Cole is often considered the first truly American artist and the founder of the American Romantic Movement in painting.

- _____
- _____
- _____

Answer Choices

(A) One example of this love of nature was the paintings of the American West by Albert Bierstadt.

(B) Although Cole himself was never well-known, his paintings influenced many other artists in the Hudson River area.

(C) The Hudson River School was similar to European Romantic painting in its emotional interpretation of nature.

(D) American Romantic painting portrayed the love of nature while understanding its power; an attitude that made it different from European painting.

(E) The Europeans were unable to show the love of nature that the Americans could.

(F) Interest in Cole's paintings of the Catskill area inspired other artists to paint in a similar style which became known as the Hudson River School.

Native American Culture

When Europeans first came to the New World, there were approximately 90 million Native Americans living on the North and South American continents. But of these, only about 10 million lived in North America. It is often assumed that the Native American population was reduced through constant wars with the new settlers. Although there is some truth in this, the real reason for their **demise** was far less dramatic but far more deadly. It was, in fact, the diseases that the Europeans brought, especially smallpox, that **decimated** their numbers. Although the population of Native Americans in North America has risen in the 20th Century, there are still fewer than two million people who qualify as Native Americans.

The story of the Native Americans probably began in Asia around 30,000 years ago. It appears from all evidence that at that time, roaming nomadic bands began crossing the Bering Sea ice bridge during the time of the great Ice Ages to hunt in North America. Populations slowly spread southward and eventually became isolated from Asia altogether when warming **did away with** all contact by land with Asia.

③→ The widespread populations of Native Americans began to develop distinct physical traits based largely on the geographic regions in which they resided. The Native Americans of the Great Plains tended to be tall and strongly built, while those of the Andes Mountains were short with broad chests, apparently enabling them to adapt to the thin air of the high mountains. In all, there are nine types of environments to which the Native American tribes had to adapt. The natural resources available and the challenges each region presented are reflected in the lifestyles and cultures that each group or tribe developed.

④→ The Southwestern United States comprised one such environment and provides a good example of how the Native American culture changed with changing conditions. Here, in the present states of Arizona, New Mexico, Colorado as well as Northern Mexico, the earliest Native American inhabitants were hunting mammoths with spears as early as 8000 B.C. As the Ice Age ended and the mammoths disappeared, the Native American inhabitants turned to the bison (or buffalo) as the main source of food. They also began to rely more heavily on plants to supplement their diet.

⑤→ There then began a long period during which the area became progressively drier. At first, the inhabitants changed to hunting deer, small game and birds. (A) ■ They relied more and more on collecting plant food such as fruits, nuts and other seeds. (B) ■ They began grinding some of these seeds into flour, which they likely used for making bread. (C) ■ This seems to indicate that they became more settled in one area and less nomadic than when they were primarily hunters. At around 300 B.C. the Native American inhabitants of the area came under the influence of culture introduced by tribes from Mexico. Maize, beans and squash became part of their diet. (D) ■ To grow such crops in such dry conditions required additional care and irrigation. This settled the residents even more, and by about 700 A.D. they had developed towns sometimes built into cliffs. This is now referred to as the Anasazi culture.

Though they were a relatively advanced culture by the time the Spanish arrived in 1540, they were no match for the invaders and were finally put under their control by 1598. During a rebellion in 1680, they managed to free themselves from Spanish control but were then subjugated first by Mexico and later the United States. Throughout **it all**, however, the Pueblo, the descendants of the Anasazi, were able to maintain their culture. For this reason there are still twenty-two Pueblo towns in existence today.

11. The word **decimated** in the passage is closest in meaning to

(A) attacked
(B) reduced
(C) influenced
(D) maintained

12. Based on the information in paragraph 3, which of the following best explains the variation in physical characteristics among Native Americans?

(A) Different cultural features produced different physical features.
(B) Different lifestyles called for different features.
(C) Different environmental factors produced different characteristics.
(D) Differences in physical features caused different cultures to develop.

Paragraph 3 is marked with an arrow [→].

13. In paragraph 3, what can be inferred about Native American culture?

(A) It is a product of physical characteristics.
(B) It is surprisingly the same despite the region.
(C) It can be divided into culture from the plains and culture from the mountains.
(D) It varies with the region and its challenges.

Paragraph 3 is marked with an arrow [→].

146

14. According to information in paragraphs 4 and 5, what was most important in the development of the culture of Native Americans in one area of the Southwest?

(A) The development of agriculture.
(B) Changing food supplies.
(C) Interaction with other tribes.
(D) Changing environmental factors.

Paragraph 4 and paragraph 5 are marked with arrows [→].

15. In paragraph 5, the author implies that towns formed

(A) in order to better care for crops.
(B) in order to build irrigation systems.
(C) to interact more effectively with other tribes.
(D) because it was easier to live together in cliffs.

Paragraph 5 is marked with an arrow [→].

16. In paragraph 5, why does the author mention the climate becoming drier?

(A) To show how changes in climate changed the type of animal that was hunted
(B) To show that climate change forced them to trade with other tribes
(C) To show how irrigation became important
(D) To show the influence of climate on culture

Paragraph 5 is marked with an arrow [→].

17. According to paragraph 5, which of the following is true about the **Anasazi**?

    (A) They were still generally nomadic.
    (B) They developed the ability to bake bread.
    (C) Their diet was influenced by tribes from Mexico.
    (D) They were forced to live in cliffs.

Paragraph 5 is marked with an arrow [→].

18. Which of the following most accurately reflects the author's opinion of the Anasazi culture?

    (A) It is surprising that it formed towns so early in its history.
    (B) It is surprising that it transformed from a hunting to an agricultural culture.
    (C) It is remarkable that it maintained its ties with other tribes.
    (D) It is remarkable that it could maintain itself after so many challenges.

19. Look at the four squares [■] that indicate where the following sentence could be added to the passage.

However, since these became more and more difficult to find, they had to change their diet even more.

Where would this sentence best fit?

20. *Directions:* An introductory sentence for a brief summary of the passage is provided below. Complete the summary by selecting the THREE answer choices that express the most important ideas in the passage. Some sentences do not belong in the summary because they express ideas that are not presented in the passage or are minor ideas in the passage. **This question is worth 2 points.**

After their arrival in America about 30,000 years ago, Native Americans faced a variety of challenges.

- _____
- _____
- _____

Answer Choices

(A) That the population of Native Americans has decreased sharply since the time of the arrival of Europeans in America.

(B) The culture was not advanced enough to resist subjugation by the Spanish in 1598.

(C) The first was the challenge of adapting to the diverse environments that they found in the New World from high altitudes to dry climates.

(D) The Anasazi culture is an example of a successful adaptation in that it adapted to both climatic change and domination by stronger cultures.

(E) Living in the mountains of the Andes and developing broad chests enabled some Native Americans to survive in an extreme environment.

(F) Despite many challenges, the Pueblo culture was able to preserve its identity and maintain its customs to the present day.

Listening Section

1. What is the man's main problem?

    (A) He's worried about the exams.

    (B) He's having trouble sleeping.

    (C) He has noisy neighbors.

    (D) He hasn't had a chance to meet anyone.

2. What advice does the man accept from the woman?

    (A) He should tell his neighbors to be quiet.

    (B) He should meet more of the students on his floor.

    (C) He should complain to the dormitory manager.

    (D) He should go to the Housing Department.

3. Why doesn't the man know more students on his floor?

(A) They are all football players.
(B) All of them are foreign students and probably don't speak much English.
(C) There really hasn't been much time to meet anyone yet.
(D) He never sees anyone.

4. Listen again to part of the conversation. Then answer the question. 🎧

Why does the man say this? 🎧

(A) He doesn't know anything about football so he really cannot talk to them.
(B) Since he doesn't look very strong they would probably not pay attention to him.
(C) They do not really care if only one person is upset.
(D) He thinks it would be better if she spoke to them.

5. Listen again to part of the conversation. Then answer the question. 🎧

What is the woman implying when she says this? 🎧

(A) She is criticizing him for being too weak in this situation.
(B) She is encouraging him to take a chance and do something risky.
(C) She is showing sympathy for his situation.
(D) She is asking him for ideas.

Economics
(Joseph Schumpeter)

6. What is the lecture mainly about?

    (A) Marxism and its influence on politics

    (B) The relationship between socialism and capitalism

    (C) The influence of economic theory on other disciplines

    (D) The innovation of entrepreneurs

7. Why does the professor mention Marxism?

    (A) Because Marx's theories are well-known

    (B) To show how economics, politics and philosophy are all connected

    (C) To show a contrast with Schumpeter's ideas

    (D) To show how Marx's ideas influenced other economists

8. Listen again to part of the lecture. Then answer the question. ∩

    What does the professor mean when he says this? ∩

    (A) Schumpeter is too difficult to understand, so he is not discussed in economics textbooks.

    (B) The professor will talk of Schumpeter even though no one has ever heard of him.

    (C) Schumpeter was influential but mainly among economists.

    (D) Schumpeter is not important enough to be mentioned in 20th century textbooks.

9. In the lecture the professor describes some ideas of Joseph Schumpeter. Indicate whether each of the following is one of his ideas. For each sentence, place a check mark in the Yes or No column.

	Yes	*No*
Capitalism depends on "creative destruction."		
Innovators must be inventors.		
Capitalism would naturally destroy itself.		
Entrepreneurs need capitalism in order to succeed.		
A wealthy class would keep capitalism strong.		

10. According to the professor, how does capitalism stimulate entrepreneurship?

Choose 2 answers.

(A) By allowing the entrepreneur to make money

(B) By allowing the entrepreneur to use "creative destruction"

(C) By allowing the entrepreneur to think of new management techniques

(D) By allowing the entrepreneur to be an innovator

11. What will the professor probably talk of next?

(A) More details of Schumpeter's economic thoughts

(B) The effect of Schumpeter's ideas on other economists

(C) A comparison of Schumpeter and Marx's ideas of socialism

(D) The negative impact of Schumpeter's ideas

Questions 12-16

12. What is the man's main problem?

(A) He has too much to read in his literature class.

(B) He's the only foreign student in his literature class.

(C) The professor's ideas are hard to follow.

(D) He's afraid to tape the professor's lecture.

13. What advice does the woman give the man?

(A) He should spend more time reading.

(B) He should ask the professor to repeat his lecture.

(C) He should tape the professor's lectures and listen to them later.

(D) He should talk to some of the American students about the problem.

14. What happened when the woman taped her professor?

(A) She was disappointed that she could only get the main idea of the lectures.
(B) American students also began taping the lectures.
(C) American students thought it was funny.
(D) An English teacher helped her understand the lectures.

15. Listen again to part of the conversation. Then answer the question. 🎧

What is the man implying when he says this? 🎧

(A) He cannot believe she could have had any trouble with listening since her English is so good.
(B) He is surprised that she had trouble with philosophy because he thinks she knows a lot about it.
(C) He is disappointed that someone with such good English also had listening problems.
(D) He can't imagine that such an optimistic person as her could ever have such problems.

16. Listen again to part of the conversation. Then answer the question. 🎧

Why does the woman say this? 🎧

(A) She thinks the man is exaggerating.
(B) She thinks it is possible that the teacher is not very good.
(C) She wants more details about the situation.
(D) She is showing how surprised she is by this situation.

History
(Explorers)

17. What is the lecture mainly about?

(A) Voyages of discovery
(B) The search for the Northwest Passage
(C) The discoveries of Henry Hudson
(D) The importance of trade with Asia

18. The professor mentions the activities of various explorers to North America. Match these activities with the correct explorer.

	Hudson	Franklin	Parry	Davis
Won an award for his explorations				
Sailed to Albany				
Disappeared while traveling to Asia				
Sighted the opening to the Northwest Passage				

19. What were two results of the search for the Northwest Passage?

Choose 2 answers.

(A) The discovery of great wealth for European countries
(B) An increase in the understanding of the geography of North America
(C) The actual discovery of the Northwest Passage
(D) The realization that there really was no Northwest Passage

20. According to the discussion, why were Europeans so interested in finding a Northwest Passage?

Choose 3 answers.

(A) Asia had many things that Europeans wanted.
(B) Magellan found it was too long and dangerous to sail around South America.
(C) They had a spirit for discovery and adventure.
(D) They thought much wealth could be found there.
(E) They wanted to make money by trading with Asia.

21. Listen again to part of the lecture. Then answer the question. ∩

What does the professor mean when she says this? ∩

(A) Though the search for the Northwest Passage was interesting, it shouldn't be looked upon as something very important.
(B) If it were not for the search for the Northwest Passage, it is unlikely that much of northern North America would have been discovered so early.
(C) It is difficult to judge how important the search for the Northwest Passage was to the understanding of North American geography.
(D) It must be stressed how important the understanding of North American geography was to Europeans.

22. Listen again to part of the lecture. Then answer the question. ∩

What can be inferred from the student's comment? ∩

(A) The student is criticizing the teacher's statement.
(B) The student is expressing how confusing the teacher's statement is.
(C) The student is expressing his surprise at the teacher's statement.
(D) The student is expressing his disagreement with the teacher's statement.

Chemistry

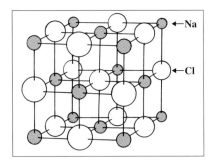

23. What is the discussion mainly about?

(A) Common table salt

(B) Acids and bases

(C) Salts

(D) Halogens

24. Why does the professor talk about table salt?

(A) Because it is an easily recognized representative of all salts.

(B) Because it is one of the most common minerals on earth.

(C) Because it is composed of an acid and a base.

(D) Because it is part of a group of elements called "halogens."

25. What are two characteristics of salts mentioned in the discussion?

Choose 2 answers.

(A) They are composed of a halogen and a metal.

(B) They are produced when acids and bases neutralize each other.

(C) They are always formed from water.

(D) They are composed of acids and bases.

26. In the discussion, the professor gives many facts about table salt. Indicate whether each of the following is or is not true of table salt.

	True	*False*
It can be dissolved in water.		
It is composed of a metal.		
It is the most abundant mineral in the oceans.		
It will not conduct electricity unless melted.		
It has a high melting point.		

27. Listen again to part of the lecture. Then answer the question. ∩

Why does the professor say this? ∩

(A) To return to the topic of table salt, since the students aren't interested in the new topic

(B) To explain something the students don't know by using table salt as an example

(C) To change the topic because he is upset that no one will answer his question

(D) To check to see if everyone understands before he continues his lecture

28. Listen again to part of the lecture. Then answer the question. ∩

What can be inferred from the student's response? ∩

(A) The student is not interested in the professor's explanation.

(B) The student wanted a different answer from the professor.

(C) The student did not fully understand the professor's explanation.

(D) The student understands very little of what the professor says.

Speaking Section

1. Independent Speaking [Paired Choice]

Listen to the following question.

Some people think that the automobile has improved people's lives, while others think it has been the source of many problems. What is your opinion?

Prepare your response after the beep.　Preparation time 15 seconds

Start your response after the beep.　Response time 45 seconds

2. Integrated Reading / Listening / Speaking Situational
—— Independent Research Paper

Now, read the passage about the Writing Requirements Registration Form. You have 45 seconds to read the passage. Begin reading now.

Reading (45 seconds):

Before beginning work on an independent research paper in order to satisfy the writing requirement, the student must receive permission from a supervising faculty member. A student may select any faculty member for supervision; however, the approval of any topic for a paper is then left solely to the discretion of that chosen member. Students are strongly encouraged to consult faculty members early in the semester in order to make any arrangements necessary to carry out the project. Once a faculty member agrees to supervise the student's work, the student must submit a Writing Requirements Registration Form which can be obtained from the Registrar's Office. The faculty member will only accept the form after meeting with the student and agreeing on an appropriate topic.

The student then must submit the Writing Requirements Registration Form with the faculty member's notes of approval to the Registrar's Office. The Registrar's Office will then submit the Writing Requirements Registration Form to the Assistant Dean for final approval. Work on the independent research paper can only begin after such approval is received.

Listening:
Now listen to a conversation between a professor and a student.

Question:
Briefly describe the process a student must go through to satisfy the writing requirement with an independent research paper.

Prepare your response after the beep. Preparation time 30 seconds

Start your response after the beep. Response time 60 seconds

3. Integrated Reading / Listening / Speaking Academic
—— Physics (Gravity)

Now, read the passage about gravity. You have 45 seconds to read the passage. Begin reading now.

Reading (45 seconds):
All the actions of all the particles and objects in the universe can be explained

by the interaction of only four forces. These forces are gravity, electromagnetism, the strong nuclear force, which holds protons and neutrons together in the nucleus of an atom, and the weak nuclear force, which is responsible for the decay of an atom's nucleus into smaller particles, and which produces radioactivity. Gravity is present in any particle, no matter how small, and the force of it is proportional to the mass of the object. Although widely distributed throughout the universe, gravity itself is the weakest of the four forces. The other forces are many times stronger, but these forces cannot be extended over a long distance. Gravity is the only force of the four that is capable of exerting its influence at long distances. However, for an object to exert any meaningful gravitational force it must be of great mass, such as a planet, moon or star.

Listening:

Now listen to part of a lecture on this topic in a physics class.

Question:

Explain what the four forces of the universe do and how they are different.

Prepare your response after the beep. | Preparation time 30 seconds

Start your response after the beep. | Response time 60 seconds

4. Integrated Listening / Speaking [Summary]
—— Oceanology (Gray Whale)

Now listen to part of a lecture in a biology class.

Question:

Explain the difficulties in understanding gray whale migration and give some possible reasons why they migrate.

Prepare your response after the beep. | Preparation time 20 seconds |

Start your response after the beep. | Response time 60 seconds |

Writing Section

1. Integrated Writing
—— Political Science

mp3
28

Directions:

For this integrated task, you have 3 minutes to read the passage. Then you will listen to part of a lecture on the topic you have just read about. Following the lecture, you have 20 minutes to plan and write your response. An ideal response will be 150 to 225 words.

Read the following passage.

Reading:

Political science is a social science which is related to the other social sciences of anthropology, history, sociology, economics and psychology. It can be argued that political science is the cornerstone of all of these other disciplines. This is because all the activity that occurs within these other disciplines is governed to some degree by the political environment in which they occur. An alternative point of view could be that political science is a study of political situations that arise from factors that are more closely linked to the other social sciences. Whatever the viewpoint of the importance of political science within the social sciences, it is clear that all of these disciplines interact, and the nature of that interaction has changed throughout history.

The idea that politics could be approached scientifically developed primarily in the 20th century. Basically, political scientists used the statistical methods developed by social scientists and applied them to politics. Using these methods, political scientists try to explain where political power comes from in a society, and how it is used.

Yet, politics is in many ways beyond the reach of true scientific investigation. The scientific method contends that the same set of conditions will produce the same outcomes. It has proven extremely difficult to make clear connections between political outcomes and the conditions from which they emerged.

Listening:
Now, listen to part of a lecture on political science, which you have just read about. You may take notes while listening to the lecture.

Now, get ready to answer the question. You may use your notes to help you answer.

Question:
The reading suggests that political science can never approach true science. However, the professor suggests ways in which it could at least be considered more scientific. Explain the reasons political science may be considered a science.

2. Writing for an Academic Discussion

Your professor is teaching a class on marketing. Write a response to the professor's question.

Please contribute your own ideas to this discussion, and support them with some details.

Your response should be at least 100 words in length.

Doctor Perez

This week we have been discussing marketing on social media. Many companies have invested in this strategy and found it successful. Others, however, have found that it is not bringing them the benefits they hoped for. This is because such advertising is not just about putting up ads on every platform. It's more about targeting specific customers which isn't always easy. I'd like to learn how you use social media and how advertising influences you. What ads seem to be most and least effective? Do you think companies should invest more on social media marketing or stay with traditional forms of advertising?

Anna

I find that most ads on social media are simply annoying. They seem to get in the way of other content that I'm more interested in. To me, such advertising seems like a waste of money. I think that traditional ads that target a specific audience would be far more cost effective. Putting money into good ads in magazines that are written for a specific type of person is the best investment.

Peter

I think Anna makes a good point. You really have to know which kind of customer you want to target. It may be that social media doesn't really target one type of person so the ads companies put there are not effective. However, people are spending much more time on social media than they were in the past, and so such advertising cannot be ignored in any marketing plan. I think with careful research, social media marketing can be very effective.

解答・解説

Reading Section

Listening Section

Speaking Section

Writing Section

Reading

1 D **2** C **3** D **4** D **5** B **6** A

7 B **8** A **9** B **10** F, C, D **11** B **12** C

13 D **14** D **15** A **16** D **17** C **18** D

19 A **20** C, D, F

Listening

1 C **2** C **3** C **4** B **5** A **6** C

7 B **8** C

9 Capitalism depends on "creative destruction." (Yes)

Innovators must be inventors. (No)

Capitalism would naturally destroy itself. (Yes)

Entrepreneurs need capitalism in order to succeed. (Yes)

A wealthy class would keep capitalism strong. (No)

10 A, D **11** B **12** C **13** C **14** B **15** A

16 B **17** B

18 Won an award for his explorations (Parry)

Sailed to Albany (Hudson)

Disappeared while traveling to Asia (Franklin)

Sighted the opening to the Northwest Passage (Davis)

19 B, C **20** A, B, E **21** B **22** C **23** C **24** A

25 A, B

26 It can be dissolved in water. (True)

It is composed of a metal. (True)

It is the most abundant mineral in the oceans. (False)

It will not conduct electricity unless melted. (False)

It has a high melting point. (True)

27 B **28** C

Reading Section　解答・解説

Questions 1-10

問題文の訳例

ハドソン・リバー派

　本当に最初のアメリカ人画家とは誰だったのか、という質問がなされることがある。この質問に対し、たぶん多くの芸術史家は、それはトーマス・コールだと答えるであろう。彼はイギリスに生まれたが、アメリカの景観に触発され、長い間その最も素晴らしい提唱者になった。しかし、彼はどんな風景にも興味を持ったわけではなく、ニューヨーク北部のハドソン川沿いのキャッツキル近辺に見られる印象的な自然の景色に特に影響を受けたようであり、その地域の風景画の制作に力を集中させたのである。多くの芸術家と異なり、彼の努力は報われずに終わることはなく、彼の絵画はむしろ急速に評価を得た。

　彼の絵画自体は、その当時ヨーロッパを広く吹き抜けていた芸術界におけるロマン主義の考え方を反映したものだったが、彼の主題はアメリカ特有のものであった。すべてのロマン主義の画家たちは、自然をインスピレーションの源とし、分析的解釈というよりはむしろ感情的な解釈に強く依存した光景を表現するために自然を使った。コールも、同様の目的のためにアメリカの風景を用いたこと以外は、ほかの画家たちと変わりはなかった。彼の名声が大きくなるにつれ、彼の風景画に表現されている場所に対する興味も大きくなっていった。この影響は画家たちの間で特に強く、多くの画家たちがキャッツキル地域に集まり始めた。彼らはともにハドソン・リバー派と呼ばれる集まりを形成した。一般的に言えば、彼らはハドソン川流域の風景画を詳細に、ロマンチックに描いた画家たちの集まりであった。

　時間が経過して彼らの影響力が大きくなるにつれ、この地域以外のほかの芸術家たちも同じようなスタイルで絵を描き始めた。ゆえに、これらの画家は、例えば、ドイツ生まれのアルバート・ビアスタットの主題は主に、アメリカ西部の風景であったにもかかわらず、彼はハドソン・リバー派に属していると見なされたのである。事実、自然への愛を表現するきめ細かい風景画を描いた、およそ 1830 年から 1880 年の間のほぼすべてのアメリカの芸術家は、ハドソン・リバー派出身であると考えられた。

　ある意味、ハドソン・リバー派の芸術家たちは、例えばヨーロッパの芸術家ではなく、アメリカの芸術家であるとはどういうことなのかを、正確に見いだそうとしていた。この試みは主に、アメリカの風景それ自体が唯一独特のもので、ヨーロッパからは消えてしまっていたある種の野生の美しさを表すものだという考えを基本にしていた。ヨーロッパにも確かに美しい自然はあったが、アメリカの未開地のような粗野な美しさには欠けていた。事実、未開の地はこれらの芸術家の作品における主要なテーマになっていった。彼らの絵画はしばしば未開の地における自然の恐ろしい力を表現しているのと同時に、その力に直面したときのある種の楽観主義、アメリカという国や新しいアメリカ人は自然がつくり出すすべてのものを圧倒するであろうというある種の信念をも、表現している。細かい部分に対する注意は、

自然の力を制御する能力があるという考えを強める傾向があった。それはまるで、詳細に描くことが自然の手当たり次第の力を制御するための方法であるかのようであった。しかし、正確に描き出すことに関する彼らのこだわりはほとんど科学的でさえあったものの、（彼らの絵画が与える）全体的な効果は感情的なものになりがちであった。

しかし、彼らが楽観的な理想を持っていたにもかかわらず、アメリカの芸術家たちがインスピレーションの源としてヨーロッパを振り返り始めたとき、その活動は魅力を失った。そのころ始まっていた印象派の活動が、画家たちに別の選択肢を提供した。印象派たちは、自分たちが過度に感情的であると考えていたロマン派絵画にうんざりしていた。印象派はロマン派の多くの主題をそのまま受け継いだが、詳細に描写する技術が絵画にもたらすものは皆無で、光を描く能力こそが重要であると考えていた。

しかし、ハドソン・リバー派の影響力はそのような批判にもかかわらず残った。象徴主義者の活動から表現主義、超現実主義、そしてフォトリアリズムへと、感情は芸術を通して表現することができる、表現されるべきであるという考えは生き続けたのである。

重要語句

☐ as if ... まるで〜かのように	☐ interpretation（名詞）解釈、理解
☐ belonging（名詞）所属するもの	☐ landscape（名詞）風景、風景画
☐ currently（副詞）広く、一般に、現在は	☐ maintain（動詞）保持する、維持する、主張する
☐ dramatic（形容詞）劇的な、躍動的な、印象的な	☐ optimism（名詞）楽観主義
☐ effect（名詞）結果、効果、影響	☐ overall（形容詞）全体の、総合的な
☐ emotional（形容詞）感情の、感情的な	☐ overly（副詞）過度に
☐ enhance（動詞）高める、強める	☐ portray（動詞）表現する、絵に描く
☐ exponent（名詞）代表的人物、提唱者	☐ recognition（名詞）認識、評価
☐ fame（名詞）名声、評判	☐ representation（名詞）表現、描写
☐ flock（動詞）集まる、群がる	☐ scene（名詞）光景、景色
☐ frighten（動詞）ぎょっとさせる、おびえさせる	☐ sentimental（形容詞）心情的な、感情的な
☐ historian（名詞）歴史学者	☐ sweep（動詞）吹き抜ける、掃く
☐ ideal（名詞）理想	☐ tend（動詞）〜する傾向がある
☐ inspiration（名詞）インスピレーション、創造的刺激	☐ unrewarded（形容詞）報酬のない
	☐ wild（形容詞）野生の、自生の
☐ inspire（動詞）（人を）奮い立たせる	☐ wilderness（名詞）未開の地、荒野

1. 解答 (D)

本文中の flock の意味に最も近いのは

(A) 塗る

(B) 会う

(C) 心引かれる

(D) 行く

解説 この言葉を文脈の中で考えてみると、「多くの芸術家たちが Catskill 地域に **flock** し始め、それで the Hudson River School をつくり、ハドソン川流域の風景画を描いた」わけなので、彼らはそこに集まり、グループをつくったことになる。従って、ここでの flock は (D) の go と同じ意味になる。ちなみに、flock to の to からも、(A) と (B) は正解ではないことがすぐにわかる。

2. 解答 (C)

第 2 パラグラフによると、画家たちはなぜキャッツキル地域に興味を持ったのか。

(A) 美しかったから。

(B) トーマス・コールがそこに住んでいたから。

(C) その地域を描いたコールの絵を見たから。

(D) ハドソン・リバー・スクールに入りたかったから。

解説 As his fame grew, so did interest in the part of the country represented in his landscapes. より、(C) が正解であるとわかる。コールの絵画が世に出るようになったわけである。

3. 解答 (D)

トーマス・コールが最初のアメリカ人画家と見なされているのはなぜか。

(A) 彼はアメリカの芸術家のためにハドソン・リバー派を作った。

(B) 彼はヨーロッパのロマン主義の伝統から離れたがっていた。

(C) 彼はヨーロッパ出身ではなかったので、アメリカの風景をよりよく理解できた。

(D) 彼はアメリカの風景を描くことでロマン主義を表現した。

解説 第 2 パラグラフの The paintings themselves reflected the ideas of the Romantic Movement in art that was currently sweeping through Europe, but his subject matter was particularly American. ... he used American landscapes to this end. という記述より、(D) が正解であるとわかる。

4. 解答 (D)

第 2 パラグラフで、なぜ著者はロマン主義運動に言及しているのか。

(A) ロマン主義を定義するために

(B) ヨーロッパの画家たちへの影響を示すために

(C) アメリカとヨーロッパの歴史を対比するために

(D) ロマン主義の絵画全体の類似点を示すために

解説 All Romantic painters looked to nature ... Cole was no different except that he used American landscapes to this end. という記述より、絵画について話していることがわかるので (A) と (C) は削除できる。さらに、前述より、ヨーロッパやアメリカを問わず All Romantic painters の絵画は似ていることがわかるため、(D) が正解となる。

5. 解答 (B)

第 3 パラグラフによると、アルバート・ビアスタットについてどんなことが推測できるか。

(A) 彼はドイツで絵を描いていたが、ハドソン・リバー派の一員と見なされていた。

(B) 彼はアメリカ西部の絵画で自然への愛情を表現した。

(C) 彼はドイツ人でありながら、ヨーロッパのロマン主義の影響を受けなかった。

(D) ハドソン・リバー派はドイツでも人気があった。

解説 以下の記述より (B) が正解であるとわかる。... Albert Bierstadt were referred to as belonging to the Hudson River School, even though his subject matter was generally scenes of the American West. ... landscapes which portrayed their love of nature was referred to as being from the Hudson River School. また、Germany とか German に関する記述は彼の生い立ちにすぎない。ここでは、彼の絵画について話している。

6. 解答 (A)

なぜ著者は第 4 パラグラフで荒野に言及したのか。

(A) アメリカとヨーロッパの芸術への自然の影響を対比するために

(B) 自然がアメリカとヨーロッパの芸術家に同様の影響を与えたことを示すために

(C) ヨーロッパ人がアメリカの芸術を決して本当には理解できないことを示唆するために

(D) アメリカ人のほうが自然により支配されていたことを示唆するために

解説 第 4 パラグラフに書いてある ... it represented a sort of wild beauty that had all but disappeared from Europe. からもわかるように、ヨーロッパと比べているので (A) が正解となる。

7. 解答 (B)

第 4 パラグラフによると、アメリカの絵画で細部の描写が重要だったのはなぜか。

(A) 荒野の概念を表現するのに役立った。

(B) 自然をコントロールする方法だった。

(C) アメリカとヨーロッパの絵画の違いを表していた。

(D) アメリカの画家たちの科学への関心を示していた。

解説 第 4 パラグラフの The attention to detail tended to enhance the idea of the ability to control nature's power. It was as if painting the details was a way of controlling nature's random forces. より、正解は (B) だとわかる。

8. 解答 (A)

第 4 パラグラフによると、アメリカの絵画はどのような対比を表そうとしたか。

(A) 自然は美しいかもしれないが、危険である。

(B) 自然は科学的であると同時に芸術的でもある。

(C) 荒野は悲観的であると同時に楽観的でもある。

(D) アメリカの風景は独特で、ヨーロッパの風景はそうではない。

解説 第 4 パラグラフの ... it represented a sort of wild beauty ... show the frightening power of the wilderness ... より、下線部は対照を成し、正解は (A) であるとわかる。

9. 解答 **(B)**

次のセンテンスの挿入箇所の候補として本文中に示された 4 つの■を見なさい。

ヨーロッパにも確かに美しい自然はあったが、アメリカの未開地のような粗野な美しさには欠けていた。

このセンテンスを挿入するのに最もふさわしい場所はどこか。

解説　挿入文の最後の部分である ... the American wilderness. に続く文を考えると、The wilderness で始まっている (B) が正解だとわかる。ちなみに、(A) の最初の部分、This attempt は前文の an attempt を指し、(C) の最初の部分、The paintings は (B) の最後にある paintings を受けたもの。従って、(A) と (C) が正解でないことはすぐにわかる。本問では、挿入文の内容を考えても (B) が正解とわかることをつけ加えておく。

10. 解答 （下の文を参照）

(F) Interest in Cole's paintings of the Catskill area inspired other artists to paint in a similar style which became known as the Hudson River School.

(C) The Hudson River School was similar to European Romantic painting in its emotional interpretation of nature.

(D) American Romantic painting portrayed the love of nature while understanding its power; an attitude that made it different from European painting.

指示文：下記に提示された導入文は本文の要約である。本文の中で最も重要な考えを選択肢から３つ選び、要約を完成させなさい。いくつかの選択肢は本文中で示されていないことを提示しているか、または重要ではない内容であるため、要約には不適切である。**この設問の配点は２点である。**

トーマス・コールは初めての真のアメリカ人芸術家であり、アメリカのロマン主義運動の創始者であると考えられている。

選択肢

(A) この自然への愛情の一例は、アルバート・ビアスタッドによるアメリカ西部の絵であった。

(B) コール自身は決して有名ではなかったが、彼の絵はハドソン川流域の大勢の芸術家に影響を与えた。

(C) ハドソン・リバー派は、自然を感情的に解釈するという点でヨーロッパのロマン派の絵画に似ていた。

(D) アメリカのロマン派の絵画は、自然の力を理解しつつ自然に対する愛情を描き、ヨーロッパの絵画とは異なる姿勢だった。

(E) ヨーロッパ人はアメリカ人のように自然への愛情を表現することができなかった。

(F) キャッツキル地域を描いたコールの絵画への関心によって刺激を受けた他の芸術家たちが、同様のスタイルで描くようになり、それがハドソン・リバー派として知られるようになった。

解説 ここでは、時間の経過に沿って要約を考えるといい。出だしの文は第１パラグラフの要約なので、次に来るのは第２パラグラフをまとめた (F) である。そしてその最後に書いてある the Hudson River School を受けて、それをさらに説明している (C) につながる。次に (C) の記述の European Romantic painting との対比を表す American Romantic painting について書かれている (D) が来る。

アメリカ先住民の文化

　ヨーロッパ人が初めて新世界に来たとき、南北アメリカ大陸にはおよそ 9,000 万人のアメリカ先住民が暮らしていた。しかしながら、そのうち北アメリカに暮らしていたのは、約 1,000 万人のみであった。アメリカ先住民の人口は、よく、新たな植民者との休む間もない戦いにより減少したと考えられている。これはある程度は正しいが、彼らが消滅した本当の理由はそれほどドラマチックなものではなく、はるかに致命的なものであった。実際は、ヨーロッパ人が持ち込んだ病気、特に天然痘が彼らの多くを死に至らしめたのである。北アメリカのアメリカ先住民の人口は 20 世紀に増えたものの、アメリカ先住民として認められているのはいまだ 200 万人にも満たない。

　アメリカ先住民の歴史は、おそらく 3 万年ほど前のアジアにおいて始まった。それは、そのときに放浪していた遊牧民族の一団が、氷河期の間、北アメリカへ狩りをするためにベーリング海のアイス・ブリッジを渡り始めたという証拠から明らかである。人口は少しずつ南方へ広がっていき、最終的に、温度上昇がアジアとの陸によるすべてのつながりを取り除いたとき、アジアから完全に分離された。

　広範囲に暮らしていたアメリカ先住民の人々は、主に彼らが住んでいた地理的条件に基づいた明らかな身体的特徴を備え始めた。大平原のアメリカ先住民は背が高く頑強な体格を持つ傾向にあったが、アンデス山脈のアメリカ先住民は、高い山々における空気の薄さに適応できなければならないという明らかな理由から、背が低く広い胸を持っていた。アメリカ先住民の部族たちが適応しなければいけない環境は、全部で 9 種類あった。それぞれの地域にあった入手可能な自然の資源と課題（問題点）が、それぞれの集団や部族が発達させた生活習慣や文化に反映されていたのである。

　合衆国南西部は、アメリカ先住民が適応しなければならなかった地域のひとつであり、彼らの文化が変わりゆく状況とともに、どのように変化したのかを見る好例となっている。現在のアリゾナ州、ニューメキシコ州、コロラド州、またメキシコ北部に当たるこの地域で、最も初期のアメリカ先住民の居住者たちは、紀元前 8000 年ごろにはすでにヤリでマンモスの狩りを行っていた。氷河期が終わりマンモスが消えていくにつれ、アメリカ先住民の居住者は主食をバイソン（またはバッファロー）に切り替えた。彼らはまた食物を補うために植物により大きく依存し始めた。

　その後、この地域は長期間にわたり次第に乾燥していった。居住者たちはまず、シカ、小動物、そして鳥を狩るように変わっていった。しかし、これらがどんどん見つけにくくなったため、居住者たちはさらに食生活を変えざるを得なくなった。彼らは果物、木の実やそのほかの種子などの植物食物を集めることにますます依存していった。彼らはこれらの種子の一部をすりつぶし、パンを作るための粉にし始めたようだ。このことは、彼らが最初狩人だったころに比べて放浪することが少なくなり、ひとつの場所に落ち着くようになったことを示しているように思われる。紀元前 300 年ごろには、この地域のアメリカ先住民居住者たちはメキシコから来た部族によってもたらされた文化の影響を受けた。トウモロコシ、豆、そしてカボチャが彼らの食事の一部分になった。このような乾燥した環境でこれらの作物を育てるためには、普通以上の手入れと灌漑（かんがい）が必要であった。このことはさらに住民

たちを住みつかせることになり、西暦 700 年ごろまでには彼らは時には崖に町をつくるようになった。これが現在アナサジ文化と呼ばれているものである。

1540 年にスペイン人がやって来るまでは、彼らの文化は比較的進んだものであったが、スペイン人にはかなわず、結局 1598 年までにはスペイン人の管理下に置かれた。1680 年に起こった反乱の間、彼らはスペイン人の管理下から離れ、なんとか自由を得ていたが、その後まずはメキシコに、そして後には合衆国に支配された。それにもかかわらず、このような状況の中でもアナサジの子孫であるプエブロは自らの文化を守ることができた。このため、今日に至っても 22 のプエブロの町が存在している。

重要語句

□ A.D.（名詞）Anno Domini（ラテン語）西暦紀元
□ advanced（形容詞）前進した、進歩的な、上級の
□ altogether（副詞）まったく、完全に
□ approximately（副詞）だいたい、おおよそ
□ as well as ...（副詞）～のみならず、～と同様に
□ assume（動詞）当然と思う、仮定する
□ available（形容詞）利用できる、手に入れられる
□ band（名詞）一隊、一団、一行
□ by（前置詞）までに（は）　no latter than
□ care（名詞）手入れ
□ cliff（名詞）崖、絶壁
□ comprise（動詞）～を構成する、～より成る
□ constant（形容詞）休みなく続く、定期的に繰り返される
□ crop（名詞）作物、収穫物
□ deadly（形容詞）致命的な、致死の、極端な、耐えられない
□ decimate（動詞）（疫病などが）多くを殺す
□ demise（名詞）消滅、終了
□ descendant（名詞）子孫、末裔
□ diet（名詞）常食、食品、食餌
□ distinct（形容詞）異なった、別個の
□ do away with 捨てる、処分する、取り除く、廃止する
□ dramatic（形容詞）劇的な、躍動的な、印象的な
□ flour（名詞）粉、粉末食品
□ game（名詞）狩猟の対象になる動物
□ geographic（形容詞）地理的な、地理学上の
□ grind（動詞）すり砕いて（つぶして、ひいて）粉にする
□ Ice Age 氷河時代
□ in all 全部で

□ inhabitant（名詞）居住者、住人
□ irrigation（名詞）灌漑（かんがい）、注水
□ isolated（形容詞）分離された、孤立した
□ maintain（動詞）保持する、保つ
□ maize（名詞）トウモロコシ
□ match（名詞）対等の人（物）、競争相手
□ nomadic（形容詞）遊牧民的な、放浪の
□ Nordic（形容詞）北方人種の、北欧人の
□ physical（形容詞）身体の、身体的な
□ primarily（副詞）初めは、第一に、主として、おおむね
□ progressively（副詞）次第に、漸次
□ qualify（動詞）認可を受ける、資格を取得する、適任である
□ rebellion（名詞）反逆、反乱
□ reside（動詞）住む、居住する
□ roam（動詞）放浪する、歩き回る
□ settle（動詞）住みつかせる、確定する、決める、処理する
□ settler（名詞）移住者、開拓者
□ smallpox（名詞）天然痘
□ spear（名詞）ヤリ
□ squash（名詞）カボチャ属の総称
□ subjugate（動詞）支配下に置く、征服する、服従させる
□ supplement（動詞）補足となる、埋め合わせる、満たす
□ throughout（前置詞）～の至る所に、～の隅から隅まで
□ trait（名詞）特徴、特色
□ tribe（名詞）部族、一族
□ warming（名詞）温度上昇
□ widespread（形容詞）広げた、広範囲に及ぶ

11. 解答 (B)

本文中の decimated の意味に最も近いのは

(A) 攻撃された

(B) 減少された

(C) 影響を受けた

(D) 維持された

解説 これも前文につながっており、smallpox（天然痘）が先住民族の人口を減少させたと言っている。取り上げられている語の意味を文脈の中で考えてみるといい。

12. 解答 (C)

第 3 パラグラフの情報に基づき、アメリカ先住民の身体的特徴の変異を適切に説明しているのは以下のどれか。

(A) 異なる文化的特徴が異なる身体的特徴を生んだ。

(B) 異なるライフスタイルが異なる特徴を生んだ。

(C) 異なる環境要因が異なる特徴を生んだ。

(D) 身体的特徴の違いにより、異なる文化が発展した。

解説 第 3 パラグラフの最初の文、... Native Americans began to develop distinct physical traits based largely on the geographic regions in which they resided. の下線部より、正解は、(A) と (D) にある culture や (B) の lifestyle ではなく、(C) の環境によるものとわかる。

13. 解答 (D)

第 3 パラグラフで、アメリカ先住民の文化について何が推測できるか。

(A) それは身体的特徴の産物である。

(B) それは地域が違っても驚くほど同じである。

(C) それは平原の文化と山脈の文化の 2 通りに分けられる。

(D) それは地域や直面する課題によって異なってくる。

解説 第 3 パラグラフの最後の文、... The natural resources available and the challenges each region presented are reflected in the lifestyles and cultures that each group or tribe developed. より、正解は (D) とわかる。

14. 解答 (D)

第4と第5パラグラフの内容によると、南西部のある地域に暮らすアメリカ先住民の文化の発展において、何が最も重要だったか。

(A) 農業の発展。

(B) 食糧供給の変化。

(C) 他の部族との交流。

(D) 環境要因の変化。

解説 第4パラグラフの最初の部分、The Southwestern United States comprised one such environment and provides a good example of how the Native American culture changed with changing conditions. や、第5パラグラフの ... This seems to indicate that they became more settled in one area and less nomadic than when they were primarily hunters. より、正解は (D) とわかる。

15. 解答 (A)

第5パラグラフで、著者はこうほのめかしている。町が出来上がったのは

(A) 作物をよりよく手入れするためである。

(B) 灌漑システムを構築するためである。

(C) 他の部族とより効果的に交流するためである。

(D) 崖で一緒に暮らすほうが楽だったからである。

解説 第5パラグラフの ... To grow such crops (= maize, beans and squash) ... required additional care ... より、正解は (A) となる。

16. 解答 (D)

第5パラグラフで、なぜ著者は気候がより乾燥することに言及しているのか。

(A) 気候の変化の中で、狩猟される動物の種類がどのように変化したかを示すために

(B) 気候の変化によって他の部族と物品を交換せざるを得なくなったことを示すために

(C) 灌漑がどれほど重要になったかを示すために

(D) 気候が文化に及ぼす影響を示すために

解説 To grow such crops in such dry conditions required ... と This settled the residents even more, ... they had developed towns ... さらに This is now referred to as the Anasazi culture. より、正解は (D) とわかる。

17. 解答 (C)

第5パラグラフによると、アナサジについて正しいものはどれか。

(A) 彼らは基本的にまだ遊牧民だった。

(B) 彼らはパンを焼く能力を身につけていった。

(C) 彼らの食生活はメキシコの部族から影響を受けた。

(D) 彼らは崖での生活を余儀なくされた。

解説 第5パラグラフの ... the Native American inhabitants of the area came under the influence of culture introduced by tribes from Mexico. Maize, beans and squash became part of their diet. を読めば、正解は (C) とわかる。ちなみに、このパラグラフには they became more settled や they had developed towns sometimes built into cliffs. といった記述もあるので、(A) や (D) が正解でないことは明らか。

18. 解答 (D)

アンサジ文化に関する著書の意見を最も正確に反映しているのはどれか。

(A) その歴史の早い時期に町を形成したことは驚きである。

(B) 狩猟から農耕文化に変わったことは驚きである。

(C) 他の部族とのつながりを維持したことは注目に値する。

(D) 非常に多くの困難を経ながらも文化を維持できたことは注目に値する。

解説 第6パラグラフの ... were finally put under their (= the Spanish) control ... were then subjugated first by Mexico and later the United States. Throughout it all, however, the Pueblo, the descendants of the Anasazi, were able to maintain their culture. といった記述より、正解は (D) とわかる。

19. 解答 (A)

次のセンテンスの挿入箇所の候補として本文中に示された 4 つの■を見なさい。

しかし、これらがどんどん見つけにくくなったため、彼らはさらに食生活を変えざるを得なくなった。

このセンテンスを挿入するのに最もふさわしい場所はどこか。

解説　まず、(B) にある grinding は次の文の初めにある This seems につながるので、(B) ではない。(D) にある such crops は前文に出てくる *Maize, beans and squash* を指すので、(D) でもない。(A) と (C) が残るが、(A) の more and more on collecting plant food such as fruits, nuts and other seeds. は挿入文の中にある their diet の例として書かれたものなので、正解は (A) となる。さらに、前文にある hunting deer, small game and birds と collecting plant food は相反するものなので、However で始まる挿入文は (A) に入れるのが自然。

20. 解答 （下の文を参照）

(C) The first was the challenge of adapting to the diverse environments that they found in the New World from high altitudes to dry climates.

(D) The Anasazi culture is an example of a successful adaptation in that it adapted to both climatic change and domination by stronger cultures.

(F) Despite many challenges, the Pueblo culture was able to preserve its identity and maintain its customs to the present day.

指示文：以下に提示された導入文は本文の要約である。本文の中で最も重要な考えを選択肢から3つ選び、要約を完成させなさい。いくつかの選択肢は本文中で示されていないことを提示しているか、または重要ではない内容であるため、要約には不適切である。**この設問の配点は2点である。**

約3万年前にアメリカに到達した後、アメリカ先住民はさまざまな課題に直面した。

選択肢

(A) アメリカ先住民の人口は、ヨーロッパ人がアメリカに到達した時期以来、激減してきている。

(B) その文化は、1598年のスペイン人による征服に抵抗できるほど発達したものではなかった。

(C) 最初の課題は、高地から乾燥気候まで、新大陸で直面した多種多様な環境に順応することであった。

(D) アナサジ文化は、気候変動とより強力な文化による支配の両方に順応した成功例の一つである。

(E) アンデス山脈に住み、広い胸部を発達させたことで、一部のアメリカ先住民は過酷な環境を生き抜くことができた。

(F) 多くの困難があったにもかかわらず、プエブロ文化は今日までその独自性を保ち、習慣を維持することができた。

解説 まず、The first で始まる (C) を選ぶが、これは第3パラグラフからもわかる。次に (C) をサポートしている文を探すと、例として挙げられている Anasazi culture、(D) であることがわかる。つまり、第3パラグラフから第4パラグラフ、第5パラグラフへと流れ、締めくくりとして第6パラグラフに書いてある内容のまとめがくる。従って、最後は (F)。ちなみに、第6パラグラフでは、Anasazi の子孫である Pueblo が多くの問題を抱えながらも自らの文化を守ることができたというのが、いちばん重要な記述である。

Listening Section　解答・解説

講義や会話を部分的に聴き直して答える問題のトランスクリプトには 🎧 マークを記してあります。このうち設問に直接対応する部分は太字で示しました（問題文ではこの部分の音声をもう一度聴くことができます）。なお、全体のトランスクリプトでは太字部分のみが示されています。

Questions **1-5**

mp3
17

トランスクリプト

Student A: Hi, how are you doing today?

Student B: Not so good.

Student A: Why? What's the problem?

Student B: I haven't been getting much sleep lately.

Student A: Why? Are you worried about the exams? Studying too late?

Student B: Well, I am worried about the exams but that's another problem. Some guys moved into the apartment next door, and it seems that every night they have parties until four in the morning. They're always shouting and playing loud music, and don't seem to care whether they keep anyone awake or not. It's just impossible to get any sleep (Q1). I've got to get some rest or I really will fail my exams.

Student A: Well, this doesn't sound like a good situation. You should do something about it.

Student B: Yeah, what?

Student A: Tell them to quiet down.

Student B: **That's easy for you to say. These guys are on the football team. Can you imagine me telling them to quiet down?** (Q4) I'm afraid they wouldn't be very understanding. I think it could even make matters worse. Believe me, that's not the solution.

Student A: Well, you've got to do something. You can't go on living like this. Where do you live anyway?

Student B: Weatherly Hall.

Student A: So it's school housing.

Student B: Yeah.

187

Student A: That's good. In this case <u>just tell the dormitory manager what's going on</u> (Q2). He's supposed to stop this kind of stuff from happening so that people can study. Besides, you can't be the only one who's upset about this. Maybe you can ask some of the other people on your floor to go to the manager with you. Do you know any other people on your floor?

Student B: No, no one. <u>Everyone seems to kind of keep to themselves</u> (Q3). I mean, <u>this is the first term, and none of us have really had much time to do more than say hello when we pass in the hall</u> (Q3). A lot of them are foreign students like me and probably just think this is the way things are at an American university. They probably just don't want to cause any trouble.

Student A: **Well, you really <u>have to</u> take some initiative here** (Q5). The more people willing to complain the more chance you'll be listened to. Just go to their rooms and introduce yourself and ask them if they have the same complaint as you have. My guess is they would be happy to do something. They can't be getting much sleep either.

Student B: But what if the manager doesn't do anything? I mean, he must know what's going on already. These are pretty loud parties.

Student A: Well, maybe, but he might just be waiting for someone like you to complain first. He may think no one really cares about these parties. And if no one cares, why should he bother doing anything about it? But if he doesn't do anything, you can always go to the Housing Department. Believe me. Someone will have to do something. You don't want to fail your exams because of this do you?

Student B: No. You're right. <u>I've got to do something.</u> OK, I'll give it a try (Q2).

Student A: Great. Let me know how it turns out.

訳例

学生A：あら、元気？
学生B：あんまり。
学生A：どうして？　何かあったの？
学生B：最近あまり眠ってないんだ。
学生A：どうして？　試験のことを心配しているの？　遅くまで勉強し過ぎ？
学生B：うん、試験のことは心配だけれど、別の問題があるんだ。アパートの隣の部屋に男が何人

か移ってきて、毎晩朝の4時までパーティーをやってるみたいなんだ。ずっと大声を上げたり大きな音で音楽をかけたりして、ほかの人がその音で眠れなくても気にしていないみたいなんだ。まったく眠れないんだよ。なんとか休まないと本当に試験で落第してしまいそうだ。

学生A： よくない状況みたいね。なんとかしなきゃ。

学生B： うん、でも何ができる?

学生A： その人たちに静かにするように言えば。

学生B： そう言うのは簡単だけれど、彼らはフットボール・チームにいるんだよ。僕が彼らに静かにしろって言っているところを想像できるかい?　わかってもらえるわけないよ。それどころかもっと状況が悪くなるかもしれない。わかるだろう、それじゃあ解決にならないよ。

学生A： うん、でもなんとかしなきゃ。そんな生活は続けていけないわよ。どこに住んでいるんだっけ?

学生B： ウェザリー・ホールだよ。

学生A： じゃあ学校の寮よね。

学生B： うん。

学生A： よかった。だったら、寮の管理人に何が起こっているか言うだけでいいわ。管理人は皆が勉強できるように、こういうことが起こらないようにしなければいけないんだから。それに、怒っているのはあなただけじゃないはずよ。同じ階のほかの人に、一緒に管理人のところに行ってくれって頼めるんじゃない。同じ階に知り合いは?

学生B： 誰もいない。皆、なんとなく人づき合いを避けているみたいなんだ。最初の学期だから、廊下で会ってもあいさつする以外の時間がある人なんて誰もいないんだよ。彼らの多くは僕みたいな留学生だから、もしかしたらアメリカの学校ではこういうものなんだと思っているのかもしれない。問題を起こしたくないと思っているだけかもしれないし。

学生A： あなたがここでイニシアチブを取らないと（駄目ね）。文句を言う人が多ければ多いほど、聞いてもらえる可能性が高くなるのよ。彼らの部屋を訪ねて、自分を紹介し、同じような不満を抱えているか聞くだけでいいのよ。私は、彼らも喜んで何かをすると思うわ。彼らもあまり眠れていないに決まっているもの。

学生B： でも、もし管理人が何もしてくれなかったら?　管理人は何が起こっているかすでに知っているはずなんだ。かなりやかましいパーティーなんだよ。

学生A： もしかしたらね。でも、あなたみたいな人がまず文句を言ってくるのを待っているだけなのかもしれないわよ。誰もパーティーのことを本当には気にしていないと思っているのかもしれないし。もし誰も気にしていないんだったら、なぜ彼がわざわざ何かしなければいけないの?　彼が何もしてくれなかったら、住居課に行けばいいのよ。信じてよ。誰かが何かをしなきゃ。このせいで試験を落第したくないでしょ?

学生B： 落第はしたくないよ。君の言うとおりだね。僕が何かしなきゃ。うん、じゃあ、やってみるよ。

学生A： そうよ。どうなったか教えてね。

1. 解答 (C)

男性の主な問題は何か。

(A) 彼は試験について心配している。

(B) 彼は睡眠に問題を抱えている。

(C) 彼の隣人が騒がしい。

(D) 彼にはまだ誰とも会う機会がない。

解説 選択肢にある (B) は、彼自身の問題で起こることである。

トランスクリプトの下線部参照。

- Some guys moved into the apartment next door, and it seems that every night they have parties until four in the morning. They're always shouting and playing loud music, and don't seem to care whether they keep anyone awake or not. It's just impossible to get any sleep.

2. 解答 (C)

男性は女性からのどのようなアドバイスを受け入れているか。

(A) 彼は隣人に静かにするよう言うべきである。

(B) 彼はもっと多くの同じ階の学生と会うべきである。

(C) 彼は寮の管理人に苦情を言うべきである。

(D) 彼は住宅局に行くべきである。

解説 (B) は、管理人の所に行くためにすることなので、正解は (C) となる。

トランスクリプトの下線部参照。

- just tell the dormitory manager what's going on.
- I've got to do something.
- OK, I'll give it a try.

3. 解答 (C)

男性はなぜもっと多くの同じ階の学生を知らないのか。

(A) 彼らは全員フットボール選手である。

(B) 彼らは全員留学生で、おそらくあまり英語を話さない。

(C) 本当に時間に余裕がなく、まだ誰とも知り合えていない。

(D) 彼はまったく誰とも出会わない。

解説 トランスクリプトの下線部参照。

- Everyone seems to kind of keep to themselves.
- this is the first term, and none of us have really had much time to do more than say hello when we pass in the hall.

4. 解答 (B)

会話の一部をもう一度聞きなさい。それから、質問に答えなさい。

男性はなぜこのように言っているのか。

(A) 彼はフットボールのことを何も知らないため、本当に彼らと話せない。

(B) 彼はあまり強そうに見えないので、彼らはおそらく彼に注目しないだろう。

(C) 一人が腹を立てているぐらいでは、彼らは特に気にしない。

(D) 彼は、彼女が彼らと話したほうがよかったのにと思っている。

解説 トランスクリプトの下線部参照。ここでは、「football team（フットボール・チーム）のメンバー」という記述から、彼らは強くて、体格もいいということが想像できる。さらに、学生は、「自分たちより貧弱な学生が苦情を言ったところで、そんなことには耳を貸さないんじゃないか」と言っている（暗示）。

Student A: Tell them to quiet down.

Student B: **That's easy for you to say. These guys are on the <u>football team</u>. Can you imagine me telling them to quiet down?** I'm afraid they wouldn't be very understanding. I think it could even make matters worse. Believe me, that's not the solution.

5. 解答 **(A)**

会話の一部をもう一度聞きなさい。それから、質問に答えなさい。

女性はこのように言うことで何をほのめかしているのか。

(A) 彼女は、この状況で弱気すぎると彼を批判している。

(B) 彼女は、彼がリスクを冒してチャンスをつかむよう促している。

(C) 彼女は、彼の状況への同情を示している。

(D) 彼女は、彼にアイデアを求めている。

解説 トランスクリプトの下線部参照。ここで使われている have to という強い表現は「〜しなければ駄目ね」という意味で、それをしていない学生を批判している。ちなみに、こういう言い方は、アドバイスをするのでなければ、聞き手を批判するときに使われる。

🎧 **Well, you really <u>have to</u> take some initiative here.** The more people willing to complain the more chance you'll be listened to.

Questions 6-11

トランスクリプト

Philosophy, politics, economics: they are all interconnected. I mean, it's hard to separate them since they seem to feed off of each other (Q6 : Q7). Well, take Marxism, for example (Q7). It's a philosophy which basically states that wealth should be evenly distributed so that a wealthy class cannot be allowed to develop or else it would be tempted to use this power to exploit the less fortunate. Now, I admit this oversimplifies things, but for the purpose of today's discussion it's close enough. The point here is that you cannot have this equal distribution of wealth without a strong and widespread system of government. This leads to power being transferred into the government rather than, say, the wealthy classes or individuals, as in capitalism. So it's only normal that in some cases, maybe many cases, you would get communist dictators. The ideas behind the philosophy tend to support it. On the other hand, capitalism, with its emphasis on individualism, tends to favor a lack of government control. I mean, the idea of a capitalist dictator doesn't really occur.

In any event, these philosophies influence government and that, in turn, influences the country's economics. I think we sometimes forget this. We think that political or economic theories are only that. That they are only theories and never really have any practical application, but I would argue that this may only seem true at the beginning. Ideas have a way of slowly influencing other areas, and in the case of economic theories, they have a way of influencing governments and they can, in turn, influence how companies conduct business.

All that I've said today is really to set up a discussion of one of the most influential economists of the 20th century, although his name is seldom found in your usual economics textbook. I'm talking about Joseph Schumpeter (Q8). Schumpeter clearly saw the interconnectedness of what I was just talking about. In his most famous book, *Capitalism, Socialism and Democracy*, Schumpeter tries to show how capitalism could naturally transform itself into socialism (Q9-c) without the proletariat revolution that

Marx always hoped for. So, let's look more closely to see how he thought this could happen.

First of all, I should make it clear that Schumpeter was a capitalist even though he thought that capitalism was logically doomed to become socialism. The hero of capitalism, according to Schumpeter, was the entrepreneur. He defines an entrepreneur as an innovator and not necessarily an inventor (Q9-b). An entrepreneur could figure out how to use market, or manufacture a new invention but, in fact, wouldn't really need a new invention at all. This is because an entrepreneur could be an innovator in, say, management. He thought that capitalism was important in stimulating entrepreneurship. Let's face it, if you can make more money by innovating, you will innovate and, in so doing, become an entrepreneur (Q10) in the sense that Schumpeter means. So it was capitalism that stimulated entrepreneurship and entrepreneurship that provided the motor for capitalism (Q9-d). In the process, however, old institutions, inventions and techniques were destroyed by innovation. Schumpeter thought this was not only necessary but good. It kept the system dynamic. He referred to this in his book as "creative destruction." (Q9-a)

But how could such a tight system deteriorate into socialism? Well, Schumpeter saw a wealthy (Q9), elite upper class developing that was somewhat removed from the entrepreneurs themselves, though they owed their own existence to them. Such a class would begin to consider the values of the entrepreneur to be low class or common (Q9-e). Since they held power, they would begin to pressure the government to curb the values that encouraged innovation. Thus, the government was encouraged to control innovation and individual initiative. In this way, a capitalist society would effectively start down the road to socialism (Q9-e).

OK, that's a little background on Schumpeter. We've seen how important he considered the role of the entrepreneur, and how innovation was a key aspect of capitalism. Now I'd like to trace the influence of his ideas on other economists that came along later in the century (Q11).

訳例

　哲学、政治学、経済学は互いに結びついています。つまり、これらは互いに情報を交換し合っているようなので、切り離して考えるのは難しいのです。そうですねえ、例えば、マルクス主義です。それは、基本的に、富裕層が発展できないように富は等しく分配されるべきだとするもので、さもないと彼らはこの権力を行使して裕福でない人々（貧乏人）からの搾取を試みたくなる誘惑を認めないとする哲学です。まあ、この説明は単純化し過ぎているのは認めますが、本日の議論の目的からするとこれでほぼ十分なのです。ここで重要なのは、この富の平等な分配は、政府の強力で広範囲に及ぶ制度なしには達成し得ないということです。これは、権力が、資本主義でもそうであるように、例えば富裕層や資産家にではなく、政府に移っていくことにつながります。ですから、いくつかのケースにおいて、おそらく多くのケースにおいて、共産主義の独裁者が生まれるのは当然なわけなのです。つまり、その哲学（マルクス主義）の背後にある考え方は、そのことを支持しがちなのです。他方、個人主義を強調する資本主義は、政府による支配が存在しないことを好む傾向にあります。つまり、資本主義の独裁者などというものは実際には存在しようがないわけなのです。

　とにかく、哲学は政府に影響を及ぼし、同様に国の経済にも影響を及ぼします。私たちはときどきこのことを忘れてしまうように感じます。私たちは政治学上の、または経済学上の理論はそれだけで存在していると考えています。それらは理論にすぎず、実際には決して使用されないのだと。しかし、私は、そう見えたのは最初だけではないかと考えています。考え方というものはゆっくりとほかの分野に影響していき、経済学上の理論の場合は、その理論は政府に影響を及ぼし、同様に会社がどのように事業を行うのかにも影響を与えることができます。

　本日、今までにお話ししたすべては、一般の経済学の教科書にはめったに名前が出てこないのですが、実際は、20世紀に最も影響力のあった経済学者のひとりの議論を基に構成したものです。私がお話ししているのは、ジョセフ・シュンペーターについてです。シュンペーターは、たった今、私がお話しした相関性という概念をはっきりと理解しています。彼の最も有名な本、『資本主義・社会主義・民主主義』でシュンペーターは、マルクスが常に望んでいたプロレタリア階級による革命がなくても、資本主義がどのようにそれ自身を社会主義へと転換させていくこともあるのかを説こうとしています。さて、それでは、どうすればこんなことが起こり得ると彼が考えたのかをもっと詳しく見ていきましょう。

　まず、シュンペーターは、資本主義は必然的に社会主義になるように運命づけられていると考えていたのですが、彼自身は資本主義者であったということをはっきりさせておいたほうがよいでしょう。シュンペーターによると、資本主義の英雄は起業家たちでした。彼は、起業家を、発案者である必要はなく、革新者であればよいと定義しています。起業家は、どのように市場を利用するか、であるとか、どのように新製品を製造するか、ということを理解しているものですが、実際にはそれが新しい発明である必要はまったくないのです。それはどうしてかというと、起業家は、言ってみれば経営における革新者であってもよいからです。シュンペーターは、資本主義は起業家精神を活性化させるのに重要であると考えていました。現実を直視しましょう。もし、革新によってより多くのお金を稼ぐことができるとしたら、革新するでしょう。そしてそうする中で、シュンペーターが言っている意味での起業家になるのです。つまり、起業家精神を活性化したのは資本主義で、資本主義の原動力となっていたのは起業家精神だったのです。しかし、その過程において古い制度や発明、技術は革新によって破壊されました。シュンペーターは、これは必要であるだけでなく、良いことだと考えていました。それは、システムを動的な状態に保ちました。彼は本の中でこれを「創造的破壊」であると述べました。

しかし、このように堅固なシステムがどのように社会主義へと堕落してしまうのでしょうか。実は、シュンペーターは、このシステムを発展させていた裕福なエリートである上流階級が、起業家たちとの間に少しずつ距離を置くようになったと考えていたのです。彼らが存在していられたのは、起業家たちのおかげだったにもかかわらずです。そのような（上流）階級では、起業家の価値は低い、もしくは平凡な存在であると考え始めるわけです。そして、彼らは権力を持っているので、革新を奨励するような考え方を抑制するように政府に圧力をかけ始めるのです。その結果、政府は革新や個人の自発性を制御するように仕向けられたのです。このようにして、資本主義社会は事実上、社会主義への道をたどり始めたのです。

というところが、シュンペーターに関するちょっとした予備知識です。彼が、起業家の役割をどれほど重要だと考えていたか、そして革新というものがどれほど資本主義にとって重要な側面であったかを見てきたわけです。では、次に、彼の考えが20世紀後半に現れてきたほかの経済学者たちにどのような影響を与えたかについてお話ししたいと思います。

6. 解答 (C)

この講義の主題は何か。

(A) マルクス主義とその政治への影響

(B) 社会主義と資本主義の関係

(C) 経済理論の他の分野への影響

(D) 起業家たちのイノベーション

解説 トランスクリプトの下線部参照。

- Philosophy, politics, economics: they are all interconnected. I mean, it's hard to separate them since they seem to feed off of each other.

7. 解答 (B)

教授はなぜマルクス主義に言及しているのか。

(A) マルクスの理論がよく知られているから

(B) 経済学、政治学、哲学のすべてがどれほど結び付いているかを示すために

(C) シュンペーターの考えとの対比を示すために

(D) マルクスの考えが他の経済学者にどのような影響を与えたかを示すために

解説 トランスクリプトの下線部参照。ここでは、Marxism はその直前にある下線部を受けて、それを説明するための具体例として使われている。

- Philosophy, politics, economics: they are all interconnected. I mean, it's hard to separate them since they seem to feed off of each other.
- take Marxism, for example.

8. 解答 (C)

講義の一部をもう一度聞きなさい。それから、質問に答えなさい。

教授はこのように発言したときに、何をほのめかしているのか。

(A) シュンペ―ターは難解すぎるので、経済学の教科書では扱われていない。

(B) 誰もシュンペーターについて聞いたことがないにもかかわらず、教授は彼について話すつもりだ。

(C) シュンペーターは影響力があったが、主に経済学者の間でだけだった。

(D) シュンペーターは 20 世紀の教科書に載るほど重要ではない。

解説 下線部より、Joseph Schumpeter は教科書などには記載はないが、経済専門家の間ではよく知られていることがわかる。

All that I've said today is really to set up a discussion of one of the most influential economists of the 20th century, although his name is seldom found in your usual economics textbook. I'm talking about Joseph Schumpeter. Schumpeter clearly saw the interconnectedness of what I was just talking about.

9. 解答 （下の表を参照）

		Yes	No
a	Capitalism depends on "creative destruction."	○	
b	Innovators must be inventors.		○
c	Capitalism would naturally destroy itself.	○	
d	Entrepreneurs need capitalism in order to succeed.	○	
e	A wealthy class would keep capitalism strong.		○

講義の中で、教授はジョセフ・シュンペーターについていくつかの見解を述べている。以下のそれぞれについて、彼の述べた見解かどうかを示しなさい。各文の Yes 欄か No 欄に印を付けなさい。

資本主義は「創造的破壊」に依存している。

革新者は発案者でなければならない。

資本主義は自然に滅びるだろう。

起業家が成功するには資本主義が必要である。

富裕層は強い資本主義を維持する。

解説 トランスクリプトの下線部参照。最後の事項である A wealthy class would keep capitalism strong. に関しての記述はない。

《Yes の根拠》

- how capitalism could naturally transform itself into socialism (c)
- So it was capitalism that stimulated entrepreneurship and entrepreneurship that provided the motor for capitalism. (d)
- In the process, however, old institutions, inventions and techniques were destroyed by innovation. Schumpeter thought this was not only necessary but good. It kept the system dynamic. He referred to this in his book as "creative destruction." (a)

《No の根拠》

- an innovator and not necessarily an inventor. (b)
- Such a class (= wealthy) would begin to consider the values of the entrepreneur to be low class or common... In this way, a capitalist society would effectively start down the road to socialism. (e)

10. 解答 (A)、(D)

教授によると、資本主義はどのように起業家精神を刺激するのか。

解答を 2 つ選びなさい。

(A) 起業家に、お金を稼がせることによって

(B) 起業家に、「創造的破壊」を利用させることによって

(C) 起業家に、新たな経営技術を考えさせることによって

(D) 起業家を革新者にさせることによって

解説 トランスクリプトの下線部参照。

- if you can make more money by innovating, you will innovate and, in so doing, become an entrepreneur

11. 解答 (B)

教授は次に何を話すと考えられるか。

(A) シュンペーターの経済思想のさらなる詳細

(B) シュンペーターの考えが他の経済学者に与えた影響

(C) シュンペーターとマルクスの社会主義に対する考え方の比較

(D) シュンペーターの考えの悪影響

解説 トランスクリプトの下線部参照。

- Now I'd like to trace the influence of his ideas on other economists that came along later in the century.

トランスクリプト

Student A: Hi, John. How are your classes going this term?

Student B: Well, pretty good overall with one exception.

Student A: What's that?

Student B: Well, in all my other classes I can understand most of what the teacher says, but in this American literature class, I'm completely lost.

Student A: How come? Is it the reading? I know literature professors expect you to read an awful lot for their classes.

Student B: No, that's not really the problem, though, it's true I have a lot to read. But when I read, I can take my time, go at my own pace, and generally get the idea of what's happening. But in class, the teacher speaks so quickly and has such complicated ideas that I can't follow him (Q12). I try to take notes, but while I'm writing, he keeps on talking and I end up missing some important comments. It's really frustrating.

Student A: **Is anyone else complaining about him?** (Q16)

Student B: No, but I'm the only foreign student in the class. The Americans seem to be enjoying his lectures. I'm sure he's a really intelligent person, it's just too difficult for me. If this keeps up, I'm afraid I might not pass the course.

Student A: I know what you mean. I had a philosophy class like that when I first started at the university, too. I had no idea what was going on half the time.

Student B: **You? Really? I can't imagine you having any trouble** (Q15).

Student A: Well, my English wasn't so great (Q15) when I first came to this country. I was having a lot of problems with my lectures, but this philosophy class was the worst.

Student B: What did you do?

Student A: Well, I remembered what an English teacher in my country told me. He said that it's always possible to control a listening situation. He

200

showed us that the first time we listen we may only get the main idea, but if we listen again we can understand more.

Student B: Well, I'm not sure how this can help. I can't ask him to repeat his lecture just for me.

Student A: But that's the point. In a way, you can. Explain your problem to him after class, and ask him if you can leave a small tape recorder on his desk during the lecture. Then you can go home and listen to it as many times as you want (Q13).

Student B: Is that what you did?

Student A: Yeah. He understood my situation and didn't mind at all if I taped him. And you know what's funny? After that, some of the American students started doing the same thing. It became kind of a fad. (Q14)

Student B: But did it help? I mean, if it's difficult in class, it may be just as difficult when you listen again.

Student A: Well, you're never going to understand everything, but I began to understand more and more. I think it really improved my listening, and I got enough of the main ideas to pass the course.

Student B: I think I'll give it a try. Anything would be better than what I understand now. Thanks for the tip.

訳例

学生A： ハイ、ジョン。今学期のクラスはどう？

学生B： うーん、ひとつの例外を除いて全体的にはなかなかいいよ。

学生A： 何なの？

学生B： ほかのクラスでは先生が言っていることの大部分はわかるんだけれど、このアメリカ文学のクラスではまったくついていけないんだ。

学生A： どうして？　リーディングのせい？　文学の教授たちって、信じられないほどの量をクラスで読ませようとするのよね。

学生B： いや、たくさん読まなきゃいけないのは事実だけれど、本当に問題なのはそれじゃないんだ。時間を使って自分のペースで読めるなら、何が起こっているかはたいていわかるんだよ。でもクラスでは、先生がすごい早口で話すし、複雑な考え方をするものだから、ついていけないんだ。ノートを取ろうとするんだけれど、僕が書いている間も先生は話し続けて、結局大事なコメントを逃すことになる。本当にイライラするよ。

学生A： 先生についてほかに文句を言っている人はいないの？

学生B： いないけれど、僕はクラスではたったひとりの留学生なんだ。アメリカ人たちは、彼の講義を楽しんでいるように見えるよ。彼がすごく知的な人なのは確かだと思うけど、とにかく僕には難し過ぎる。このまま続くと僕は単位を取れないかもしれない。

学生Ａ：あなたが言っていることはよくわかるわ。私も大学に入ってすぐに、それに似たような哲学のクラスを取ったのよ。クラスの時間の半分くらいは何が起こっているのかまったくわからなかったわ。

学生Ｂ：君が？　本当に？　君がそんな問題を抱えていたなんて想像できないよ。

学生Ａ：最初にこの国に来たころの私の英語力は大したことはなかったのよ。講義はいつも大変だったけれど、この哲学のクラスは最悪だったわ。

学生Ｂ：それで、どうしたの？

学生Ａ：母国のある英語の先生が私に言ってくれたことを思い出したの。リスニングの状況をコントロールすることは常に可能だって。最初に聞いたときはメイン・アイデアしかつかめないとしても、もう一度聞けば、もっと理解できるってことを教えてくれたの。

学生Ｂ：それがどう助けになるのかわからないよ。僕だけのために講義を繰り返してくれって先生には頼めないだろう。

学生Ａ：でも、そこがポイントなの。ある意味では、できるのよ。授業の後で先生にあなたの問題を説明して、講義の間、先生の机の上に小さなテープレコーダーを置かせてもらうことはできるかって聞いてみるの*。そうすれば、家に帰って聞きたいだけ何度でも聞き直すことができるわ。

学生Ｂ：君はそうしたのかい？

学生Ａ：そうよ。先生は私の状況を理解してくれて、私が彼の講義を録音してもまったく気にしなかったわ。それに、おかしなことになったのよ。その後、何人かのアメリカ人学生が同じことをやり始めたの。ある種の流行になったわ。

学生Ｂ：でも、それが助けになったのかい？　授業で難しいことは、もう一度聞いても同じように難しいと思うけど。

学生Ａ：ええ、全部を理解できることは絶対にないけど、だんだん理解できるようになったわ。そのおかげで私のリスニング力は本当に上達したと思うし、単位を取るのに必要なだけの重要なアイデアは理解したもの。

学生Ｂ：やってみるよ。僕の今の理解力に比べれば、何だってましさ。アドバイスをありがとう。

注：＊ 講義を録音させてもらうときは、必ず教授に相談して許可を得なくてはならないことを覚えておいてほしい。アメリカの大学では誰もが心得ている最低限のマナーである。

12. 解答 (C)

男性の主な問題は何か。

(A) 彼には、文学の授業で読まなければならないものが多すぎる。

(B) 彼は文学の授業で唯一の外国人留学生である。

(C) 教授の考えについていくのが難しい。

(D) 彼は教授の講義を録音することをためらっている。

解説 トランスクリプトの下線部参照。

- in class, the teacher speaks so quickly and has such complicated ideas that I can't follow him.

13. 解答 (C)

女性は男性にどのようなアドバイスをしているか。

(A) 彼は読むことにもっと時間を費やすべきだ。

(B) 彼は講義を繰り返してくれるよう教授に頼むべきだ。

(C) 彼は教授の講義を録音して、後で聞くべきだ。

(D) 彼は何人かのアメリカ人の学生にその問題を相談すべきだ。

解説 トランスクリプトの下線部参照。

- Explain your problem to him after class, and ask him if you can leave a small tape recorder on his desk during the lecture. Then you can go home and listen to it as many times as you want.

14. 解答 (B)

女性が教授の話を録音したら、何が起こったか。

(A) 彼女は講義の要点しか理解できず、がっかりした。

(B) アメリカ人の学生たちも講義を録音し始めた。

(C) アメリカ人の学生たちがそれを面白がった。

(D) ある英語の教員が、彼女が講義を理解できるよう手助けした。

解説 トランスクリプトの下線部参照。

- After that, some of the American students started doing the same thing. It became kind of a fad.

15. 解答 (A)

会話の一部をもう一度聞きなさい。それから、質問に答えなさい。

男性はこのように言うことで何をほのめかしているのか。

(A) 彼には、彼女が聞き取りに問題を抱えていたとは信じられない。彼女が非常に英語を得意としているからだ。

(B) 彼は、彼女が哲学に苦労したことに驚いている。彼女が哲学に詳しいと思っていたからだ。

(C) 彼は、これほど英語が得意な人でも聞き取りに問題を抱えていたことにがっかりしている。

(D) 彼には、彼女のように楽観的な人がそのような問題を抱えているとは想像できない。

解説 トランスクリプトの下線部参照。ここでは "Really?" という表現を使い、「信じられない」と言っている。

- Well, my English wasn't so great
- Student A: I know what you mean. I had a philosophy class like that when I first started at the university, too. I had no idea what was going on half the time.

  Student B: **You? Really? I can't imagine you having any trouble.**

16. 解答 (B)

会話の一部をもう一度聞きなさい。それから、質問に答えなさい。

彼女はなぜこのようなことを言うのか。

(A) 彼女は、男性が大げさに言っていると思っている。

(B) 彼女は、その教員があまりよくない可能性があると思っている。

(C) 彼女は、状況をもっと詳しく知りたがっている。

(D) 彼女は、自分がこの状況にどれほど驚いているかを示そうとしている。

解説 トランスクリプトの下線部参照。ここでは、「ほかにも苦情を言っている学生がいれば、先生がよくないという可能性もある」ということを暗示している。

- Student A: **Is anyone else complaining about him?**

  Student B: No, but I'm the only foreign student in the class. The Americans seem to be enjoying his lectures.

トランスクリプト

Professor: OK, let's get started. Now we've been talking for some time about the early explorers in America and the effect their discoveries had on their own countries and the rest of Europe. But let's not forget why Columbus sailed west in the first place. Why was that?

Student A: To prove the world was round?

Professor: Well, not exactly, though this would certainly have made it easier for him to get more support for future expeditions.

Student B: He was hoping to get to India?

Professor: Sure, he wanted to get to India. And why was that?

Student B: It would ... maybe ... be easier to trade with India by going this way than by going all around Africa.

Professor: Exactly. Asia had a lot of good stuff, and Europe wanted it (Q20). The problem was it was really hard to bring back any great amount of anything without using ships, and the ships had to make long dangerous journeys around Africa (Q20). It was bad enough that it was so far away and took so long, but many times the ships were lost in rough seas, and investors lost all their money. It was a real risky business venture.

Student A: So it was really business that stimulated exploration more than, say, adventure or discovery (Q20).

Professor: Yeah, and you'll find that business was behind a lot of major events in history. But, to get back to what I was saying, although the discovery of a "New World" was interesting and promised some financial returns, for many it was just a big obstacle in the way of getting to Asia. Well, about 30 years after Columbus's voyage, Magellan proved you could sail west to Asia, but to do it you had to sail around South America which, as it turned out, was even worse than sailing around Africa (Q20). That's when attention began to turn to the north, or more specifically, to the idea of finding a Northwest Passage (Q17) to Asia. **I really can't emphasize**

205

enough (Q21) **how important this goal was to the Europeans, or the contributions that the searches for this passage made to the geographical understanding of the northern regions of North America** (Q19 : Q21). I really doubt if anyone would have wasted their time in these cold regions if it wasn't for the chance to earn a lot of money by sailing more directly to Asia.

Student B: But it's sort of like Atlantis, isn't it? I mean, there was never any Northwest Passage (Q17) to find, right?

Professor: Well, a lot of people still think so, but, no, there really is a Northwest Passage (Q17 : Q19) and it was actually discovered in the 1580's by an explorer named John Davis (Q18 : Q19). Unfortunately, he didn't sail completely through it and so it was really no more than an enlightened guess on his part.

But turning more to the geographical contributions of these searches, let's look at what these explorers found. In 1609, even before the Pilgrims landed, the Englishman Henry Hudson explored Chesapeake Bay and sailed up the Hudson River all the way to Albany (Q18). A year later, he was back exploring Hudson Bay when he was frozen in. This trip cost him his life as most of his crew rebelled and put him, his young son, and a few loyal crewmembers into a small boat and sent them on their way, never to be heard from again.

But Hudson was only one of many that died trying to find or get through this passage (Q17). A man named William Parry penetrated the passage far enough to win a reward for the act from the British Parliament (Q18). He was only 200 miles from making the passage to the Pacific when the ice stopped him.

Student A: Excuse me, when was that?

Professor: Oh, sorry, let me check my notes. Yeah, that was in 1820. Anyway, Parry came so close that the British were now sure they could make it through and finally, in 1845, actually packed two ships full of trading goods and sent them off to Asia captained by a man named John Franklin with a crew of 130 sailors. This was to turn out to be one of the greatest disasters in the attempt to make it through the Northwest Passage (Q17). <u>After hearing nothing from Franklin for two years</u> (Q18), the British Navy set off to try to find him and his crew in 1847. It kind of became a national cause. In all, something like 40 separate expeditions were sent off to look for Franklin over the next nine years.

Student B: Well, what do you think happened?

Professor: Well, no one can be sure of course but many people think that Franklin didn't have the proper equipment for arctic survival. I mean, like the right clothes and so on.

Student B: **But <u>how is that possible?</u> They had to know it was cold in the Arctic. It doesn't seem to make any sense** (Q22).

Professor: I agree. My only guess is that they expected Franklin to sail right on through the Northwest Passage with few problems and head on to Asia. It somehow never occurred to them that he might end up in some sort of survival situation.

訳例

教　授： はい、それでは始めましょう。さて、昔のアメリカ探検家たちと彼らの発見が、彼ら自身の国やヨーロッパのほかの地域に及ぼした影響についてしばらくの間話してきたわけですが、そもそも、なぜコロンブスが西へ航海したのかを忘れないでおきましょう。それはなぜでしたか。

学生Ａ： 地球が丸いことを証明するためですか。

教　授： それは確かに彼のそれ以降の探検に対してより多くの支持を得ることを容易にしましたが、厳密には違います。

学生Ｂ： インドに行きたかったのですか。

教　授： 確かに彼はインドに行きたかったのです。でも、それはなぜ？

学生Ｂ： それはたぶん、アフリカをぐるっと回って行くよりも、その方向で行くほうがインドと貿易しやすかったからでは。

教　授： そのとおりです。アジアにはたくさんの良い品物があり、ヨーロッパはそれが欲しかった。問題は、船を使わないで何か大量の物を持ち帰ることは大変に難しく、しかも船はアフリカを回るのに長く危険な旅をしなければいけなかったということでした。こんなに離れていて、こんなに時間がかかっただけでも良くないことを言うには十分でしたが、それに加えて船は何度も荒波にのまれて沈没し、投資家たちはすべての財産を失ったのです。それは本当に危険な投機事業でした。

学生Ａ： それでは、探検という行為を実際に促したのは、例えば、それが冒険とか発見だったとかいうよりも、ビジネスだったのですね。

教　授： ええ、歴史上、多くの主要な出来事の背後にビジネスがあったのだということがわかるようになりますよ。でも、このあたりで、話を戻しましょう。「新大陸」の発見は興味深く、またある程度の金銭的見返りも期待できましたが、多くの人にとってそれはアジアに行くときの大きな障害でしかなかったのです。コロンブスの航海から約30年後、マゼランは西に航

海すればアジアに行くことができる、しかし、そうするためには南アメリカを回って航海しなければならず、それはアフリカ回りの航海をするよりももっと危険だったということを証明したのです。それからは北に、より具体的にはアジアまでの北西方向の航路を見つけることに人々の注意が向き始めたのです。この目的がヨーロッパ人にとってどれほど重要だったか、また、この航路を探そうとしたことが北アメリカ北部地域の地理的理解にどれほど貢献したかは、どんなに強調しても強調しきれないほどです。もし、より直接的にアジアに航海することによって多くのお金を稼げる見込みがなければ、彼らがこれらの寒冷地で時間を無駄にしたかどうか疑わしいと思います。

学生Ｂ：でも、それはアトランティスみたいなものではないですか。つまり、そこには見つけるべき北西航路なんかなかったんですよね？

教　授：多くの人はいまだにそう考えていますが、違うのです。北西航路は本当にあって、1580 年代にジョン・デイビスという探検家によって実際に発見されました。不運にも彼はその航路を完全に通り抜けて航海しなかったので、それは、結局、彼の見聞の広さからきた推測以上のものにはなりませんでした。

　　　でも、ここでそれらの探索の地理学への貢献に、より注目して、探検家たちが何を発見したのかを見てみましょう。1609 年、ピルグリムたちの上陸よりずっと前に、イギリス人のヘンリー・ハドソンがチェサピーク湾を探検し、ハドソン川をずっとアルバニーまで航行しました。１年後、彼はハドソン湾を探検するために戻り、氷のせいで動けなくなりました。この旅により彼は命を失ってしまいました。多くの乗組員がハドソンに反抗し、彼と彼の幼い息子と、彼に忠実だった何人かの乗組員を小さなボートに乗せて送り出してしまったので、消息を絶ちました。

　　　しかし、ハドソンはこの航路を見つけて通り抜けようとして死んだ多くの人のひとりでしかありませんでした。ウィリアム・パリーという人は、この航路を十分に遠くまで突き抜けたので、それによってイギリス議会から褒美を勝ち取ったのです。氷によって止まらざるを得なくなったとき、彼は太平洋まで抜けるのにあとたった 200 マイルのところでした。

学生Ａ：すみません、それはいつでしたか。

教　授：ああ、ごめんなさい、ノートを見てみます。ええ、1820 年のことでした。とにかく、パリーはとても近くまで来ていたので、イギリス人たちはそこを通り抜けることができると確信し、ついに 1845 年には実際に 2 隻の船に貿易品を満杯に積み、ジョン・フランクリンという男を船長にして、130 人の乗組員とともにアジアへと送り出しました。これは、北西航路を通り抜けようとした試みの中で、最も大きな惨事のひとつとなりました。２年間フランクリンから音沙汰がなかったので、イギリス海軍は 1847 年に彼と乗組員を見つけるために出発しました。それはある意味で国家的な大儀になりました。その後の 9 年間で、合計 40 ほどの異なる捜索隊がフランクリンを探すために送り出されたのです。

学生Ｂ：先生は、何が起こったと思われますか。

教　授：もちろん、誰も確かなことはわかりませんが、多くの人はフランクリンが北極で生き残るために必要な備品を持っていなかったのではないかと考えています。つまり、適切な衣類などをですね。

学生Ｂ：しかし、そんなことがあり得るでしょうか。北極は寒いということを彼らは知っていたはずです。まったくわけがわかりません。

教　授：そうですね。私の唯一の推測では、人々はフランクリンが北西航路をほとんど問題なく真っすぐに通り抜け、アジアへ向かうと考えていたのだと思います。彼が生死をかけなければいけないような状況に陥るかもしれないとは、なぜかまったく考えなかったのです。

17. 解答 **(B)**

この講義の主題は何か。

(A) 発見の旅

(B) 北西航路の探索

(C) ヘンリー・ハドソンの発見

(D) アジアとの交易の重要性

解説 トランスクリプトの下線部参照。

- to the idea of finding a Northwest Passage
- Northwest Passage
- this passage
- through the Northwest Passage

18. 解答 （下の表を参照）

	Hudson	*Franklin*	*Parry*	*Davis*
Won an award for his explorations			○	
Sailed to Albany	○			
Disappeared while traveling to Asia		○		
Sighted the opening to the Northwest Passage				○

教授は、さまざまな探検家たちの北アメリカへ向けた活動について述べている。これらの活動と探検家を正しく結び付けなさい。

いくつかの探検について賞を受けた

アルバニーへ航海した

アジアへの移動途中で姿を消した

北西航路への入り口を発見した

解説 トランスクリプトの下線部参照。

《Hudson の根拠》

• Henry Hudson explored Chesapeake Bay and sailed up the Hudson River all the way to Albany.

《Franklin の根拠》

• After hearing nothing from Franklin for two years

《Parry の根拠》

• William Parry penetrated the passage far enough to win a reward for the act from the British Parliament.

《Davis の根拠》

• it (= Northwest Passage) was actually discovered in the 1580's by an explorer named John Davis.

19. 解答 (B)、(C)

北西航路の探索の 2 つの結果とは何か。

解答を 2 つ選びなさい。

(A) ヨーロッパ諸国における巨万の富の発見

(B) 北アメリカの地理の理解の向上

(C) 北西航路の実際の発見

(D) 北西航路は実在しなかったという認識

解説 トランスクリプトの下線部参照。

- the contributions that the searches for this passage made to the geographical understanding of the northern regions of North America.
- there really is a Northwest Passage
- it was actually discovered in the 1580's by an explorer named John Davis.

20. 解答 (A)、(B)、(E)

講義によると、ヨーロッパ人はなぜ北西航路の発見にそれほど興味を抱いたのか。

解答を 3 つ選びなさい。

(A) アジアにはヨーロッパ人が望むものがたくさんあった。

(B) マゼランが、南アメリカを回る航海は長すぎて危険であることを発見した。

(C) 彼らには発見と冒険への情熱があった。

(D) 彼らはそこに膨大な富があると考えた。

(E) 彼らはアジアとの交易でお金をもうけたかった。

解説 トランスクリプトの下線部参照。

- Asia had a lot of good stuff, and Europe wanted it.
- the ships had to make long dangerous journeys around Africa.
- it was really business that stimulated exploration more than, say, adventure or discovery.
- Magellan proved you could sail west to Asia but to do it you had to sail around South America which, as it turned out, was even worse than sailing around Africa.

21. 解答 (B)

講義の一部をもう一度聞きなさい。それから、質問に答えなさい。

教授はこのように発言することで、何を言おうとしているのか。

(A) 北西航路の探索は興味深いものだったが、それほど重要だったと捉えるべきではない。

(B) 北西航路の探検がなかったら、北アメリカ北部の大部分がこれほど早く発見されることはなかっただろう。

(C) 北西航路の探索が北アメリカの地理の理解にどれほど重要だったかを評価するのは難しい。

(D) ヨーロッパ人にとって北アメリカの地理を理解するのがどれほど重要だったかを強調しなければならない。

解説 トランスクリプトの下線部参照。「その探検がいかに重要であるかということはどんなに強調しても、強調しきれないほどだ」。つまり、それがなかったら北アメリカの北部がそんなに早くに発見されることはあり得なかっただろう、と言っている。

🎧 That's when attention began to turn to the north, or more specifically, to the idea of finding a Northwest Passage to Asia. **I really can't emphasize enough how important this goal was to the Europeans, or the contributions that the searches for this passage made to the geographical understanding of the northern regions of North America.**

22. 解答 (C)

講義の一部をもう一度聞きなさい。それから、質問に答えなさい。

この学生の意見から何が推測できるか。

(A) この学生は教授の発言を批判している。

(B) この学生は教授の発言がいかに混乱しているかを伝えている。

(C) この学生は教授の発言に対する驚きを表明している。

(D) この学生は教授の発言に異を唱えている。

解説 トランスクリプトの下線部参照。学生は「そんなことがあるんですか」と言って驚いている。ここでは、北米の学生は教師を批判したり、教師に異論を唱えたりはしない傾向にあるという事実を背景知識として頭に入れておこう。

Professor: Well, no one can be sure of course but many people think that Franklin didn't have the proper equipment for arctic survival. I mean, like the right clothes and so on.

Student B: **But how is that possible? They had to know it was cold in the arctic. It doesn't seem to make any sense.**

トランスクリプト

Professor: So to begin today's lecture I'm going to assume that you all know what salt is (Q23). But do you all know what a salt is? I mean, in chemical terms; what does it take for a chemical compound to qualify as a salt? No one? OK, so who knows the chemical composition of common table salt?

Student A: It's sodium chloride, right? Or in chemical terms N-A-C-L.

Professor: **Good. So does anyone know why it qualifies to be placed in the group of compounds called "salts?"** (Q23) **No? OK, then let's look more closely at this common compound that we use as a seasoning, common table salt. Let's start with what we all know** (Q24 : Q27). It commonly occurs as a white, crystalline solid, and is soluble in water (Q26-a). This, of course, is how it occurs in the oceans. Actually it makes up about 3 percent of the oceans by weight (Q26-c), so it's quite an important component. Much of the salt we are familiar with comes from ancient seas that have simply dried up and left their salt behind. We actually call such massive types of salt "halite."

Student B: Why not just call it "salt?" Why do we need another word for it?

Professor: Well, that's a fair question. I suppose that mineralogists want to differentiate it from the chemical idea of salt. And after all, in the form of rock salt, it is more of a rock than a chemical. But to continue on with the properties of salt, it is composed of two elements, it conducts electricity well when it is dissolved in water (Q26-d), and it has a high melting point (Q26-e). I mean, if you for some reason wanted to melt salt, you'd have to get a temperature of around 1,500 degrees Fahrenheit.

Now, the fact that table salt is composed of two elements is very important, because it is a characteristic of all other salts. One of these elements must be an acid and the other a base (Q25). To us, acids, like vinegar, taste sour and bases taste, well, if you want to taste soap or baking soda you'll soon find they have a kind of bitter taste. But the important point is that they are opposites, and if you combine them in a chemical reaction, **they** will neutralize each other. The products formed by this neutralization are salt and water (Q25).

Student A: OK, so they are opposites but in terms of chemistry, is there an easy way to understand why they are opposites?

Professor: Well, nothing's ever easy in chemistry, but in a simple way, you can say that acids are anything that produce hydrogen ions when dissolved in water, and bases or alkali produce hydroxide ions when dissolved in water. In other words, acids produce positive ions and bases produce negative ions. Does that answer your question?

Student A: **Well, kind of. So these chemical reactions always occur in water and always produce salts?** (Q28)

Professor: They mainly, but not always, occur in water and always produce salts (Q28). And some acids produce more hydrogen ions than others, and some bases accept these ions more easily than others. So you have stronger and weaker acids and bases. But salts are always a product of their reactions. So let's look more closely at this reaction. Chlorine is one of a group of elements called the "halogens." (Q25) Interestingly enough, the term "halogen" comes from Greek and means "salt former." They all carry a negative electric charge, and they are all very reactive. They will readily combine with metals, which have a positive charge, to form salts (Q25 : Q26-b).

Student B: So this means that sodium is a metal.

Professor: That's right.

Student B: But I've never heard of sodium metal. I've never heard of anything made of sodium metal. Is it so rare?

Professor: Actually sodium is the seventh most abundant element on earth, but you will never find it in its natural, elemental state. And the reason for this is because it is so reactive. Basically, it reacts with nearly everything and so you never see it in its pure form.

215

Student A: And you said all halogens are reactive, too. So can we find any of them in their pure form?

Professor: Yes, but it's not very common. I mean, all of you have probably heard of chlorine bleach or you've used iodine on a cut. These are solutions of halogens, basically, and they are used as antiseptics. They have the ability to kill microorganisms that can cause infections.

Student A: So that's why they use chlorine in water and in swimming pools.

Professor: Exactly. And when you dissolve any compound with chlorine and then add any compound with sodium their ions will strongly attract and you will get NaCl or common table salt.

訳例

教　授：今日の講義を始めるに当たって、当然、皆さん全員が塩とは何かを知っていると思いますが、皆さんは塩とは何かを知っていますか。ここで取り上げているのは、化学用語としてです。ある化合物が塩であると認められるためには何が必要なのでしょうか。誰もわかりませんか。いいでしょう、では一般的な食卓塩の化学組成が何か、誰か知っていますか。

学生A：塩化ナトリウムですか。化学用語では、N-A-C-L。

教　授：よろしい。それでは、なぜそれが「塩」と呼ばれる化合物のグループの一員として認められているのか誰か知っていますか。知りませんか。わかりました。では、私たちが調味料として使っている一般的な化合物、つまり一般的な食卓塩についてもっと詳しく見ていきましょう。まず、私たち皆が知っていることから始めましょう。食卓塩は、普通、白い結晶性固体であり、水に溶けます。これは、もちろん海の中でもそうです。実際、それは重さで言うと海の約3パーセントを構成しているので、非常に重要な構成要素なのです。私たちがよく知っている塩の多くは、干上がった後に塩を残した太古の海から来ているのです。私たちは実際、そのような大きな塩の塊を「岩塩」と呼んでいます。

学生B：なぜ、単なる「塩」と言わないのですか。なぜ、ほかの言葉が必要なのでしょうか。

教　授：ええ、いい質問ですね。鉱物学者たちが、化学で言う塩と区別したかったのだと思います。そして結局、岩塩の形では、それは化学物質というよりは岩に近かったのです。しかし、塩の性質について続けると、塩は2つの成分により構成され、水に溶けると電気をよく通し、高い融点を持っています。つまり、皆さんがなんらかの理由で塩を溶かしたいと思ったら、カ氏で約1500度の温度が必要です。

　　　　　さて、食卓塩が2つの成分から構成されているという事実はとても重要です。どうしてかというと、それは、ほかのすべての塩の特性だからです。これらの成分のひとつは酸で、もうひとつは塩基でなければなりません。私たちには、酸は、酢のように酸っぱく感じますし、もしもせっけんか重曹を味わってみれば、塩基はなんとなく苦い味がするとすぐにわかるでしょう。でも、重要なのは、酸と塩基が正反対のもので、混ぜ合わせて化学反応を起こすと、それらは互いに中和するということです。この中和によって形成される生成物は、塩と水です。

学生A：わかりました。つまり、それらは正反対なのですね。けれども、化学的に見てそれらがなぜ正反対であるか理解する簡単な方法はありますか。

教　授：化学においては、簡単ということはまったくありませんが、単純な言い方をすると、酸とは

水に溶けたとき水素イオンをつくり出すすべてのものであり、塩基またはアルカリは水に溶けたとき水酸化物イオンをつくり出すものだと言えます。ほかの言い方をすれば、酸は陽イオンをつくり、塩基は陰イオンをつくり出すのです。これで、質問の答えになりましたか。

学生 A：はい、まあ。つまり、そういう化学反応は常に水の中で起こり、常に塩をつくり出すのですか。

教　授：たいていはそうですが、常に水の中で起こるわけでもなく、常に塩をつくり出すわけでもありません。ある酸はほかの酸よりも多くの水素イオンをつくり、ある塩基はほかの塩基よりもより容易にこれらのイオンを受け入れます。つまり、より強かったり弱かったりする酸や塩基があるのです。いずれにしても、塩は常にこれらの反応による生産物です。それでは、より詳しくこの反応を見てみましょう。塩素は、「ハロゲン」と呼ばれているグループの成分のひとつです。大変興味深いことに、「ハロゲン」という言葉はギリシャ語から来ており、「塩をつくるもの」という意味です。ハロゲンはすべて負電荷を帯びており、非常によく反応します。それらは正電荷を帯びている金属と直ちに結合し、塩を形成します。

学生 B：つまり、ナトリウムが金属であるという意味ですね。

教　授：そのとおりです。

学生 B：でも、金属酸ナトリウムだなんて一度も聞いたことがありません。金属酸ナトリウムからできている何かなんて一度も聞いたことがありません。そんなに珍しいものなのですか。

教　授：実際のところ、ナトリウムは地球上で 7 番目に豊富な元素です。しかし、皆さんがそれを、自然の、元素の状態で見つけることは決してないでしょうね。なぜかといえば、ナトリウムはとても早く反応するからです。基本的に、ナトリウムはほとんどすべての物と反応するので、純粋な状態でそれを見ることは決してありません。

学生 A：すべてのハロゲンは反応が早いとおっしゃいましたね。ハロゲンのうちの何かを純粋な形で見ることはできますか。

教　授：はい、ですが、あまり一般的ではありません。つまり、皆さん全員がたぶん、塩素系漂白剤のことを聞いたことがあるか、切り傷にヨードを使ったことがありますね。それらはハロゲンの溶液であり、基本的には防腐剤として使われます。それらは感染症を引き起こす微生物をやっつける能力を持っています。

学生 A：だから、水の中やスイミング・プールで塩素を使うのですね。

教　授：そのとおりです。そして、塩素を含む化合物を溶かしてからナトリウムを含む化合物を加えると、それらのイオンは強く引き合い、NaCl、つまり一般的な食卓塩ができるのです。

23. 解答 (C)

この講義の主題は何か。

(A) 一般的な食卓塩

(B) 酸と塩基

(C) 塩

(D) ハロゲン

解説 トランスクリプトの下線部参照。

- So to begin today's lecture I'm going to assume that you all know what salt is.
- So does anyone know why it qualifies to be placed in the group of compounds called "salts?"

24. 解答 (A)

教授はなぜ食卓塩について話しているのか。

(A) あらゆる塩の代表として簡単に目にとまるから。

(B) 地球上で最も一般的な鉱物の一つだから。

(C) 酸と塩基で構成されているから。

(D) 「ハロゲン」という元素のグループの一部だから。

解説 トランスクリプトの下線部参照。下記の "common" という表現より、食卓塩は誰もが知っている「塩」であるとわかる。

- No? OK, then let's look more closely at this common compound that we use as a seasoning, common table salt. Let's start with what we all know.

25. 解答 (A)、(B)

講義の中で述べられた塩の 2 つの特徴は何か。

解答を 2 つ選びなさい。

(A) ハロゲンと金属で構成されている。

(B) 酸と塩基が互い中和するときに作られる。

(C) 常に水から作られる。

(D) 酸と塩基で構成される。

解説 トランスクリプトの下線部参照。ここでは「酸と塩基の中和」と「ハロゲンは金属と結合し塩を形成する」ということが大切であることがわかる。

- the fact that table salt is composed of two elements is very important, because it is a characteristic of all other salts. One of these elements must be an acid and the other a base.
- if you combine them (= acids and bases) in a chemical reaction, they will neutralize each other. The products formed by this neutralization are salt and water.
- Chlorine is one of a group of elements called the "halogens."
- They (= halogens) will readily combine with metals, which have a positive charge, to form salts.

26. 解答 （下の表を参照）

		True	*False*
a	It can be dissolved in water.	○	
b	It is composed of a metal.	○	
c	It is the most abundant mineral in the oceans.		○
d	It will not conduct electricity unless melted.		○
e	It has a high melting point.	○	

講義の中で、教授は食卓塩に関する多くの事実を述べている。次の各文が食卓塩について当てはまるか否かを示しなさい。

水に溶かすことができる。

金属で出来ている。

海の中で最も豊富な鉱物である。

溶けていなければ電気を通さない。

高い融点を持つ。

解説 トランスクリプトの下線部参照。ここで、注意しなければならないのは "melt" と "dissolve" は違うということである。

《True の根拠》

- soluble in water (a)

- it has a high melting point. (e)

- They will readily combine with metals, which have a positive charge, to form salts. (b)

《False の根拠》

- Actually it makes up about 3 percent of the oceans by weight (c)

- it conducts electricity well when it is dissolved in water (d)

27. 解答 (B)

講義の一部をもう一度聞きなさい。それから、質問に答えなさい。

教授はなぜこのようなことを言うのか。

(A) 学生が新しい話題に興味がないので、食卓塩に話を戻すために

(B) 食卓塩を例に取って学生が知らないことを説明するために

(C) 誰も質問に答えそうもないので腹を立て、話題を変えるために

(D) 講義を続ける前に、全員が理解しているかを確認するために

解説 トランスクリプトの下線部参照。ここでは "No?" という発言から、まず学生が質問の解を知らないことがわかり、その後「食卓塩についてもっと詳しく見ていこう」と続くので、正解は (B) とわかる。

🎧 Student A: It's sodium chloride, right? Or in chemical terms N-A-C-L.

Professor: **Good. So does anyone know why it qualifies to be placed in the group of compounds called "salts?" No? OK, then let's look more closely at this common compound that we use as a seasoning, common table salt. Let's start with what we all know.**

28. 解答 (C)

講義の一部をもう一度聞きなさい。それから、質問に答えなさい。

この学生の反応から何が推測できるか。

(A) この学生は教授の説明に興味がない。

(B) この学生は教授とは異なる答えを求めていた。

(C) この学生は教授の説明を完全には理解していなかった。

(D) この学生は教授の言うことをほとんど理解していない。

解説 トランスクリプトの下線部参照。学生は「はい、まあ」と答えた後、確認の質問をしているので、完全に理解していないだろうとわかる。

🎧 Professor: Well, nothing's ever easy in chemistry, but in a simple way, you can say that acids are anything that produce hydrogen ions when dissolved in water, and bases or alkali produce hydroxide ions when dissolved in water. In other words, acids produce positive ions and bases produce negative ions. Does that answer your question?

Student A: **Well, kind of. So these chemical reactions always occur in water and always produce salts?**

1. 比較選択に関する問題
[15 秒で準備して、45 秒話す]

質問の訳

自動車が人々の生活を改善してきたと思う人もいれば、自動車がさまざまな問題の原因になってきたと考える人もいる。あなたの意見はどうか。

模範解答（一例）

mp3
29

　Personally, I've lived with and without an automobile and I have to say that it really does make things more convenient. I mean, before when I had to go places I would have to take a bus or a train. Many times I would be waiting and waiting for buses or trains that weren't on time. Even when you finally get on a bus you don't even get a seat and you have to stand up for two hours. At least this is true in my country. But when I got a car I was able to go whenever I chose. I think it has made my life more efficient because I don't lose all that time I would have spent waiting. If it's true for me, then it must also be true for others. So, altogether, I think when people have cars the whole society is improved, at least in terms of efficiency.

訳例

　個人的には自動車のある生活とない生活を経験してきましたが、自動車のおかげで物事の利便性が大変高まることは間違いありません。例えば、以前は、どこかへ行く必要があると、バスや電車に乗らなければなりませんでした。何度となく、時間通りに来ないバスや電車を待ち続けたものです。ようやくバスに乗っても席に座ることもできず、2 時間立っていなければなりません。少なくともこれが私の国での現実です。でも、車を手に入れると、いつでも好きなときに出かけられるようになりました。自分の生活の効率が上がったと思います。待つことに費やしていたあれだけの時間を失わずにすむからです。私がそうなのですから、他の人たちにもそれは当てはまるはずです。だから、結局のところ、人々が車を持てば、少なくとも効率面で、社会全体が改善されると思います。

ポイント

　本問は「自動車によって人々の暮らしが改善されたと思うか、それともそれが多くの問題をもたらす源になってしまったと思うか」という問題である。短い時間内に答えなくてはならないので、まず設問に答え、その理由をつけていく。最初に自分の考えを述べ、それに理由を加えていくという話の展開をとるといい。具体例をつけるに当たっては、模範解答にあるように、短所と長所を比べていく方法を使って自分の見解をサポートしてもいい。時間が許せば、最後に簡単なまとめを入れて締めくくる。また、これは短いスピーチなので、模範解答ではその目的に合わせて、つなぎ言葉として Personally、I mean、Even when、At least、But、I think、So などが使われている。

45 秒の構成

与えられたトピックに対する解答（設問に答えて）

理由・具体例（短所）

理由・具体例（長所）

意見（理由に基づく）

まとめ

話の組み立て方

① いちばん大きな概念（トピックに対する解答：**the automobile has improved people's lives**〈車は人々の暮らしを向上させた〉のかどうかに対する意見）：

Personally, I've lived with and without an automobile and I have to say that it really does make things more convenient.

② 自己の見解をサポートする具体例：

車の購入前　▶ I mean, before when I had to go places I would have to take a bus or a train. Many times I would be waiting and waiting for buses or trains that weren't on time. Even when you finally get on a bus you don't even get a seat and you have to stand up for two hours. At least this is true in my country.

車の購入後　▶ But when I got a car I was able to go whenever I chose.

③ 具体例に基づいたトピックをサポートする意見：

I think it has made my life more efficient because I don't lose all that time

I would have spent waiting. If it's true for me, then it must also be true for others.

④ まとめ：

So, altogether, I think when people have cars the whole society is improved, at least in terms of efficiency.

2. 読む・聴く・話す問題
——自由研究論文
［30秒で準備して、60秒話す］

質問の訳

質問：
学生が自由研究論文の執筆要件を満たすために必要な手順について、簡単に述べなさい。

模範解答（一例）

mp3 30

　　First of all, the student should talk to a faculty member because someone has to supervise the paper. He* needs the faculty member's agreement before he can begin his work. Next, he and the faculty member should decide on a topic. When this is done, the student needs to pick up a form at the Registrar's Office and bring it to the faculty member. If they have agreed on a topic, the faculty member will write a few notes on the form to explain why writing this paper would be good for the student. After the faculty member signs it, the student must take it back to the Registrar. Finally, the Registrar sends it to the Assistant Dean for approval. If he thinks it's OK, he signs it and the student can begin work.

注：＊これは一例なので "He" としてあるが、もちろん "She" としてもいい。

訳例

　　まず、この学生は教官に相談するべきでしょう。誰かが論文を指導しなければならないのですから。論文に取り掛かる前に、指導教官との合意が必要です。次に、学生と指導教官はテーマを決めます。これが終わったら、学生は教務課で用紙を受け取り、教官に渡さなければなりません。テーマについて合意が取れていれば、教官は用紙に二、三記入し、なぜこの論文を書くことが学生にとって適当なのかを説明します。教官が署名した後、学生は用紙を教務課に戻さなければなりません。最後に、教務課が用紙を学部長補佐に回して承認を取ります。学部長補佐は、問題なしと判断すればそれに署名し、学生が論文に取り掛かれるようになります。

ポイント

　　これまでと同様に、聞かれていることに答える形で解答の組み立てを考えよう。まず設問に対する解答を最初に述べ、それをサポートする理由をつけていくという英

語式の答え方がいいだろう。また、答えるときは、読んだことや聴いたことを、まったくそのままの文章で使うのではなく、言い換えていくことが大切だ。具体的には、Briefly describe the process a student must go through ... という質問なので、物事の過程（the process）を説明していくことになる。つまり、本問では自由研究論文を書くに当たってしなければならないことを順を追って説明していくわけだ。従って、まず何をして、次にこれ、その次は〜、という答え方をするといい。

話の組み立て方

① 最初にすべきこと：

First of all, the student should talk to a faculty member because someone has to supervise the paper.

その理由 ▶ He needs the faculty member's agreement before he can begin his work.

② 次にすべきこと：

Next, he and the faculty member should decide on a topic.（学生と指導教官が納得できるトピックが決まって初めて教授は指導を引き受ける）

それで ▶ When this is done, the student needs to pick up a form at the Registrar's Office and bring it to the faculty member.（前出のトピックに関して、学生と指導教官が納得できるトピックであれば、指導教官が学生をサポートしてくれる、つまり）

③ それが順調に進むと：

If they have agreed on a topic, the faculty member will write a few notes on the form to explain why writing this paper would be good for the student.（指導教官のサインをもらって正式な手続きができる）

④ つまり：

After the faculty member signs it, the student must take it back to the Registrar.

⑤ 最後に：

Finally, the Registrar sends it to the Assistant Dean for approval.（承認されて、初めてそのペーパー*に取り組むことができる）If he thinks it's OK, he signs it and the student can begin work.

注：＊ ここでいうリサーチ・ペーパーとは、「図書館リサーチ」とか「セカンダリー・リサーチ」と呼ばれるもので、

リサーチのトピックに関する文献を読んで自分なりに分析しまとめて、ペーパーを書くものである。

読むテクスト

Before beginning work on an independent research paper in order to satisfy the writing requirement, the student must receive permission from a supervising faculty member. A student may select any faculty member for supervision (解答では *First of all, the student should talk to a faculty member because someone has to supervise the paper. He needs the faculty member's agreement before he can begin his work*); however, the approval of any topic for a paper is then left solely to the discretion of that chosen member. Students are strongly encouraged to consult faculty members early in the semester in order to make any arrangements necessary to carry out the project. Once a faculty member agrees to supervise the student's work, the student must submit a Writing Requirements Registration Form which can be obtained from the Registrar's Office (解答では *When this is done, the student needs to pick up a form at the Registrar's Office and bring it to the faculty member*). The faculty member will only accept the form after meeting with the student and agreeing on an appropriate topic. The student then must submit the Writing Requirements Registration Form with the faculty member's notes of approval to the Registrar's Office (解答では *If they have agreed on a topic, the faculty member will write a few notes on the form to explain why writing this paper would be good for the student. After the faculty member signs it, the student must take it back to the Registrar*). The Registrar's Office will then submit the Writing Requirements Registration Form to the Assistant Dean for final approval (解答では *Finally, the Registrar sends it to the Assistant Dean for approval*). Work on the independent research paper can only begin after such approval is received (解答では *If he thinks it's OK, he signs it and the student can begin work*).

訳例

　学生は、自由研究論文（独自で進めるリサーチペーパー）に取り掛かる前に、そのコースを取るための条件を満たすため、指導教官の許可を得なければならない。学生は各自で指導教官を決めることができるが、論文のトピックの承認は各自の指導教官の判断に委ねられている。（自由研究論文の）プロジェクトに取り掛かるのに必要な手はずを整えるために、学期の早いうちに教官に相談することを強く奨励する。教官がいったん学生を指導することに同意したら、学生は教務課に置いてある、コースを取る条件を満たすための登録用紙（Writing

227

Requirements Registration Form）を提出しなければならない。教官は、学生に会って話し合い、適切なトピックに合意して初めてその登録用紙を承認する。学生はそれから、指導教官の承認を得たその登録用紙を教務課に提出しなければならない。教務課は、最終的な承認を得るために、学生が提出した登録用紙を学部長補佐に提出しなければならない。学部長補佐による最終承認が得られて初めて、自由研究論文に取り掛かることができる。

mp3
24

聴くテクスト

Student: A friend of mine told me it might be possible to satisfy the writing requirement for the course by writing an independent research paper. I guess I'd just like to know if this is really true or not.

Professor: Well, yeah, it is possible, but there are a few things you'd have to do first. It's not as easy as just writing some kind of paper and handing it in.

Student: So what exactly is it that I'd have to do?

Professor: Well, first of all, you'd have to receive permission to do this from a faculty member（解答では *First of all, the student should talk to a faculty member because someone has to supervise the paper. He needs the faculty member's agreement before he can begin his work*）.

Student: Yeah, I guess I was hoping you'd agree to this.

Professor: No, I don't mind supervising it but you've got to do a few things first, and the most important thing is to select a topic that we both agree will reflect what you've learned（解答では *Next, he and the faculty member should decide on a topic*）. Naturally, I hope you'll choose something you're interested in but that you can also learn from.

Student: Well, I've got a few ideas I'd like to discuss with you. But what else do I have to do before I get started?

Professor: OK, then assuming I agree on your topic, you'll have to go get a writing requirements form from the Registrar's Office（解答では *When this is done, the student needs to pick up a form at the Registrar's Office*）.

Student: So I just fill out this form and hand it back to them, right?

Professor: Well, not exactly. You bring it to me（解答では *and bring it to the faculty member*）and we agree on what topic you're going to write about. Then I write a few notes on why I think the topic would be a good one for you and what I expect you to accomplish, sign it, and give it to you to take back to the Registrar（解答では *If they have agreed on a topic, the faculty member will write a few notes on the form to explain why writing this paper would be good for the student. After the faculty member signs it, the student must take it back to the Registrar*）.

Student: Yeah, and then I start working on the paper. I know I came in to ask you about this a little late but I didn't know it was possible at all until recently.

Professor: Wait a minute. Don't get ahead of yourself. You can't really begin writing until the Assistant Dean approves the topic（解答では *... If he thinks it's OK, he signs it and the student can begin work*）. That's why I have to write notes on the form. I sort of have to convince him that your topic is valid or he won't approve it. You see what I mean?

Student: Oh, OK, I think I get the picture.

訳例

学生：友人のひとりが教えてくれたのですが、自由研究論文を書くことによって、コースのライティングの必要条件を満たすことができるかもしれないということなのですが。本当かどうか知りたいだけなのですが。

教授：なるほど。そう、できることはできるのだけれど、まずしなければならないことがいくつかあるんだよ。ただ、論文を書いて出せばいいというようなたやすいものではないよ。

学生：それで、正確には何をしなければならないのですか。

教授：ええと、まず、それをするための許可を教官からもらわなくてはならないんだよ。

学生：そうですか。先生が同意してくだされば、と考えていたんですが。

教授：いやあ、指導するのは一向に構わないんだけれど、まずいくつかのことをしてもらわなければならないんだ。その中でもいちばん大切なのが、君が学んできたことを反映し、かつ、君と私が合意できるようなトピックを選ぶことなんだよ。当然のことながら、君が興味のあるもので、それから何かを学べるようなトピックを選ぶのを期待しているんだが。

学生：そうですねえ。先生にご相談したいいくつかの考えがあるんですが。それより、（自由研究論文に）取り組む前に、ほかにはどんなことをしなければならないのですか。

教授：よし、わかった。じゃあ、君のトピックに合意したと考えて、教務課から自由研究論文でのコースを取るのに必要な条件を満たすための登録用紙をもらって来なくてはならないよ。

学生：それで、その用紙に書き込んで教務課に提出すればいいんですね。

教授：ううん、そうじゃないんだ。それを僕のところに持って来て、君がどんなトピックで（自由研究）論文を書くかに合意するわけなんだよ。合意したら、僕がなぜ、そのトピックが君にとってためになるものと考えられるのか、そのトピックから何を学んでほしいかを書いて、サインをして、教務課に持っていくために君に渡すんだ。

学生：そうですか。それで、（自由研究）論文に取り掛かるわけですね。このことに関して伺いに来るのがちょっと遅くなってしまいましたが、こんな方法があるなんて最近まで知らなかったんです。

教授：ちょっと待ちたまえ。まだ取り掛からないでくれよ。学部長補佐がトピックを承認するまでは、（自由研究論文に）取り掛かることはできないんだ。だから、その用紙に僕があれこれ書き込むんだ。言ってみれば、君のトピックは妥当であると、僕が彼を説得しなければならないんだ。さもないと学部長補佐はトピックを承認しないからね。というわけなんだ。

学生：そうなんですか。わかりました。状況がつかめました。

注：＊ 北米の大学ではいくつかのライティングのコースを取るのが卒業条件のひとつになっていて、学生はそれらのコースに出席してコースの課題などをこなして単位を取っていく。ここでは、あるライティングのコースの単位が、クラスに出なくても自由研究論文を書くことによって取得できることがテーマとなっている。

重要語句

- [ ] accomplish 成し遂げる、達成する
- [ ] approval 承認、賛成、同意
- [ ] approve 承認する、賛成する、同意する
- [ ] Assistant Dean 学部長補佐
- [ ] carry out 行う、実行する
- [ ] discretion 判断力、決定権、判断の自由
- [ ] encourage 奨励する、促進する、助長する
- [ ] expect 期待する、要求する、求める
- [ ] get ahead 取り掛かる、着手する
- [ ] get the picture 状況を把握する
- [ ] hand in 提出する、手渡しする
- [ ] independent research paper 自由研究論文（指導教官の指示を仰ぎながら独自に進めるリサーチ・ペーパー）
- [ ] permission 許可
- [ ] reflect 反映する、思案する
- [ ] Registrar's Office 教務課
- [ ] submit 提出する
- [ ] supervise 指導する
- [ ] supervising faculty member 指導教官
- [ ] Writing Requirements Registration Form 必要条件を満たすための文書による登録用紙

3. 読む・聴く・話す問題
──物理学（重力）
［30秒で準備して、60秒話す］

質問の訳

質問：
宇宙にある4つの力がどんな作用をするのか、またどのように異なるのかを説明しなさい。

模範解答 （一例）

mp3
31

　There are four forces that hold the universe together. These are gravity, electromagnetism, the strong nuclear force and the weak nuclear force. Gravity is the force that is most important for large objects such as planets and stars. It holds these objects together. Every object has some gravity, but it has to be really big for gravity to make any impact. The strong nuclear force holds the parts of an atom together. The weak nuclear force also occurs in atoms and is responsible for radioactivity. Both of these forces are very strong compared to gravity but operate only at very small distances. Gravity is the only force that can work at great distances.

訳例

　宇宙を形成する4つの力があります。それは重力、電磁気力、強い核力、弱い核力です。重力は、惑星や恒星などの大きな物体にとって最も重要な力です。これが、そうした物体をまとめています。あらゆる物体に重力がありますが、重力が影響を与えるには物体が非常に大きくなければなりません。強い核力が原子の各部分を結び付けています。弱い核力も原子内で発生し、これが放射線の要因です。この2つの力は重力に比べると非常に強いものですが、ごく短い距離でのみ作用します。重力は遠く離れていても作用できる唯一の力です。

ポイント

　宇宙における4つの力（the four forces of the universe）についての講義なので、まずその4つの力があることを述べてから、それらは何かを列挙する（一般的なことから具体例へという話の枠組みをつくる）。そのうえで、what the four forces of the universe do の解として、それぞれの力について話す。それにより、おのおのがどういう役目を果たしているのか、そしてどう違うのかについて述べることになり、2つ目の設問である how they are different に答えることになる。また、本問では、gravity

に関しての情報が至る所に出てくるので、それらをまとめて言い換えたものが解となっ
ていることにも注目しよう。

話の組み立て方

① **トピックの提起（4 つの力について）：**

There are four forces that hold the universe together. These are gravity, electromagnetism, the strong nuclear force and the weak nuclear force.

② **最初の力について：**

Gravity is the force that is most important for large objects such as planets and stars. It holds these objects together.

③ **次の発話とのつなぎ：**

Every object has some gravity, but it has to be really big for gravity to make any impact.

④ **ほかの力について：**

The strong nuclear force holds the parts of an atom together. The weak nuclear force also occurs in atoms and is responsible for radioactivity.

⑤ **最初の力との比較：**

Both of these forces are very strong compared to gravity but operate only at very small distances.

⑥ **最初の力の特徴（比較詳細）：**

Gravity is the only force that can work at great distances.

読むテクスト

All the actions of all the particles and objects in the universe can be explained by the interaction of only four forces（解答では *There are four forces that hold the universe together*）. These forces are gravity, electromagnetism, the strong nuclear force, which holds protons and neutrons together in the nucleus of an atom, and the weak nuclear force, which is responsible for the decay of an atom's nucleus into smaller particles and which produces radioactivity（解答では*These are gravity, electromagnetism, the strong nuclear force and the weak nuclear force*）. Gravity is present in any particle, no matter how small and the force of it is proportional to the mass of the object. Although widely distributed throughout the universe, gravity itself is the weakest of the four forces. The other forces are many times stronger but these forces cannot be extended over a long distance. Gravity is the only force of the four that is capable of exerting its influence at long distances（解答では*Gravity is the only force that can work at great distances*）. However, for an object to exert any meaningful gravitational force it must be of great mass, such as a planet, moon, or star（解答では*Gravity is the force that is most important for large objects such as planets and stars. It holds these objects together. Every object has some gravity, but it has to be really big for gravity to make any impact.* 以下の「聴くテクスト」も参照のこと）.

訳例

　宇宙にあるすべての粒子と物体のありとあらゆる活動は、たった4つの力の相互作用によって説明することができる。これらの力とは、重力、電磁気力、陽子と中性子をともに原子核の中にとどめておく強い核力、そして、原子核をより小さな粒子に変質させ、放射能をつくり出す（役目を担う）弱い核力、である。重力はどんなに小さな粒子にも存在し、その力はその物体の質量に比例する。宇宙の至る所に存在するものの、重力そのものは4つの力の中で最も弱い。ほかの力はこの何倍も強いが、その力を長距離にわたって拡張することはできない。重力は、4つの力の中で唯一、長距離にわたってその影響力を及ぼすことができる。しかし、ある物体が大きな重力を発揮するためには、惑星、月、または星のように大きな質量を持っていなければならない。

聴くテクスト　mp3 **26**

　OK, let's look a little closer at gravity, which, of course, is one of the four forces of the universe and the one that we are probably most aware of. Now you may find it surprising that both you and I produce this gravitational force, and it is the same gravitational force that the earth or the sun has. But I wouldn't depend much on trying to use this force yourself because it is so weak that it is nearly nonexistent. That's the problem with gravity. It has an influence, and a huge influence, only on very big objects or groups of objects（解答では*Gravity is the force that is most important for large objects such as planets and stars. It holds these objects together.*）, but it is incredibly weak when compared to the other forces. It is the force that holds much of the universe together, moons and planets, planets and stars, stars and galaxies（解答では*Gravity is the force that is most important for large objects such as planets and stars. It holds these objects together.*）, but its influence on small objects is negligible. It is more than a quintillion times weaker than the weak nuclear force, a number that can be expressed by 10 followed by 36 zeroes.

The case is just the opposite for the other forces. They are incredibly strong but they have an extremely limited range. <u>Both the strong and weak nuclear forces are hardly detectable beyond one million-millionth of a centimeter. Yet, without them, all of the universe would be destroyed in an instant. We try to harness some of this energy when we make nuclear reactors or nuclear weapons</u> （解答では *The strong nuclear force holds the parts of an atom together. The weak nuclear force also occurs in atoms and is responsible for radioactivity. Both of these forces are very strong compared to gravity but operate only at very small distances*）. Einstein thought all the forces were simply different parts of, let's say, the same spectrum. His idea was that they could all be manifestations of some kind of deeper process. He called this Unified Field Theory.

訳例

　それでは、宇宙にある４つの力のひとつであり、おそらく私たちが最もよく知っている力である重力についてもう少し詳しく見ていきましょう。皆さんも私も、地球や太陽が持っているのと同じ重力をつくり出しているのだということがわかると驚かれるかもしれませんね。もちろん、皆さんがこの力を使うことをそんなに当てにしているとは思いませんが。なぜかといえば、私たちの力はほとんど存在しないのと同じくらい弱いものですから。それが重力の持つ問題点なのです。重力は影響力を、巨大な影響力を持っていますが、それは非常に大きな物体や物体の集合においてのみであり、ほかの力に比べると信じられないほど弱いのです。重力は、月と惑星、惑星と星、星と銀河系など、宇宙の大部分を結びつけている力ですが、小さな物体に対する影響力は無視してもよい程度です。これは弱い核力よりも 100 京倍、つまり 10 の後にゼロが 36 個続くことによって表される数ですが、それ以上に弱いのです。

　そのほかの力の場合はちょうど逆になります。それらは途方もなく強力ですが、非常に限られた範囲でのみ働きます。強い核力も弱い核力も１兆分の１センチでも移動するとほとんど探知できません。しかし、それらがなければ宇宙のすべてが一瞬にして破壊されるでしょう。私たちは原子炉や核兵器をつくるためにこのエネルギーを利用しようとしています。アインシュタインは、すべての力は、単に、言ってみれば、同じスペクトルの異なった部分であると考えていました。彼の考えは、すべての力はなんらかの複雑なプロセスが表面に出てきたものだというものでした。彼はこれを統一場理論と呼んだのです。

重要語句

- □ atom 原子
- □ decay 崩壊、腐食
- □ depend on ... ～を信頼する、当てにする
- □ detectable 発見できる、探知できる
- □ distribute 分配する、分布する
- □ electromagnetism 電磁気力、電磁気現象
- □ exert 発揮する、働かせる、出す
- □ extend 伸ばす、拡張する
- □ gravitation 重力、引力
- □ gravitational force 重力
- □ harness 役立てる、生かす
- □ in an instant 一瞬のうちに
- □ incredibly 信じられないほど
- □ interaction 相互作用
- □ let's say まあ言ってみれば
- □ manifestation 明示、表明、現れ
- □ mass 質量、塊
- □ meaningful 意味のある、重要な
- □ negligible 無視してよい、取るに足らない、ごくわずかな
- □ neutron 中性子
- □ no matter how ... どんなに～であろうとも
- □ nonexistent 存在しない
- □ nuclear force 核力
- □ nuclear reactor 原子炉
- □ nuclear weapon 核兵器
- □ nucleus 原子核、核心
- □ object 物体
- □ opposite 正反対の、逆の
- □ particle 粒子
- □ physics 物理学
- □ planet 惑星
- □ present 存在している、そこにある
- □ proportional 比例する、比例の
- □ proton 陽子
- □ quintillion 10 の 18 乗、100 京の
- □ radioactivity 放射能
- □ spectrum スペクトル、連続体
- □ throughout ... ～の至る所に
- □ unified field theory 統一場理論

4. 聴く・話す問題
——海洋学（コククジラ）
[20秒で準備して、60秒話す]

質問の訳

質問：
コククジラの移動に関する理解の難しさについて説明し、彼らが移動する理由として
考えられるものをいくつか挙げなさい。

mp3
32

模範解答 （一例）

It is difficult to explain why a whale living in an area with lots of food would decide to leave it and travel 6,000 miles. We know that they travel this great distance to have babies, but the main question is: why don't they just have their babies in the Bering Sea, where they have lots of food to eat? Scientists also know that when they leave the Bering Sea, they don't eat anything for about six months. It seems strange that they need to make such a long trip without food just to have babies.

Apparently, there is a good reason for their long migration. As long as they live in the Arctic, they have to use a lot of energy just to keep warm. When they move south, they move to the warmer waters south of California. By moving here they can save a lot of energy. Scientists also know that when the babies are born, they have very little fat to protect them from the cold. They think that if these whales were born in the Arctic, they may not be able to survive in the cold waters.

訳例

　餌が豊富な海域に暮らすクジラが、なぜそこを離れて 6,000 マイルも移動するかを説明するのは難しいことです。クジラがこれほどの長距離を移動した後に子どもを産むことはわかっていますが、一番の疑問は、なぜ食べ物が豊富なベーリング海で出産しないのかということです。科学者たちは、クジラがベーリング海を離れると約 6 カ月間、何も食べないことも突き止めています。子どもを産むだけのために、何も食べずにこれほどの長旅をしなければならないというのは奇妙に思えます。

　どうやら、クジラの長い移動には相応の理由があるようです。北極に住んでいる限り、ただ体温を維持するためだけに多くのエネルギーを使わなければなりません。南へ移動すれば、カリフォルニア州の南の暖かい海域に入ることになります。ここへ移動することで、クジラは多くのエネルギーを節約できるのです。科学者たちはまた、生まれたばかりのクジラの子

どもがほとんど脂肪をまとっておらず、寒さから身を守れないことも把握しています。科学者たちの考えによると、もしクジラが北極で生まれたら、冷たい海水の中で生き残れないかもしれないというのです。

ポイント

　要約をすることで設問に答える、という形で解答の組み立てを考えよう。まず設問に答え、それをサポートする理由をつけていく。聴いたことを自分の言葉に言い換えて話すことも大切。この設問では、まず講義のテーマとしての問題提起をした後、それを明確にし、解答の主題を述べる。それから、問題の解明を試みる。ここでもやはり、まずトピックを提起して、それをサポートする具体例をつけていくという方法で話を展開させていくことが重要だ。

話の組み立て方

① 設問への答え（コククジラの移動が理解しがたいのはなぜか）:

　　問題提起 ▶ It is difficult to explain why a whale living in an area with lots of food would decide to leave it and travel 6,000 miles.

　　問題点の明確化（問題提起の絞り込み） ▶ We know that they travel this great distance to have babies, but the main question is: Why don't they just have their babies in the Bering Sea, where they have lots of food to eat?

　　問題提起をサポートする具体例（つなぎ [connecting information]） ▶ Scientists also know that when they leave the Bering Sea, they don't eat anything for about six months.

　　解答の主題 ▶ It seems strange that they need to make such a long trip without food just to have babies.

② トピック（理由）:

　Apparently, there is a good reason for their long migration.

　　トピックをサポートする具体例 ▶ As long as they live in the Arctic, they have to use a lot of energy just to keep warm. When they move south, they move to the warmer waters south of California. By moving here they can save a lot of energy.

　　2つ目の具体例 ▶ Scientists also know that when the babies are born, they have very little fat to protect them from the cold. They think that if these whales were born in the Arctic, they may not be able to survive in the cold waters.

聴くテクスト

The gray whale migrates farther than any other mammal. The main question is, why? Well, on the surface it may seem like an easy answer, because we know that other species migrate either for reasons of food or mating. And this pattern seems to fit the gray whale. In the summer, it feeds heavily in the Bering Sea off of Alaska, and when it starts to get cold it migrates south of California to have its babies. But this still doesn't answer the question, why? Think of it this way: the whale is fat and healthy, and there's lots of food in the Bering Sea. Why not have the baby there? Why travel 6,000 miles to have a baby? Another thing you should know is that they stop feeding after they start to migrate. I mean, they hardly eat anything for about six months. So they use all of this energy to go south to have a baby that it seems they could have had in the Bering Sea.

（最初からここまでの重要なポイントを設問に答える形で要約すると、*It is difficult to explain why a whale living in an area with lots of food would decide to leave it and travel 6,000 miles. We know that they travel this great distance to have babies, but the main question is: Why don't they just have their babies in the Bering Sea, where they have lots of food to eat? Scientists also know that when they leave the Bering Sea, they don't eat anything for about six months. It seems strange that they need to make such a long trip without food just to have babies.* となる）

Well, scientists were confused about this for a long time. But now it seems they have an answer. When the whales live in the Arctic, they use a lot of their energy simply to keep warm. Moving to warmer water means they use less energy in the long run. Also their babies are born with very little fat to protect them. It is now thought that if these babies were born in the cold Arctic waters, they might not be able to survive.

（次の段落の最初からここまでの重要なポイントを要約すると、*As long as they live in the Arctic, they have to use a lot of energy just to keep warm. When they move south, they move to the warmer waters south of California. By moving here they can save a lot of energy. Scientists also know that when the babies are born, they have very little fat to protect them from the cold. They think that if these whales were born in the Arctic, they may not be able to survive in the cold waters.* となる） And you have to remember that the survival of the young, of the species, is the number one priority for most animals. It ensures biological success.

訳例

　コククジラは、ほかのどのほ乳類よりも遠くへ移動します。（われわれの持つ）主な疑問は、それは、なぜなのかということです。一見、それに答えるのは簡単なようです。なぜかというと、私たちはほかの動物が、食物か交配か、いずれかのために移動することを知っているからです。この傾向は、コククジラにも当てはまるようです。夏には、コククジラはアラスカ沖のベーリング海で大量の餌を捕っています。そして、寒くなると子どもを産むためにカリフォルニアの南に移動します。でも、これではまだなぜという質問に対する答えにはなっていませんね。では、このように考えてみてください。クジラは太っていて、健康です。そしてベーリング海には多くの食物があります。なぜそこで子どもを産まないのでしょうか。なぜ、子どもを産むのに 6,000 マイルも移動するのでしょうか。皆さんが知っておくべきもうひとつのことは、彼らが移動を始めると餌を捕るのをやめるということです。つまり、彼らは約 6 カ月間ほとんど何も食べないのです。ベーリング海にいてもできることかもしれないのに、彼らは子どもを産むために南に移動することにすべてのエネルギーを使うのです。

　さて、科学者たちはこのことについて長い間困惑していました。しかし、現在では彼らは答えを見つけたようです。北極地域に住んでいるとき、クジラはただ体を温めるためだけに多くのエネルギーを使います。より暖かい海へと移動することは、長い目で見れば使うエネルギーが少なくなることを意味します。また、彼らの子どもたちは自分を守る脂肪をほとんど持たずに生まれてきます。子どもたちが寒い北極地域の水中で生まれていたとしたら、生き残ることができないだろうと現在では考えられています。多くの動物にとって、種の生き残り、つまり子どもが生き残ることが最優先事項であることを覚えておかなければいけません。それが、生物学的な成功を保証するのです。

重要語句

□ arctic 北極地域
□ Bering Sea ベーリング海
□ biological 生物学の
□ confuse 混乱させる、困惑させる
□ gray whale コククジラ
□ in the long run 長い目で見れば、結局
□ insure 保証する、約束する

□ mating 交配
□ migrate 移動する、移住する
□ off of ... 〜から
□ on the surface 一見すると、外観は
□ priority 優先すること
□ species 種

239

1. 読む・聴く・書く問題（20分で書き上げるエッセイ）
——政治学

指示文・質問の訳

指示文：

このタスクでは、3分間でパッセージを読みます。その後、読み終えた文章の話題に関する講義の一部を聞きます。講義の後、20分間で解答を考え、作成します。理想的な解答は 150 から 225 語です。

次のパッセージを読みなさい。

リスニング：

では、読み終えた政治学の話題に関する講義の一部を聞きなさい。講義を聞きながらメモを取ることができます。

では、次の質問に答えなさい。メモを使って解答できます。

質問：

この読み物では、政治学が真の科学にはなりえないことを示唆している。しかし教授は、政治学が多少なりともより科学的だと認識される方法をいくつか提案している。政治学が科学として認められるかもしれない理由を説明しなさい。

模範解答（一例）

　　Political science, like all the social sciences, is not a true science because it cannot always predict, with 100 percent accuracy, the outcomes of every political situation. This is because political science deals with the behavior of people which is not always so predictable. On the other hand, in true sciences, like chemistry, the outcome of mixing two chemicals can always be predicted.

　　Then why should we even call this study "political science"? The reason is that political science tries to analyze data to predict outcomes through a mathematical system called statistics. The better the data is analyzed, the more accurate the predictions. These predictions may not always be 100 percent accurate, but with proper analysis they can begin to approach scientific certainty.

If all true sciences are supported by mathematical proof, then so is political science. Political science is supported by statistics. Statistics is a branch of mathematics which deals with the analysis of data. Without statistics we would only have data, which would have little meaning on its own. The more skill that is applied in the use of statistics, the more likely it is that meaningful conclusions can be drawn from the data.

As statistical methods become more sophisticated, computers make data easier to manipulate. Political science will continue to become more and more scientific.

訳例

　政治学は、あらゆる社会科学と同様に、真の科学とは言えない。それは、どんな政治状況の行く末をも、常に 100 パーセントの精度で予測することができないからだ。これは、政治学が、必ずしも予測可能ではない人間の行動を扱っているからである。一方、真の科学では、例えば化学の場合、2 つの化学物質を混合した結果は常に予測可能である。

　では、なぜこの学問を political science と呼ぶべきなのか。その理由は、政治学では統計という数学的体系を通じてデータを分析し、結果を予測しようと試みるからだ。データが適切に分析されるほど、予測の精度が上がる。こうした予測は必ずしも 100 パーセント正確ではないものの、適切な分析によって科学的な確実性に近づけるのだ。

　真の科学がどれも数学的証明によって裏付けられるものであるとすれば、政治学も同様である。政治学は統計に支えられている。統計学は数学の一分野で、データ分析を扱う。統計がなければ、手にするのはデータだけであり、それ自体にほとんど意味はない。統計に多くの技法を使えば使うほど、データから有意義な結果を引き出せる可能性が高まる。

　統計学的手法がより高度になるに従って、コンピューターがデータを処理しやすくする。政治学はこの先ますます科学的になっていくだろう。

ポイント

　20 分で構想をまとめ、読んだこと（3 分間で与えられたトピックについて読む）と聴いたことに基づいて解答を書き上げる。聞かれていることに答える形で解答の組み立てを考えよう。ここで大切なのは、アカデミック・ライティングの基本を踏まえて書くこと。つまり、最初のパラグラフでは、一般的概念を書いてからそれをサポートする理由を書く。次のパラグラフでは、レトリカル・クエスチョン*をトピック・センテンスとして、例題などを使って、それをサポートする具体例を書くことにより設問に答える。ここでも、英語式の理論展開（具体例やさらなる説明をつけ加えてトピッ

ク・センテンスをサポートする方式）が使われている。また、読んだことや聞いたことは、言い換えをして要約していくことが大切だ。具体的には、まず **The reading suggests that political science can never approach true science.** という記述を明確にし、なぜ **"political science"** がいわゆる「科学」でないのかを書く。次に、それに対する教授の反論をサポートするために **Explain the reasons political science may be considered a science.** に答える。時間があれば、簡単に全体のまとめを書いてもいい（下記参照）。

注：＊「レトリカル・クエスチョンと」は聞き手の返答を要求しない質問のこと。

エッセイの組み立て方　※**Q**は設問からの引用です。

Q **The reading suggests that political science can never approach true science.**

① まず大きな概念を書く：

Political science, like all the social sciences, is not a true science because it cannot always predict, with 100 percent accuracy, the outcomes of every political situation.

② それをサポートする理由を記す：

This is because political science deals with the behavior of people which is not always so predictable. On the other hand, in true sciences, like chemistry, the outcome of mixing two chemicals can always be predicted.

Q **Explain the reasons political science may be considered a science.**

③ 本論に入る前のトピック提起：

Then why should we even call this study "political science"?

④ レトリカル・クエスチョンで提起したトピックに答える（ような形で書き進める）：

The reason is that political science tries to analyze data to predict outcomes through a mathematical system called statistics. The better the data is analyzed, the more accurate the predictions.

⑤ 反論と論駁（counterargument and refutation）：

These predictions may not always be 100 percent accurate, but with proper analysis they can begin to approach scientific certainty.

⑥ レトリカル・クエスチョンの解答をさらにサポートする理由：

If all true sciences are supported by mathematical proof, then so is political science. Political science is supported by statistics.

⑦ ⑥の下線部のサポートの詳細を記す：

Statistics is a branch of mathematics which deals with the analysis of data. Without statistics we would only have data, which would have little meaning on its own.

⑧ ⑥⑦の簡単なまとめ：

The more skill that is applied in the use of statistics, the more likely it is that meaningful conclusions can be drawn from the data.

⑨ 全体のまとめ：

As statistical methods become more sophisticated, computers make data easier to manipulate. Political science will continue to become more and more scientific.

読むテクスト

最初の2パラグラフより本講義のトピックである "political science" について学ぶ

　Political science is a social science which is related to the other social sciences of anthropology, history, sociology, economics and psychology. It can be argued that political science is the cornerstone of all of these other disciplines. This is because all the activity that occurs within these other disciplines is governed to some degree by the political environment in which they occur. An alternative point of view could be that political science is a study of political situations that arise from factors that are more closely linked to the other social sciences. Whatever the viewpoint of the importance of political science within the social sciences, it is clear that all of these disciplines interact, and the nature of that interaction has changed throughout history.

　The idea that politics could be approached scientifically developed primarily in the 20th century. Basically, political scientists used the statistical methods developed by social scientists and applied them to politics. Using these methods, political scientists try to explain where political power comes from in a society, and how it is used.

> **The reading suggests that political science can never approach true science.**

Yet, politics is in many ways beyond the reach of true scientific investigation. The scientific method contends that the same set of conditions will produce the same outcomes. It has proven extremely difficult to make clear connections between political outcomes and the conditions from which they emerged.

訳例

政治学は、人類学、歴史学、社会学、経済学、そして心理学といったほかの社会科学に関連を持つ社会科学のひとつである。それ（政治学）は、これらのほかの学問分野すべての基礎となるものであるといえる。なぜならば、これらのほかの学問分野で扱われるすべての活動は、それらが起こる政治環境によりある程度支配されるからである。別の視点から見れば、政治学とは、ほかの社会科学とより密接に結びついている要因から起こる政治的状況の研究であるともいえる。社会科学における政治学の重要性についてどのような視点に立ったとしても、これらの学問分野のすべては互いに影響し合い、その相互作用の本質は歴史を通して変化することは明白である。

政治学が科学的に研究できるという考え方は、そもそも 20 世紀に発展した。基本的に、政治学者は社会科学者によって開発された統計的手法を使い、政治にそれを応用した。これらの手法を使い、政治学者は社会において政治的権力はどこからくるのか、そしてどのように使われるのかを説明しようとしている。

しかし、政治はさまざまな意味で、本当の意味での科学的調査の領域を超えたところにある。科学的手法は、一連の同じ状況があれば、同じ結果が生じると主張するが、政治的な結果とそれが現れた状況との関係を明確にすることは極めて困難であると証明されているのである。

mp3
28

聴くテクスト

> リーディングの内容 (political science can never approach true science) を受けて

Today, I'd like to continue our look at the role of political science within the context of the other disciplines of social science and ask the basic question as to why it is called "political science" at all. I mean, what makes political science "scientific?" Maybe it's only a name and has nothing to do with science at all. Certainly it isn't scientific in the way that, say, physics or chemistry are scientific.

> The professor suggests ways in which it could at least be considered more scientific. Explain the reasons political science may be considered a science. 以下の 3 つのパラグラフを要約することで設問に答える

Now, most scientific theories have to rely on mathematical proof to validate them. Gravity would be only an idea if Newton hadn't supported it with mathematical proof. The same goes for Einstein's Theory of Relativity. So mathematics seems to be vital to any real science. But what about statistics? It is certainly a discipline based on mathematics. I mean, you get a bunch of data and numbers and, so what? What does it all mean? Well, you've got to organize all that raw data, and to do it, you must use statistical methods, mathematical techniques, to give all those numbers meaning.

> The professor suggests ways in which it could at least be considered more scientific. Explain the reasons political science may be considered a science.

So to get back to political science, there are times when we make surveys or polls, and we collect a lot of data and we apply statistics to it to see what it all means. If we apply the statistics correctly we should be able to get something meaningful from our data. We may be able to predict, with reasonable accuracy, say, the outcome of an election before the election actually takes place.

> The professor suggests ways in which it could at least be considered more scientific. Explain the reasons political science may be considered a science.

It's not as easy as it sounds. You've got to design the original poll correctly or you will get results that, no matter how good your statistics are, will really be of no use and will not make accurate predictions. Then, when you get your data, and let's suppose it has the potential to be useful, you've got to know precisely which statistical techniques to use to give you the best predictions. However, with better predictions, you can at least approach real science.

訳例

今日は、社会科学のほかの学問分野との関係における政治学の役割について引き続き見ていき、なぜそれが「政治学」と呼ばれているのかという基本的な質問について解明していき

たいと思います。つまり、何が政治学を「科学的」にしているのでしょうか。もしかしたら、これはただの名前であり、科学とは何の関係もないのかもしれません。確かに、政治学は物理学や化学が科学的であるという意味では、科学的ではないのです。

　さて、多くの科学的理論は、正当性を立証するために数学的証明に頼らなければなりません。もしニュートンが数学的に証明しなければ、重力はただのアイデアにすぎませんでした。同じことがアインシュタインの相対性理論にもいえます。従って、数学はどのような真の科学にとっても極めて重要なものと思われます。しかし、統計学はどうでしょうか。それ（統計学）は確かに数学を基礎にする学問です。皆さんはたくさんのデータや数値を得ますが、それが何なのでしょうか。それはいったい何を意味するのでしょうか。皆さんは統計的手法や数学的手法を用いて生のデータを整理し、これらの数値に意味を与えなければならないのです。

　政治学の話に戻りましょう。私たちは、調査や世論調査を行い、たくさんのデータを集めることがあります。そして、それがいったい何を意味するのかを見るために統計学を利用します。もし、私たちが統計学を正確に利用すれば、データから意味のある何かを得ることができるでしょう。例えば、ある程度の正確さをもって実際の選挙が行われる前に選挙結果を予測することができるかもしれません。

　しかし、それは言うほど容易なことではありません。皆さんは世論調査の要となる調査用紙を正確に書き上げなければなりません。さもないと、どれほど立派な統計を使っても、まったく役立たなかったり、正確な予測ができないような調査結果を得たりすることになるでしょう。皆さんがデータを得たとき、それが潜在的に役に立つ可能性があるとすれば、皆さんはどの統計的手法を使えば最も正確な予測が得られるかを知っていなければなりません。よりよい予測が得られれば、少なくとも本物の科学に近づくことができるわけですから。

重要語句

- a bunch of たくさんの、かなりの数の
- accuracy 正確さ、精度
- alternative 代わりとなるもの
- anthropology 人類学
- apply 応用する、利用する
- arise 起こる、生じる
- contend 強く主張する、競争する
- cornerstone 土台、基礎、要
- discipline 専門分野、研究分野
- economics 経済学
- election 選挙
- emerge 現れる、出現する
- govern 支配する、治める
- gravity 引力、重力
- interact 互いに影響し合う、相互に作用する
- investigation 調査、研究
- meaningful 意味のある、重要な
- nothing to do with ... 〜とは無関係な
- outcome 結果、結末
- point of view 視点、観点
- political science 政治学
- politics 政治学、政治
- poll 世論調査、投票
- potential 可能性がある、起こり得る
- proof 証拠、証明
- psychology 心理学
- reasonable 正当な、妥当な
- social science 社会科学
- sociology 社会学
- statistical 統計の、統計に基づく
- survey 調査
- theory of relativity 相対性原理
- validate 正当性を立証する
- vital 肝要な、極めて重要な

2. オンライン投稿文

この課題では、オンラインのディスカッションを読みます。教授が質問を投稿しており、クラスメートがディスカッション掲示板に回答を寄せています。あなたは自分自身の回答を書き、ディスカッションに貢献することが求められています。読むのも含めて 10 分間で自分の意見を書いてください。

指示文と質問・議論の訳

教授がマーケティングの授業をしています。教授の質問に答える自分の意見を書いてください。

解答では、自分の言葉で意見を述べ、その裏付けをしておきます。

効果的な解答は、最低でも 100 語が必要です。

ペレス博士

　今週はソーシャルメディアでのマーケティングについて議論してきました。多くの企業がこの戦略に投資し、成功を見いだしています。しかし、期待していた利益がもたらされていないと感じている向きもあります。これは、その種の広告手法が、あらゆるプラットフォームに広告を掲載するだけではないからです。それよりむしろ、特定の顧客をターゲットにすることを指しており、それが必ずしも簡単ではないのです。私が知りたいのは、皆さんがソーシャルメディアをどのように使い、広告からどんな影響を受けているかです。どのような広告が最も効果的で、どのような広告が最も効果が薄いと考えられるでしょうか。企業はソーシャルメディアでのマーケティングにもっと投資すべきだと思いますか、あるいは従来型の広告に留まるべきだと思いますか。

アンナ

　私は、ソーシャルメディア上のほとんどの広告が単に迷惑だと感じます。広告は、自分が興味を持っている他のコンテンツの邪魔をしているように思います。私には、そういう広告はお金の無駄のように見えます。特定の顧客をターゲットにした従来型の広告のほうが、はるかに費用対効果が高いと思います。特定の層の人向けに書かれた雑誌に載せる優れた広告にお金を払うことが、最良の投資です。

ピーター

　アンナさんは良い指摘をしていると思います。どのような種類の顧客をターゲットにしたいかをよくわかっておく必要があります。ソーシャルメディアは、実際のところある特定の人をターゲットにしているわけではないので、そこに企業が打つ広告は効果的ではないのかもしれません。でも、人々はかつてよりもはるかに多くの時間をソーシャルメディアに費やしているので、いかなるマーケティング計画においても、そうした広告を無視することはできません。慎重に調査すれば、ソーシャルメディアでのマーケティングは非常に効果的なものになると思います。

模範解答 （一例）

　I agree with Peter that we can no longer leave out social media in any marketing strategy. On the other hand, Anna is correct in pointing out that most ads are simply ignored. I read one study that showed that 82 percent of online ads were ignored, which was far more than in traditional media. Therefore, it seems to me that investing in platforms that will help you target specific customers will bring the most benefits. Social media platforms collect a lot of personal data on their users, and this will help you reach those users that may be most interested in your product. Sure, you may have to pay more money for such a service, but I believe this would be the most lucrative approach in the long run.

訳例

　いかなるマーケティング戦略においても、もはやソーシャルメディアを除外できないという点で、私はピーターさんに同意します。他方で、ほとんどの広告は単に無視されるというアンナさんの指摘は正しいものです。私が読んだ研究論文によると、オンライン広告の82パーセントが無視されており、それは従来のメディアにおける割合よりもはるかに大きいものでした。したがって、特定の顧客層に訴求する助けとなるようなプラットフォームへの投資が最大の利益をもたらすように思います。ソーシャルメディアのプラットフォームはユーザーの個人データをたくさん収集しており、それが自社製品に最も関心があるかもしれないユーザーに訴求するのに役立ちます。確かに、そうしたサービスにはより多くの投資が必要になるかもしれませんが、長い目で見ればこれが最も利益を上げる方法だろうと思います。

ポイント

議論の参加者 2 人の意見が異なるので、まず、自分の意見を考える。そして、書き出しでは、どちらか一方の意見を参考にして自分の見解も述べる "I agree with Peter that we can no longer leave out social media in any marketing strategy." という形がいい。次に、もう一方の意見も尊重して "On the other hand, Anna is correct in pointing out that most ads are simply ignored." と述べ、具体例 "I read one study that showed that 82 percent of online ads were ignored, which was far more than in traditional media" を使いその論拠を書いて裏付けをする。それから、最初に述べた自分の意見を言い換えて "it seems to me that investing in platforms that will help you target specific customers will bring the most benefits" とし、その意見の裏付けをして "Social media platforms collect a lot of personal data on their users, and this will help you reach those users that may be most interested in your product." と簡単にまとめ、結論 "Sure, you may have to pay more money for such a service, but I believe this would be the most lucrative approach in the long run." につなげていく。なお、話に一貫性を持たせるために、「つなぎ言葉（転換語）」"on the other hand"（2 行目）、"therefore"（5 行目）"sure"（8 行目）などを、うまく使うことが大切である。

大きな枠

1. 議論の参加者 2 人の意見が異なるときには、どちらかの意見を踏まえて自分の意見を述べる。
2. 次に、もう一方の意見も踏まえて参加者を尊重し、そこから具体例（自分の意見の裏付け）も含めて自分の意見を述べる。
3. その後、話の流れの中で、意見を簡単にまとめ、おちをつけて結論とする。

Test

3

Reading Section

Listening Section

Speaking Section

Writing Section

解答・解説

Reading Section

Questions 1-10

Dialects

A dialect is a version of a language which differs in some aspects of grammar, pronunciation or vocabulary from other forms of the same language. A dialect can be restricted to a certain area or it can be spoken by a specific group of people within the same area as other dialects. So it is that the British may refer to American English as American dialect, but in America itself, American English is often broken into southern dialect, New England dialect, African American dialect and so on. It is very often difficult to determine when a version of the language is at such a stage in its development that it qualifies as a dialect. The basic rule is that a dialect can noticeably differ from the basic language but cannot **do so** to the point that it is incomprehensible to speakers of the basic language. It may be the case that some dialects are nearly incomprehensible in the spoken form, but the written form should maintain enough similarities to make understanding clear. If it did not, then it would, perhaps, begin to be qualified as a separate language.

The evolution of a dialect can best be seen in the formation of American English with its gradual **differentiation** from British English. In its early history, to about 1800, Americans spoke British English. (A) ■ Noticeable differences in the two dialects steadily increased, however, for in 1828 Noah Webster felt the necessity to write *The American Dictionary of the English Language*, which pointed out the variations between the two dialects. (B) ■ Webster showed that there were many new words used in America that were either not used at all in Britain or were used there but were used differently. (C) ■ Many new words in American English came from the settlers' contacts with local Native Americans.

(D) ■ Such words as moose, squash, canoe and hickory, which came from a variety of Native American languages made their way into common usage. Webster also noted spelling differences such as -er replacing the British -re (center, centre) and or replacing our (behavior, behaviour).

③→ Since America was settled during the time of Shakespeare, it is interesting to note that some aspects of American English became frozen in time and are closer to Shakespearean English than are many aspects of British English. The British may no longer use the American word *trash* for *rubbish* or *fall* for *autumn*, but Shakespeare probably would have. There are certain regions of the United States in which even more aspects of Shakespeare's Elizabethan English are maintained. This is particularly evident in the Appalachian Mountains from Virginia to the Ozarks.

④→ But as America grew and came into contact with other languages, such as French and Spanish, the language began to break into its own dialects. Black slaves from Africa also introduced new vocabulary and speech patterns into the language. Today some experts recognize as many as 24 regional dialects in the U.S. In truth, these could be broken into two dialects that can simply be called **northern and southern dialects**. Oddly enough, northern dialects can be found stretching from New England to the Pacific Northwest, and down to California and the Southwest. This is because these regions were largely settled by people from New England and the East Coast who brought their dialects with them. The southern dialect, however, has remained **confined** to an area from the southern East Coast to Texas.

⑤→ There is some evidence that dialects are decreasing. Mass media and mass communication have inadvertently set up a standard of English for people to follow. Those not following such a standard may be subjected to a stigma of speaking something less than correct English. The same communications have made speakers of British English more aware of American English and vice versa. Words that were once confined to one dialect are now finding their ways more and more into the other.

1. Why did Noah Webster feel it was necessary to write *The American Dictionary of the English Language*?

    (A) British dictionaries did not contain American vocabulary.

    (B) He saw that American English was becoming a new language.

    (C) He saw enough differences between the two dialects to make a dictionary useful.

    (D) He wanted to include many new words used from contact with Native Americans.

2. Why does the author mention Shakespeare in paragraph 3?

    (A) He is interested in Shakespearean English.

    (B) He wants to show the similarities between American and Shakespearean English.

    (C) He wants to show that British and American English are quite similar.

    (D) He wants to show how languages change over time.

Paragraph 3 is marked with an arrow [→].

3. According to paragraph 3, why do the British not use the word trash?

    (A) It's an American word.

    (B) It's an old word.

    (C) It sounds too formal.

    (D) It was used by Shakespeare.

Paragraph 3 is marked with an arrow [→].

4. Why does the author mention **northern and southern dialects**?

    (A) To describe the two dialects of the U.S.
    (B) To show how widespread they are
    (C) To contrast them with British English
    (D) To simplify the number of dialects

5. The word **confined** in the passage is closest in meaning to

    (A) limited
    (B) found
    (C) spoken
    (D) alive

6. According to paragraph 4, why is the northern dialect so widespread?

    (A) Because it extends from New England to California.
    (B) Because New Englanders settled in much of the West.
    (C) Because the southern dialect was spoken only in the southern U.S.
    (D) Because of contact with the French and Spanish languages.

Paragraph 4 is marked with an arrow [→].

7. According to paragraph 5, why could the number of dialects be decreasing?

    (A) Dialects are influenced by the standard language used in media.
    (B) British and American English are becoming more similar.
    (C) Speaking a dialect can lead to a stigma.
    (D) Speakers use words from many dialects.

Paragraph 5 is marked with an arrow [→].

8. According to the passage, what is true of dialects?

    (A) They eventually become separate languages.

    (B) Several dialects could be spoken in the same area.

    (C) They will soon disappear.

    (D) They differ mainly in vocabulary.

9. Look at the four squares [■] that indicate where the following sentence could be added to the passage.

There were several types of variations that he deemed important.

Where would this sentence best fit?

10. *Directions:* An introductory sentence for a brief summary of the passage is provided below. Complete the summary by selecting the THREE answer choices that express the most important ideas in the passage. Some sentences do not belong in the summary because they express ideas that are not presented in the passage or are minor ideas in the passage. **This question is worth 2 points.**

There are several reasons for the development and evolution of dialects.

- _____
- _____
- _____

Answer Choices

(A) Dialects have developed in the U.S. though under pressure from media some may begin to disappear.

(B) The main differences between British and American English are in vocabulary and spelling.

(C) Shakespeare's English is more similar to American English than British English.

(D) One of the main reasons for the development of a dialect is geographic isolation from the basic language.

(E) The differences between American and British dialects became apparent in the early 1800s.

(F) Native American, French and Spanish languages have all influenced the development of American dialects.

U.S. Political Parties

①→ The founders of the United States constitution were against the formation of political parties. They believed that political parties were destined to become sources of corruption. They also believed that people should decide individually on issues according to their own merit, not on the basis of which party supported them. Yet, it was the very nature of the government that the Constitution produced that in a short time led to the formation of political parties. This was because it quickly became clear that no president could govern effectively without support from the legislative branches: the Senate and the House of Representatives. In order to get such support it was easier to organize legislators of similar beliefs than for the president to approach each of them separately on each issue that was proposed.

The first political parties to form were the Federalists, named after their belief in a strong central government, and the Republicans, who believed in a limited role for government, especially in economics. After some early turmoil, the Republican Party gained power with the election of Thomas Jefferson and remained in control of the government for 28 years.

③→ For a while it seemed that the country would only have one political party, but as is often the case in politics, individuals within the party began to quarrel among themselves. One **faction** of this party began to promote a more active role of the government in economics. To distinguish themselves from their opponents in the Republican Party they referred to themselves as National Republicans. However, their opponents in the Republican Party prevailed and elected Andrew Jackson president. These original Republicans also wanted to distance themselves from their opponents within the Republican Party and first called themselves Democratic Republicans and later in 1828 referred to themselves as the Democratic Party. **The policies and behavior of Jackson were so controversial that the National Republicans, seeing little hope for themselves within the Republican Party, renamed their party the Whig Party.**

④→ But it was the Democratic Party that generally controlled the government, at least until 1860. However, major issues in politics and society were **looming**. (A) ■ Slavery, primarily in the South, was becoming an issue that was splitting the country. (B) ■ Over time the Democrats became more associated with the South and the defense of slavery, while the Whig Party split into two camps. (C) ■ The situation became more confusing with the passing of the Kansas-Nebraska Act which allowed for the possibility of slavery being extended into the new western territories. (D) ■ This act, signed by a Democratic president, caused a split within that party as well. So strong was this split that it caused the formation of two distinct Democratic parties, not surprisingly called the Northern Democratic Party and the Southern Democratic Party. It became impossible to refer to them as belonging to the same party when in 1860 **both** put forth their own presidential candidate.

⑤→ The outcome of all of this political confusion was the formation of a new anti-slavery party called the Republican Party. They were not unchallenged in their anti-slavery stance, however. The previously formed Know-Nothing Party had gained great support for its anti-slavery views. Unfortunately for its future success, it also held strongly anti-Catholic and anti-immigrant views. When the Know-Nothings seemed to be weakening their anti-slavery position, many of their supporters with those from the remnants of the Whig Party and some northern Democrats **crossed over** to the Republican Party. When the Democrats put forth two candidates, it virtually assured the election of Abraham Lincoln as the first Republican president.

From this time to the present, the United States has generally been a two-party nation. Although other parties have arisen from time to time and occasionally enjoyed some degree of success, none has been able to maintain public interest for as long as the Democrats and Republicans.

11. Based on the information in paragraph 1, why did political parties begin to form?

(A) They were encouraged by the Constitution.
(B) They were forced to do so by the nature of the government.
(C) They needed to avoid corruption.
(D) The president needed to approach individuals separately.

Paragraph 1 is marked with an arrow [→].

12. According to the information in paragraph 3, what can be inferred about politicians in general?

(A) They usually form political parties.
(B) They are often confused.
(C) They often disagree with each other.
(D) Their ideas often change.

Paragraph 3 is marked with an arrow [→].

13. Based on the information in paragraph 3, which of the following is true about the Republican Party?

(A) It broke into four parts.
(B) It was replaced by the Democratic Party and the Whig Party.
(C) It disappeared completely.
(D) It first became the Democratic Republicans and later became the Whig Party.

14. According to paragraph 4, what can be inferred about the two main political parties?

(A) They favored the passage of the Kansas-Nebraska Act.
(B) They were confused on the meaning of the Kansas-Nebraska Act.
(C) They did not take a strong stand against slavery.
(D) They were surprised that a Democratic president signed the Kansas-Nebraska Act.

Paragraph 4 is marked with an arrow [→].

15. Which of the sentences below best expresses the essential information in the highlighted sentence in the passage? *Incorrect choices change the meaning in important ways or leave out essential information.*

The policies and behavior of Jackson were so controversial that the National Republicans, seeing little hope for themselves within the Republican Party, renamed their party the Whig Party.

(A) The National Republicans were upset by the way Jackson ran the country and, since they had no chance to influence the party, changed the name of the party to the Whig Party.
(B) The Whig Party was formed because it saw the National Republicans and their leader, Jackson, as being hopeless.
(C) The Republican Party was tired of the National Republicans so Jackson forced them into forming a new party called the Whig Party.
(D) The National Republicans had no respect for Jackson or the Republicans so they decided to form their own party called the Whigs to have a chance of success.

16. In paragraph 5, why does the author mention the Know-Nothing Party?

(A) To show how they were transformed into the Republican Party
(B) To show that other parties besides the two main parties existed
(C) To show how popular an anti-slavery position was
(D) To show why there were two Democratic candidates for president

Paragraph 5 is marked with an arrow [→].

17. The phrase **crossed over** in the passage is closest in meaning to

(A) fought against
(B) joined
(C) replaced
(D) composed

18. Which of the following statements most accurately reflects the author's views on Lincoln's becoming president?

(A) He became president by pure luck.
(B) He would have won the election whether or not the Democratic Party had split.
(C) The Know-Nothings would have won but they changed their views on slavery.
(D) It would have been a much closer election if the Democratic Party had not split.

19. Look at the four squares [■] that indicate where the following sentence could be added to the passage.

Though neither side wanted to be seen as directly supporting it, neither did they want to alienate Southern voters.

Where would this sentence best fit?

20. *Directions:* An introductory sentence for a brief summary of the passage is provided below. Complete the summary by selecting the THREE answer choices that express the most important ideas in the passage. Some sentences do not belong in the summary because they express ideas that are not presented in the passage or are minor ideas in the passage. **This question is worth 2 points.**

Today's two major political parties have had a long and difficult history.

- _____
- _____
- _____

Answer Choices

(A) The Federalists believed in a strong central government while the Republicans did not.

(B) The founding fathers were against political parties but soon two parties, the Federalists and the Republicans, formed anyway.

(C) Though the Republican Party held dominance during the early 1800s, it was soon split by internal quarrels.

(D) The issue of slavery caused a crisis within all political parties and led to the formation of the current Republican Party.

(E) The Whig Party formed as an opponent of the Republican Party but failed to have a significant influence on the politics of the U.S.

(F) The Know-Nothing Party was another party that influenced politics in the mid 1800s.

Listening Section

1. What problem is the man having?

   (A) He has too much studying to do.

   (B) He cannot adjust to life in the U.S.

   (C) He has no time for anything but studying.

   (D) He only has friends from his own country.

2. What advice does the woman give the man about meeting Americans?

   (A) He should go to a movie with them.

   (B) He should talk to them first.

   (C) He should be more patient and wait for them to speak to him.

   (D) He should first try to meet Asian Americans.

3. What mistake did the woman make when she first came to America?

(A) She only had friends from her own country.
(B) She never used English.
(C) She was wasting her time studying.
(D) She was afraid to speak because no one could understand her.

4. Listen again to part of the conversation. Then answer the question. ∩

What can be inferred about foreigners in Asia when the woman says this? ∩

(A) There aren't many foreigners in Asia.
(B) In Asia it is easy to see that a person is a foreigner.
(C) It is not so unusual to see foreigners in Asia.
(D) In Asia people can easily avoid foreigners.

5. Listen again to part of the conversation. Then answer the question. ∩

Why does the woman say this? ∩

(A) She's tired of hearing the man complain.
(B) She's criticizing the man's attitude.
(C) She's asking for the man's advice.
(D) She's sympathizing with the man.

Art
(Van Gogh vs. Picasso)

6. What main idea is the professor talking about in this lecture?

(A) the life of Picasso
(B) the difference in artistic styles between Van Gogh and Picasso
(C) misleading stereotypes of artists
(D) artistic inspiration

7. What were the two main reasons behind Picasso's fame?

Choose 2 answers.

(A) He was treated as a gifted artist when he was only 15 years old.
(B) His technique appealed to the general public.
(C) He changed styles many times.
(D) He lived for 93 years.

8. Listen again to part of the lecture. Then answer the question. ⋂

What does the professor imply when he says this? ⋂

(A) He's implying that the younger you are taken seriously as an artist, the more likely it is that you will become famous.
(B) He's saying that you have to display talent when you are young or no one will pay attention to you later.
(C) He's implying that you are either born with artistic talent or you are not.
(D) He's saying that Picasso would have become famous even if he was not discovered at the age of 15.

9. The professor tells an anecdote about Picasso's creative process. Summarize this process by putting the events in order.

- He traced the bones in red pencil.
- He prepared the fish skeleton.
- He took out a sheet of paper.
- He used a yellow pencil.

1.	
2.	
3.	
4.	

10. Listen again to part of the lecture. Then answer the question. ∩

Why does the professor say this? ∩

(A) He wants a student to give an opinion.

(B) He's emphasizing Picasso's understanding of his fame.

(C) He's hoping students will now discuss the importance of fame.

(D) He's criticizing Picasso's behavior.

11. What will probably be the next topic in the lecture?

(A) The influence of Picasso on the art world

(B) A criticism of Picasso's work

(C) A history of Picasso's artistic style

(D) The reaction of critics to Picasso's early fame

Questions 12-16

mp3 35

12. Why does the man visit the woman?

(A) He's looking for a better apartment.

(B) He wants to live in the new dorm.

(C) He is interested in finding a sleeping room.

(D) He can't find a place to live.

13. Why does the woman mention sleeping rooms?

(A) She knows the man has very little money.

(B) She has no other housing available.

(C) They are off campus.

(D) They have recently been remodeled.

14. What is the biggest problem with living in a sleeping room?

(A) Students must share the bathroom.

(B) The rooms have no TVs.

(C) Students are not allowed to eat in the rooms.

(D) Cooking is not allowed.

15. Listen again to part of the conversation. Then answer the question. 𝛺

What does the woman mean when she says the following? 𝛺

(A) She's not completely sure whether students can cook or not.

(B) She really doesn't know the details about what students can have in their rooms.

(C) She's not sure if the rooms have hot water.

(D) She must ask the building manager to find out if anything is available.

16. Listen again to part of the conversation. Then answer the question. 𝛺

What can be inferred from the following? 𝛺

(A) The woman is not very enthusiastic about the sleeping rooms.

(B) The sleeping rooms may be better than one would think.

(C) The woman is hinting that the man should really consider living somewhere else.

(D) The building is quite old so the man should not expect the rooms to be very good.

Psychology

17. What is the main topic of this lecture?

(A) Whether or not psychology is a science

(B) When to prescribe drugs for psychological problems

(C) The use of drugs in psychology

(D) Brain chemistry

18. In the lecture, the professor gives information about elements of psychology. Indicate whether each of the following is one of these elements or not.

	Yes	No
Depends on statistical analysis		
Aims for psychological changes that are long lasting and drug-free		
Needs to understand brain chemistry		
Sometimes prescribes alcohol as a psychological drug		
Is closer to a social science than a science		

19. Why does the professor mention alcohol?

(A) She wants to joke with the class.

(B) She wants to show that alcohol can be considered a psychological drug.

(C) She wants to show students how bad alcohol can be for their brain.

(D) She wants to compare alcohol to serotonin.

20. Listen again to part of the lecture. Then answer the question. ∩

What does the professor mean when she says this? ∩

(A) Drugs used to change personality do not have a lasting effect.

(B) Taking alcohol should not be considered a joke.

(C) Drugs are useful in changing behavior.

(D) Psychology and psychiatry use drugs to make people return to their old self.

21. According to the professor, what is the result of using lithium?

Choose 2 answers.

(A) A person will become happier.

(B) A person's personality will stabilize.

(C) Serotonin will be created in the brain.

(D) Chemical balance will occur in the brain.

22. Listen again to part of the lecture. Then answer the question. ∩

Why does the professor say this? ∩

(A) To introduce a summary of the lecture

(B) To emphasize a key point

(C) To clarify a point

(D) To explain how difficult the topic is to discuss

Biology
(Evolution)

23. What is the main topic of this lecture?

    (A) Successful organisms

    (B) Elements of adaptation

    (C) Adaptation to extreme environments

    (D) Variety in nature

24. What are the three main parts of adaptation?

    (A) Amplitude, duration and efficiency

    (B) Reproduction, efficiency and distribution

    (C) Distribution, reproduction and amplitude

    (D) Duration, reproduction and efficiency

25. Why does the professor mention the cockroach?

Choose 2 answers.

    (A) It is an example of a widespread organism.

    (B) It is an example of an organism that can successfully reproduce.

    (C) It is an example of efficiency.

    (D) It is an example of an organism tolerant of many environments.

26. The professor describes features of adaptation for various organisms. Match these features with the organism.

	Alpine Trees	Toad	Cockroach	Coral
High amplitude, high efficiency				
High amplitude, low efficiency				
High amplitude, low duration				
Low amplitude				

27. What does the professor say about alpine trees that only exist in harsh environments?

(A) They demonstrate successful reproduction.

(B) They are limited by extremes in their environment.

(C) They are tough but cannot reproduce efficiently.

(D) They are not confined to narrow zones.

28. Listen again to part of the lecture. Then answer the question. ∩

Why does the professor say this? ∩

(A) To emphasize that he's now sure the students understand

(B) To check the students' understanding

(C) To encourage the students to ask questions

(D) To point out the students' misunderstandings

Speaking Section

1. **Independent Speaking** [Paired Choice]

Listen to the following question.

Do you agree or disagree with the following statement? Watching TV can have a bad influence on children. Give specific examples to support your answer.

Prepare your response after the beep. | Preparation time 15 seconds |

Start your response after the beep. | Response time 45 seconds |

2. **Integrated Reading / Listening / Speaking Situational**
—— Information in a College Catalog

Now, read the passage about information in a college catalog. You have 45 seconds to read the passage. Begin reading now.

Reading (45 seconds):

Probation

Students who fail a course or who earn a cumulative grade point average below 2.0 are automatically placed on probation. A student who is on probation will have one term in which to show that he or she is capable of doing university-level work. In general, this is shown by either retaking and passing the failed course or by finishing the semester with a grade point average above 2.0, whichever is appropriate.

In general, students on probation are expected to earn a grade point average of at least 2.0 while taking at least 12 credit hours of courses during the semester following the imposition of probationary status. Any student who fails to meet all of these conditions may be suspended or dismissed at the end of the following semester. Students have the right to appeal any such decisions. Please note that no notation of academic probation is made on the student's transcript.

Listening:

Now listen to a conversation between two students.

Question:

The woman gives her reasons why she is on probation. State her reasons and tell what she expects to happen.

Prepare your response after the beep. | Preparation time 30 seconds |

Start your response after the beep. | Response time 60 seconds |

3. Integrated Reading / Listening / Speaking Academic

—— Economics (Business Cycles)

Now, read the passage about business cycles. You have 45 seconds to read the passage. Begin reading now.

Reading (45 seconds):

Business activity and the economy in general seem to follow distinct four-part cycles. The four parts are known among economists as prosperity, liquidation, depression and recovery. During prosperity, there is a rise in productivity, employment and wages. Optimism runs high and investment, in order to expand productivity, is common. Unfortunately, the natural outgrowth of such high productivity is an increase in prices, which at some point inhibits consumer spending. As demand declines, so does productivity and then employment. The result is a pessimistic period known as liquidation, when little investment occurs. If liquidation worsens, unemployment will grow, demand for products — even at lower prices — decreases and factories are forced to shut down. Such severe economic times are referred to as depressions. The fourth stage of the cycle, recovery, may take some time, and it is not clear what factors may most influence it.

mp3
42

Listening:

Now listen to part of a lecture on this topic in a business class.

Question:

Explain the four stages in the economic cycle and why they are often difficult to identify in practice.

Prepare your response after the beep. | Preparation time 30 seconds |

Start your response after the beep. | Response time 60 seconds |

4. Integrated Listening / Speaking [Summary]

—— History (Alcohol in the early 1900s)

Now listen to part of a lecture in a history class.

Question:

Summarize the history of Prohibition in the early part of the 20th century in the U.S.

Prepare your response after the beep. | Preparation time 20 seconds

Start your response after the beep. | Response time 60 seconds

Writing Section

1. Integrated Writing
—— Linguistics Lecture (Pidgin)

mp3
44

Directions:

For this integrated task, you have 3 minutes to read the passage. Then you will listen to part of a lecture on the topic you have just read about. Following the lecture, you have 20 minutes to plan and write your response. An ideal response will be 150 to 225 words.

Read the following passage.

Reading:

A pidgin is a language which is created when two separate language groups live in close proximity to each other. For this reason, pidgins are sometimes referred to as contact languages. In some cases, however, as when different language groups have an economic relationship, the pidgin is used as a means of negotiating business and does not need continuous contact as do other pidgins. Because the nature of a pidgin is to expedite communication, in linguistic form, it often consists of simple grammar patterns, reduced phonology, and is often highly dependent on vocabulary to transmit meaning. But communication is the nature of all language and is generally considered its main role.

In order for pidgins to develop, several factors must be present. The contact between the language groups must be persistent. In other words, contact must prevail for an extended period of time. Secondly, there must be a mutual need for the groups to communicate with each other. Without this need, language groups can live in complete isolation despite living in close physical contact with each other. Thirdly, it is important that the groups do not share some third language. In other words, if two groups living in close proximity and sharing a need to communicate both speak a third language, it is likely that the development of a pidgin will be suppressed by this third language. Pidgins are not generally learned as a first language, however, in the cases where this occurs, it is referred to as creolization.

Listening:
Now, listen to part of a lecture on pidgins, which you have just read about. You may take notes while listening to the lecture.

Now, get ready to answer the question. You may use your notes to help you answer.

Question:
Summarize the main points concerning the development and form of pidgins. Explain how the professor's view of communication contrasts with the view expressed in the reading.

2. Writing for an Academic Discussion

Your professor is teaching a class on information science. Write a response to the professor's question.

Please contribute your own ideas to this discussion, and support them with some details.

Your response should be at least 100 words in length.

Doctor Lee

This week, we've been discussing the various ways of digitally storing information. But we often forget that information storage has been around for centuries. Libraries have existed in even the first civilizations and have traditionally been an important part of any town and city. Yet, nowadays, people are questioning whether we really have any need for libraries since so much information is available online. Do you think we really have any need to maintain large, expensive libraries in this digital age?

Anna

I rarely go to the library anymore. Most of the materials in the university library have been digitalized so that I can access them online. Sure, maybe there are a few rare books that I can only read by going to the library, but how often do I really need to use them? Times have changed. It is simply more convenient to find what I need from anywhere by simply using my cell phone. So, maybe there's a place for libraries, but we shouldn't be spending as much money on them as we used to.

Peter

I have to disagree with Anna. Of course, we can get most of the information we need online, but there's more to libraries than books. They offer us a quiet place to study without being interrupted. Besides, I can get access to ebooks, films, and music in one place without having to pay any extra money like I do online. I think this far outweighs the effort it takes to go to the local library. I think libraries will continue to be important no matter how much information we can get online.

解答・解説

Reading Section

Listening Section

Speaking Section

Writing Section

Reading

1 C　　**2** B　　**3** B　　**4** D　　**5** A　　**6** B

7 A　　**8** B　　**9** B　　**10** D, E, F　　**11** B　　**12** C

13 B　　**14** C　　**15** A　　**16** C　　**17** B　　**18** D

19 B　　**20** B, C, D

Listening

1 C　　**2** B　　**3** A　　**4** B　　**5** B　　**6** C

7 A, D　　**8** A

9 1. He prepared the fish skeleton.

2. He took out a sheet of paper.

3. He traced the bones in red pencil.

4. He used a yellow pencil.

10 B　　**11** C　　**12** D　　**13** A　　**14** D　　**15** B

16 B　　**17** C

18 Depends on statistical analysis (Yes)

Aims for psychological changes that are long lasting and drug-free (Yes)

Needs to understand brain chemistry (Yes)

Sometimes prescribes alcohol as a psychological drug (No)

Is closer to a social science than a science (Yes)

19 B　　**20** A　　**21** B, D　　**22** A　　**23** B　　**24** A

25 A, D

26 High amplitude, high efficiency (Cockroach)

High amplitude, low efficiency (Alpine Trees)

High amplitude, low duration (Toad)

Low amplitude (Coral)

27 C　　**28** B

Reading Section　解答・解説

Questions **Questions** 1-10

問題文の訳例

> ### 方言
>
> 　方言とは、同じ言語のほかの形と、文法、発音や語彙の一部が異なっているひとつの言語のバージョンである。方言の使用は、ある地域に限定されたり、他の方言として同じ地域の中の特定の集団によって話されたりする。だから、イギリス人はアメリカ英語をアメリカ方言ととらえるかもしれないが、アメリカ国内ではアメリカ英語がしばしば南部方言やニューイングランド方言、アフリカン・アメリカン方言などに分類されているのである。言語のあるバージョンがその発展過程において、いつ方言としての特質を得るまでになるのかを決めることは、しばしば非常に困難である。基本的な決まりは、方言とは基となる言語と著しく異なってはいるものの、その礎となる言語の話者たちに理解されないほどの違いはない、ということである。例えば、話し言葉ではほとんど理解不可能であったとしても、書き言葉は十分に共通点を維持しており、それによって理解を深めることができる状態でなければ方言とはいえない。そうでなければ、その方言はその時点で別の言語としての特質を持ち始めるであろう。
>
> 　方言の進化は、イギリス英語から段階的に分化したアメリカ英語の形成において最もよく見られる。1800年ごろ、アメリカ史の初期においては、アメリカ人はイギリス英語を話していた。しかし、2つの方言における著しい違いは着実に増加していき、そのため1828年にはノア・ウェブスターは2つの方言の間の変化を指摘する *The American Dictionary of the English Language* を書く必要性を感じていた。いくつもの種類の変化が存在し、彼はそれらを重要視した。ウェブスターは、アメリカで使用されている新しい単語で、イギリスではまったく使用されていないか、使用されてはいるものの、異なった形で使用されている単語を掲示した。アメリカ英語の新しい単語の多くは、入植者たちが地元のアメリカ先住民たちと接触することによりもたらされたものであった。ムース、スカッシュ、カヌー、ヒッコリーといったような単語は、さまざまなアメリカ先住民の言語からもたらされ、共通の言葉として使用されるようになった。ウェブスターはまた、イギリス英語の -re が -er に（center、centre）、-our が -or に（behavior、behaviour）取って代わられているといったつづり上の違いをも指摘した。
>
> 　アメリカは、シェークスピアの時代に入植されたため、興味深いことにアメリカ英語の特徴の一部はそのころのまま変化せず、イギリス英語の多くの特徴に比べてシェークスピア英語に近いままで残っている。イギリスではもはや、アメリカ英語の単語である trash や fall を rubbish や autumn の代わりには使わないかもしれないが、シェークスピアなら使うだろう。アメリカ合衆国のある地域には、シェークスピアが生きたエリザベス女王時代の英語に見られる特徴が多く維持された英語が残っている。このような英語は特にバージニアからオザー

クにかけてのアパラチア山脈地方において顕著である。

　しかし、アメリカが大国となり、フランス語やスペイン語といったほかの言語と接触するようになるにつれ、アメリカ英語自体がいくつかの方言に分かれ始めた。アフリカから来た黒人奴隷たちは、アメリカ英語に新たな語彙と言語形態を持ち込んだ。今日、アメリカ合衆国において24の地域方言を認めている専門家もいる。実際のところ、これらの方言は、北部方言と南部方言と単純に呼ばれる2つの方言に分類することができる。奇妙なことに、北部方言はニューイングランド地方から太平洋岸北西部、カリフォルニア、そして南西部にかけて見受けられる。これは、ニューイングランド地方や東海岸の人々が自分たちの方言とともにこれらの地域に住むようになったからである。しかし、南部方言は東海岸の南部からテキサスにかけての地域に限定されたままであった。

　方言が減少しているといういくつかの証拠がある。マスメディアやマスコミは、無意識のうちに人々が従うべき標準英語をつくり上げてきた。それで、このような標準英語に従わない人々は、正確さで劣る英語を話しているという汚名を着せられるかもしれない。同様にして、イギリス英語の話者はアメリカ英語により敏感になり、アメリカ英語の話者はイギリス英語により敏感になってきている。かつてひとつの方言に限定されていた単語は、現在ではどんどんほかの方言へと広がりを見せている。

重要語句

- □ aspect（名詞）様子、外見、面
- □ British（名詞）イギリス人
- □ canoe（名詞）カヌー
- □ common（形容詞）共通の、共用の、一般的な
- □ confine（動詞）限定する
- □ dialect（名詞）方言
- □ differ（動詞）異なる、相違する
- □ differentiation（名詞）区別、差別化、分化
- □ Elizabethan（形容詞）エリザベス女王時代の
- □ evident（形容詞）明白な、明らかな、はっきりわかる
- □ evolution（名詞）進化、展開
- □ expert（名詞）専門家
- □ formation（名詞）形成、成立
- □ gradual（形容詞）段階的な、徐々の
- □ hickory（名詞）ヒッコリー（クルミ科の木の名称）
- □ inadvertently（副詞）不注意に、気づかずに、ふと
- □ incomprehensible（形容詞）理解しにくい
- □ moose（名詞）ヘラジカ、ムース
- □ note（動詞）〜に言及する、指摘する、気づく
- □ noticeably（副詞）著しく、目立って
- □ oddly（副詞）奇妙にも
- □ pronunciation（名詞）発音
- □ qualify（動詞）資格（資質）を得る
- □ recognize（動詞）認める、認識する、承認する
- □ replace（動詞）取り替える、取って代わる
- □ restrict（動詞）制限する、限定する、禁止する
- □ settle（動詞）入植する、定住する
- □ settler（名詞）開拓者、移住者
- □ spelling（名詞）語のつづり、スペリング
- □ squash（名詞）スカッシュ、カボチャ
- □ steadily（副詞）着実に、堅調に
- □ stigma（名詞）汚名、汚点、不名誉
- □ usage（名詞）使用（法）、利用（法）
- □ variation（名詞）変化、ばらつき
- □ version（名詞）種類、版、バージョン
- □ vocabulary（名詞）ボキャブラリー、語彙

1. 解答 (C)

ノア・ウェブスターはなぜ *The American Dictionary of the English Language* が必要だと感じたのか。

(A) イギリスの辞書にはアメリカ英語の語彙が含まれていなかった。

(B) 彼はアメリカ英語が新たな言語になろうとしていると思った。

(C) 彼は 2 つの方言に十分な違いを見いだし、辞書が役立つと思った。

(D) 彼はアメリカ先住民との接触で使われるようになった新しい単語をたくさん含めたいと考えた。

解説 第 2 パラグラフの <u>Noticeable differences</u> in the two dialects <u>steadily increased</u>, ... という記述を言い換えている (C) が正解となる。

2. 解答 (B)

なぜ著者は第 3 パラグラフでシェークスピアに言及しているのか。

(A) 彼はシェークスピアの英語に興味があった。

(B) 彼はアメリカ英語とシェークスピア英語の類似点を示したかった。

(C) 彼はイギリス英語とアメリカ英語がとても似ていることを示したかった。

(D) 彼は時間の経過とともに言語がどのように変わるかを示したかった。

解説 第 3 パラグラフの <u>some aspects of American English</u> became frozen in time and <u>are closer to Shakespearean English</u> than are many aspects of British English. から、アメリカ英語とシェークスピア英語の類似点に焦点を当てている (B) が正解であるとわかる。

3. 解答 (B)

第 3 パラグラフによると、なぜイギリス人は trash という語を使わないのか。

(A) アメリカの言葉だから。

(B) 古い言葉だから。

(C) あまりにも堅苦しく聞こえるから。

(D) シェークスピアが使っていたから。

解説 第 3 パラグラフの The British may no longer use ..., but Shakespeare probably would have. から、シェークスピア英語がどのような位置にあるのかを考えると、まず出てくるのが「古い」ということである。従って、正解は (B) となる。

4. 解答 (D)

なぜ著者は北部と南部の方言に言及しているのか。

(A) アメリカの2つの方言を説明するために

(B) どれほど幅広く使われているかを示すために

(C) それらをイギリス英語と対比するために

(D) 方言の数を単純化するために

解説 第4パラグラフの Today some experts recognize as many as 24 regional dialects in the U.S. In truth, these could be broken into two dialects that can simply be called northern and southern dialects. から、下線部を言い換えている (D) が正解とわかる。

5. 解答 (A)

本文中の confined の意味に最も近いのは

(A) 限定された

(B) 見つかった

(C) 話された

(D) 現存する

解説 この語の意味を文脈において考えてみると、いろいろな地域に広まった northern dialects に比べて（however に注目）、southern dialects はどうかということで、The Southern dialect, however, has remained **confined** to an area from the southern East Coast to Texas. となっているので、northern dialects と対照的になっていると考えると、(A) が正解とわかる。

6. 解答 (B)

第4パラグラフによると、なぜ北部の方言がこれほど広まっているのか。

(A) ニューイングランドからカリフォルニアまで広がっているから。

(B) ニューイングランドの住民が西部の大部分に定住したから。

(C) 南部の方言はアメリカ南部でのみ話されていたから。

(D) フランス語とスペイン語に接していたから。

解説 第4パラグラフの This is because these regions were largely settled by people from New England and the East Coast who brought their dialects with them. から、正解は (B) となる。

7. 解答 (A)

第5パラグラフによると、なぜ方言の数が減少していると考えられるのか。

(A) 方言はメディアで使われる標準語に影響を受けている。

(B) イギリス英語とアメリカ英語がいっそう似てきている。

(C) 方言で話すことが不名誉につながる。

(D) 話者が多くの方言からの単語を使っている。

解説 第5パラグラフの Mass media and mass communication have inadvertently set up a standard of English for people to follow. から、正解は (A) となる。

8. 解答 (B)

本文によると、方言に当てはまることは何か。

(A) 最終的には別々の言語となる。

(B) 複数の方言が同一地域で話される可能性がある。

(C) すぐに消えてなくなる。

(D) 主に語彙が異なる。

解説 第1パラグラフの ... it can be spoken by a specific group of people within the same area as other dialects. などという記述から、同一地域でもさまざまな dialects が見られることがわかる。

9. 解答 (B)

次のセンテンスの挿入箇所の候補として本文中に示された4つの■を見なさい。

いくつもの種類の変化が存在し、彼はそれらを重要視した。

このセンテンスを挿入するのに最もふさわしい場所はどこか。

解説 挿入文には he という代名詞が入っているので、それに当たる人物名が前文のどこかに出てきている必要がある。従って、前文に人物の記述がない (A) は正解ではないとわかる。さらに読み進めると、(B) の前文に Noah Webster と the variations が出てきて、それらを受けて ... several types of variations that he ... となるので、正解は (B) とわかる。

10. 解答

(D) One of the main reasons for the development of a dialect is geographic isolation from the basic language.

(E) The differences between American and British dialects became apparent in the early 1800s.

(F) Native American, French and Spanish languages have all influenced the development of American dialects.

指示文：以下に提示された導入文は本文の要約である。本文の中で最も重要な考えを選択肢から3つ選び、要約を完成させなさい。いくつかの選択肢は本文中で示されていないことを提示しているか、または重要ではない内容であるため、要約には不適切である。**この設問の配点は2点である。**

方言の発展や進化にはいくつかの理由がある。

選択肢

(A) アメリカでは方言が発達してきたが、メディアからの圧力によって、一部は消え始めているかもしれない。

(B) イギリス英語とアメリカ英語の主な違いは語彙と綴りにある。

(C) シェークスピア英語はイギリス英語よりもアメリカ英語に似ている。

(D) 方言が発達する主な理由の一つは、元の言語からの地理的な孤立である。

(E) アメリカ英語とイギリス英語の方言の違いは 1800 年代初頭に明らかになった。

(F) アメリカ先住民の言葉、フランス語、スペイン語のどれもがアメリカの方言の発達に影響を与えてきた。

解説　与えられた出だしのセンテンスに several reasons for ... とあるので、理由が続くことがわかる。(D) One of the main reasons ... が適している。次に (D) にある geographic isolation の例として American and British dialects が出てくる。さらに、American dialects（このパッセージのトピック）に関する発達の過程が詳しく書いてある (F) が続く。ちなみに、(A)(B)(C) に関してであるが、本問では reasons for the development and evolution of dialects. についての記述を選択するので、正解とはならない。

問題文の訳例

アメリカ合衆国の政党

　アメリカ合衆国憲法の創始者たちは、政党の設立には反対であった。彼らは政党が汚職の源になる運命にあると信じていた。彼らはまた、人々がどの政党が自分たちを助けてくれるかではなく、自分たち自身の利益を考えて個人としてさまざまな物事を決定すべきであると信じていた。しかし、憲法の制定がすぐに政党の形成につながるというのは、政治の性質上、当然であった。これは、上院と下院という立法部門からのサポートを受けることなくしては、効果的に統治を行うことができる大統領はいないということがすぐに明確になったためである。このようなサポートを得るためには、大統領が提案された問題ごとにそれぞれの国会議員と交渉するよりも、よく似た考えを持った国会議員を組織化するほうがより簡単だったのである。

　最初に形成された政党は、強力な中央政府を持つべきだという考え方から名づけられた連邦主義党と、特に経済において政府の役割は制限されているべきだと考えていた共和党であった。初期に多少の混乱はあったが、共和党はトーマス・ジェファソンを選出する力を持ち、28年間政治を支配したのである。

　しばらくの間、アメリカにはひとつの政党しか存在しないようであった。しかし、政治の世界ではよくあるように、政党の中の個人の間で口論が始まった。そして、この政党の中のある派閥が、経済における政府のより活発な役割を推進し始めた。それで、自分たちと共和党内の敵対者たちとを区別するために、彼らは自分たちを国民共和党と呼ぶようになった。しかし、共和党内の彼らの敵対者たちは勢力を広げ、アンドリュー・ジャクソンを大統領に選出した。元の共和党議員たちもまた、自分たちと共和党内の敵対者たちの間に距離を置きたかったため、まず自分たちを民主共和党と呼び、その後1828年には民主党と呼ぶようになった。ジャクソンの政策や行為が物議を醸すものであったため、国民共和党は共和党にいては望みがないと考え、ホイッグ党と政党の名前を変えた。

　少なくとも1860年までは政府を支配していたのは民主党であったが、政界と社会における主要な問題が迫ってきていた。主に南部で行われていた奴隷制が、国を2分するほどの問題になっていた。どちらの側も、この問題を直接支持していると見なされることを望んでいなかったが、どちらも南部の有権者たちを遠ざけたくはなかった。時間とともに民主党は南部と強いかかわりを持つようになり、奴隷制を擁護していたが、ホイッグ党ではこの問題について意見が分かれていた。西部の新たな地域へも奴隷制を拡張できる可能性を認めたカンザス・ネブラスカ法が通過したことで、当時の状況はより混乱した。民主党出身の大統領によって署名されたこの法案は、民主党をも分裂させた。この分裂は非常に根深く、当然のように北部民主党と南部民主党と名づけられた2つの異なる民主党の形成につながった。1860年に双方がそれぞれ大統領候補を出したとき、これら2つが同じ政党に属していると考えることは不可能になった。

　これらすべての政治的混乱の結果、反奴隷制を支持する共和党と呼ばれる新しい政党が形成された。しかし、彼らの反奴隷制の立場は確固としたものではなかった。これより以前に形成されたノウ・ナッシング党はその反奴隷制の信念により多くの支持を得た。将来の成功のため、不幸にもこの政党は反カトリックと反移民という考えをも強く支持した。ノウ・ナッ

シング党が反奴隷制の立場を弱めたかに見えたとき、多くの支持者はホイッグ党の残党と北部民主党員とともに共和党へと移った。民主党が2人の候補者を立てたとき、事実上、このことが、初めての共和党大統領としてのエイブラハム・リンカーンの選出を確実にしたのである。

このときから現在まで、アメリカ合衆国は通常二大政党制となった。ほかの政党がときどき現れ、ある程度の成功を収めることもあったが、民主党や共和党と同じほど長きにわたり一般市民の関心を維持することはできなかった。

重要語句

- □ according to ... 〜に従って、〜によれば
- □ act（名詞）法令
- □ approach（動詞）話を持ち掛ける、交渉する、近づく
- □ assure（動詞）保証する、確実にする
- □ be destined to (do) 〜する運命にある
- □ belonging（名詞）所属するもの
- □ constitution（名詞）憲法
- □ controversial（形容詞）異論のある、議論の
- □ corruption（名詞）汚職、腐敗
- □ cross over 〜に乗り換える
- □ defense（名詞）防御、擁護
- □ democratic（形容詞）民主主義の
- □ distinct（形容詞）異なった、相違する
- □ distinguish（動詞）区別する、識別する
- □ effectively（副詞）効果的に、効率的に
- □ election（名詞）選挙、選択
- □ faction（名詞）派閥、党派
- □ Federalists（名詞）フェデラリスト、連邦主義者
- □ formation（名詞）形成、設立、成立
- □ founder（名詞）創始者、設立者
- □ from time to time ときどき、折々
- □ generally（副詞）一般に、通常、おおむね
- □ govern（動詞）治める、支配する
- □ government（名詞）政治、政府、政治体制
- □ House of Representatives（名詞）下院
- □ immigrant（名詞）移民、移住者
- □ individually（副詞）個別に、個人的には
- □ issue（名詞）問題、論点
- □ legislative（形容詞）立法上の
- □ legislator（名詞）国会議員
- □ looming（形容詞）迫ってくる、ぼんやり見えてくる
- □ merit（名詞）功績、素晴らしさ、実力
- □ nature（名詞）自然、性質、本質
- □ occasionally（副詞）時々、時折
- □ opponent（名詞）競争相手、敵対者
- □ organize（動詞）組織化する
- □ outcome（名詞）結果、結末
- □ over time 時間がたてば、時間とともに
- □ political party（名詞）政党
- □ politics（名詞）政治、政治学
- □ prevail（動詞）広がる、普及する
- □ previously（副詞）前に、以前に
- □ primarily（副詞）主として、最初は、第一に
- □ promote（動詞）進める、推進する
- □ put forth（考え・案など）を出す
- □ quarrel（名詞）けんか、口論、紛争
- □ remnant（名詞）残り、残党
- □ Republicans（名詞）共和党
- □ Senate（名詞）議会、立法機関、上院
- □ slavery（名詞）奴隷制
- □ turmoil（名詞）混乱、不安、騒ぎ
- □ unchallenged（形容詞）確固たる、揺るぎない
- □ view（名詞）意見、見解、信念
- □ virtually 実質的には、事実上
- □ Whig Party（名詞）ホイッグ党

11. 解答 (B)

第 1 パラグラフの情報に基づくと、なぜ政党が結成され始めたのか。

(A) 憲法によって奨励されていた。

(B) 政府の性質上、そうせざるを得なかった。

(C) 汚職を防ぐために必要だった。

(D) 大統領が個々人に対して別々に働きかける必要があった。

解説 第 1 パラグラフの it was the very nature of the government that the constitution formed that in a short time led to the formation of political parties. から、正解は (B) とわかる。

12. 解答 (C)

第 3 パラグラフの情報によると、政治家全般について何が推測できるか。

(A) 彼らは通常、政党を結成する。

(B) 彼らはしばしば、混乱している。

(C) 彼らはしばしば、互いに意見が合わない。

(D) 彼らの考えは、しばしば変わる。

解説 第 3 パラグラフの ... individuals within the party began to quarrel among themselves. から、意見などの食い違いがあったことがわかり、正解は (C) となる。

13. 解答 (B)

第 3 パラグラフの情報に基づくと、次のうち共和党についてあてはまるのはどれか。

(A) 4 つに分かれた。

(B) 民主党とホイッグ党に取って代わられた。

(C) 完全に消滅した。

(D) 最初は民主共和党になり、後にホイッグ党となった。

解説 第 3 パラグラフから 2 つの流れがわかる。Republican Party から National Republican、Whig Party になったものと Republican Party から Democratic Republican、そして Democratic Party になったものがある。

14. 解答 (C)

第4パラグラフによると、2つの主要政党について何が推測できるか。

(A) いずれもカンザス・ネブラスカ法の可決に賛成した。

(B) いずれもカンザス・ネブラスカ法の意味について混乱していた。

(C) いずれも奴隷制度に対して強い態度を取らなかった。

(D) いずれも民主党の大統領がカンザス・ネブラスカ法に署名したことに驚いた。

解説 第4パラグラフの ... the Whig Party split into two campus ... the Kansas-Nebraska Act which allowed for the possibility of slavery being extended into the new western territories. This act, signed by a Democratic president, caused a split within that party as well. から、この問題（slavery）に関して Whig Party も Democratic Party もそれぞれの内部で意見が分かれたことになる。これにより、どちらの政党も slavery に強く反対したわけではないとわかる。

15. 解答 (A)

以下のセンテンスのうち、本文中で強調されたセンテンスにある重要な情報を最もよく表しているのはどれか。誤った選択肢は意味合いを致命的に変えてしまうか、必要な情報を削除してしまうものである。

ジャクソンの政策や行為があまりにも物議を醸すものだったので、国民共和党は、共和党の内部にいてはほとんど望みがないと考え、党名をホイッグ党に改めた。

(A) 国民共和党はジャクソンの国政運営の方法に腹を立て、また、自分たちが党に影響を与えられる可能性がなかったので、党名をホイッグ党に変えた。

(B) ホイッグ党が結成されたのは、国民共和党とその指導者ジャクソンを絶望的だと見限ったからである。

(C) 共和党は国民共和党にうんざりしていたので、ジャクソンはホイッグ党と呼ばれる新党を結成するように強要した。

(D) 国民共和党はジャクソンや共和党に敬意を抱いていなかったので、ホイッグ党と呼ばれる独自の政党を結成することに決め、成功の機会を得ようとした。

解説 消去法を使って正しくない記述を消していこう。選択肢にある (B) The Whig Party was formed because it saw the National Republicans and their leader, Jackson, as being hopeless. (C) ... Jackson forced them into forming a new party called the Whig Party. (D) ... had no respect for Jackson ... などの記述を第3パラグラフと照らし合わせて考えると、それらは正しくないことがわかり、(A) が正解となる。

16. 解答 (C)

第5パラグラフで、なぜ著者はノウ・ナッシング党に言及しているのか。

(A) 彼らがどのように共和党に変わっていったかを示すために

(B) 二大政党以外とは別の政党が存在していたことを示すために

(C) 反奴隷制の立場がどれほど高く支持されていたかを示すために

(D) なぜ2人の民主党の大統領候補者がいたのかを示すために

解説 第5パラグラフの The previously formed Know-Nothing party had gained great support for its anti-slavery views. という記述から、正解は (C) とわかる。

17. 解答 (B)

本文中の crossed over の意味に最も近いのは

(A) 対戦した

(B) 加わった

(C) 取って代わった

(D) 構成した

解説 文脈の中で考え、第5パラグラフの ... many of their (Know-Nothings') supporters with those from the remnants of the Whig Party and some northern Democrats crossed over to the Republican Party. を読むと、人々が Republican Party に移ったとわかるので、(B) が正解となる。また、Republican は下線部の党派によって新たに構成されたものではないので、(C) や (D) ではないこともわかる。

18. 解答 (D)

以下の記述のうち、リンカーンの大統領就任に関する著者の意見を最も正確に反映しているものはどれか。

(A) 彼はまったくの幸運から大統領になった。

(B) 彼は民主党が分裂してもしなくても、選挙に勝っただろう。

(C) ノウ・ナッシング党が勝っていたはずだが、彼らは奴隷制についての立場を変えた。

(D) 民主党が分裂していなければ、選挙はもっと接戦になっていただろう。

解説 第 5 パラグラフの When the Democrats put forth <u>two candidates,</u> it virtually assured the election of Abraham Lincoln as the first Republican president. という記述から、(D) が正解とわかる。

19. 解答 (B)

次のセンテンスの挿入箇所の候補として本文中に示された 4 つの■を見なさい。

どちらの側も、この問題を直接支持していると見なされることを望んでいなかったが、どちらも南部の有権者たちを遠ざけたくはなかった。

このセンテンスを挿入するのに最もふさわしい場所はどこか。

解説 第 4 パラグラフの最初の文にある major issues は、次の文 (A) の Slavery ... splitting the country につながり、それが挿入文にある neither side ..., neither did <u>they</u>（Democrats and Whig）へとつながる。ちなみに、(C) の The situation は、その前文である (B) の記述を指し、(C) の the Kansas-Nebraska Act は、(D) の This act につながる。

20. 解答 （下を参照）

(B) The founding fathers were against political parties but soon two parties, the Federalists and the Republicans, formed anyway.

(C) Though the Republican Party held dominance during the early 1800s, it was soon split by internal quarrels.

(D) The issue of slavery caused a crisis within all political parties and led to the formation of the current Republican Party.

指示文：下記に提示された導入文は本文の要約である。本文の中で最も重要な考えを選択肢から 3 つ選び、要約を完成させなさい。いくつかの選択肢は本文中で示されていないことを提示しているか、または重要ではない内容であるため、要約には不適切である。**この設問の配点は 2 点である。**

現在の二大政党は、長く困難な歴史を歩んできた。

選択肢

(A) 連邦主義党は強い中央政権を信奉していたが、共和党はそうではなかった。

(B) 建国の父たちは政党に反対していたが、すぐに連邦主義党と共和党という 2 つの政党が結成された。

(C) 1800 年代初頭には共和党が優勢だったが、すぐに内輪もめによって分裂した。

(D) 奴隷制度の問題はあらゆる政党内に危機をもたらし、現在の共和党の結成につながった。

(E) ホイッグ党は共和党の対抗勢力として結成されたが、アメリカの政治に大きな影響を与えることはできなかった

(F) ノウ・ナッシング党は 1800 年代半ばに政治に影響を及ぼしたもう一つの政党だった。

解説 まず、与えられたセンテンスにある major political parties が (B) の下線部につながる。次に、そこにある Republicans が (C) の下線部の the Republican Party につながり、その文の後半の下線部、it was soon split by internal quarrels. の原因として (D) がきている。本問では、Today's two major political parties have had a long and difficult history. を考えて、歴史の流れの中で政党を追っていくとよい。つまり、Federalists と Republicans → Republicans → current Republicans となったわけである。

Listening Section　解答・解説

講義や会話を部分的に聴き直して答える問題のトランスクリプトには🎧マークを記してあります。このうち設問に直接対応する部分は太字で示しました（問題文ではこの部分の音声をもう一度聴くことができます）。なお、全体のトランスクリプトでは太字部分のみが示されています。

Questions 1-5

トランスクリプト

Student A: Hey, it's been a while. How've you been doing? How do you like university life?

Student B: Oh, it's OK, I guess. I'm just wondering if going to school in the U.S. was such a good idea after all.

Student A: Why? Are the classes too difficult?

Student B: No, it's not that. I'm doing well enough in my classes. <u>It's just seems that I'm spending all my time studying. I don't go anywhere. I don't meet anyone</u> (Q1). I'm not sure it even matters that I'm in the U.S. I could be doing the same thing back in my own country.

Student A: Well, I know grades are important and all but you just can't study all the time. You've got to take a break every once in a while. Go to a movie. Go out for a meal at a restaurant. After all, you've come all this way you should get to know a little about the U.S. Maybe you can go out with some of your friends from class.

Student B: That's just it. I haven't met anyone. No one even talks to me. I thought that by going to the U.S. I would be able to make a lot of American friends, but they just don't seem interested in meeting foreigners.

Student A: I think you're wrong there. I think they're interested, but they're not going to go out of their way to meet you. I learned long ago that <u>you'll have to make the first move</u> (Q2).

Student B: Me? But I'm the foreigner. In my country, people go out of their way to speak to foreigners.

Student A: **Yeah, because you're from Asia and <u>in Asia it's obvious when a person is a foreigner.</u> Here, there are so many foreigners**

that it's not such a big thing (Q4). You also have to remember that there are a lot of Asian Americans here. They probably don't even know you're a foreigner. Even if they know you're a foreigner, and they're interested in you, they may be afraid to approach you because they don't know how well you understand English. Believe me, I met all of my American friends by speaking to them first. After that, I had no problem.

Student B: But I'm kind of afraid they may not understand me. I'm a little nervous about that.

Student A: It's normal to feel that way, but your English is fine. **Unless you want to waste your time in the U.S., you have to stop thinking like that. It's all up to you** (Q5). And don't make the mistake I did at first (Q3).

Student B: What was that?

Student A: Well, and I guess it's normal, I began meeting people from my own country and hanging around with them in my free time (Q3). But then I realized that I was hardly using any English at all. I mean, I came all this way to the U.S., and my goal was to improve my English and all, and here I was speaking more of my native language than English.

Student B: So you left all your friends from your country?

Student A: No, nothing so dramatic. I just tried to balance out my life a little more. I'd still meet with my old friends, but I tried to develop new friendships, too. I think it was the best thing I could have done.

訳例

学生 A : あら、久しぶりね。元気だった？　大学生活はどう？

学生 B : ああ、まあまあだと思うけど。アメリカで学校に行くっていうのは本当にいい考えだったのかなって思っているんだ。

学生 A : どうして？　授業が難し過ぎるの？

学生 B : いや、そうじゃないんだ。授業では十分によくやっているんだけど。ただ、自分の時間のすべてを勉強に費やしているような気がするんだ。どこにも行かない。誰にも会わない。アメリカにいることが重要なのかさえわからないよ。自分の国でも同じことだったらできただろうからね。

学生 A : 成績が大事なのはわかるけど、ずっと勉強はできないわ。たまには休みを取らなきゃ。映画に行くのよ。レストランで食事するのもいいわ。せっかくここまで来たんだから、アメリカについて少しは知るべきよ。クラスの友達の何人かと出掛けることもできるかもしれないじゃ

ない。

学生 B ： そこなんだよ。僕は誰にも出会ってないんだ。誰も僕と話さえしてくれない。アメリカに来たらたくさんのアメリカ人の友達ができると思ってたのに、アメリカ人は外国人と出会うことに興味がないみたいだ。

学生 A ： それが間違ってるのよ。興味はあると思うけど、あなたに出会うために彼らがわざわざ心を砕くことはないのよ。まず自分から動かなければいけないってことをずいぶん前に学んだわ、私は。

学生 B ： 僕が？　でも、僕は外国人なんだよ。僕の国では、みんなわざわざ外国人と話そうとするよ。

学生 A ： ええ、それはあなたがアジアから来ていて、アジアでは誰かが外国人だったら目立つからよ。ここでは、外国人がたくさんい過ぎて、外国人であることはそんなに大したことではないの。ここにはアジア系アメリカ人もたくさんいるしね。彼らはもしかしたらあなたが外国人だということさえ知らないのかもしれない。仮に彼らが、あなたが外国人だということを知っていて、あなたに興味を持っていたとしても、あなたがどれくらい英語ができるかわからないから怖がって近づいてこないのかもしれないわ。信じてよ、私はアメリカ人の友達全員に、自分から話し掛けたことで出会ったのよ。その後は、何の問題もなかったわ。

学生 B ： でも、僕の言うことが理解してもらえないんじゃないかとちょっと怖いんだ。ちょっと神経質になっているのかもしれない。

学生 A ： そんなふうに感じるのは普通のことだけど、あなたの英語は問題ないわ。アメリカで時間を無駄にしたくないのなら、そんなふうに考えるのはやめなきゃ。全部あなた次第なのよ。私が初めのころにしたのと同じ過ちを繰り返さないで。

学生 B ： 何だいそれは？

学生 A ： 自然なことだとは思うけど、自分の国から来た人たちと会うようになって、自由時間には彼らとたむろしていたわけよ。でも、そうしたら自分が英語をほとんど使っていないことに気づいたわ。わざわざアメリカまで来て、目標は英語力を向上させることだったのに、英語よりも母語をたくさん話しているなんて。

学生 B ： それで、同じ国からの友達みんなから離れたの？

学生 A ： いいえ、そんなに劇的なものではないわ。ただ自分の人生をもう少しバランスの取れたものにしただけ。昔からの友達とはずっと会っていたし、でも新しい友達もつくるように努力したの。それが私にできた最善の策だったと思うわ。

1. 解答 (**C**)

男性はどのよう問題を抱えているか。

(A) 彼にはやるべき勉強の量が多すぎる。

(B) 彼はアメリカでの生活に適応できない。

(C) 彼には勉強以外のことに割ける時間がない。

(D) 彼には自分と同じ国出身の友達しかいない。

解説 トランスクリプトの下線部参照。

- It's just seems that I'm spending all my time studying. I don't go anywhere. I don't meet anyone.

2. 解答 (**B**)

女性は男性に、アメリカ人と知り合えるようどのようなアドバイスをしたか。

(A) 彼は彼らと一緒に映画へ行くべきだ。

(B) 彼はまず、彼らと話してみるべきだ。

(C) 彼は、彼らが話してかけてくるまで、もっと忍耐強く待つべきだ。

(D) 彼はまず、アジア系アメリカ人と会ってみるべきだ。

解説 トランスクリプトの下線部参照。

- you'll have to make the first move.

3. 解答 (**A**)

女性は初めてアメリカへ来たときにどんな間違いを犯したか。

(A) 彼女は自分と同じ国の出身者としか友達にならなかった。

(B) 彼女はいっさい英語を使わなかった。

(C) 彼女は勉強に時間を費やしていた。

(D) 彼女は、誰も自分の言うことを理解できなかったので、話すことを怖がっていた。

解説 トランスクリプトの下線部参照。

- And don't make the mistake I did at first.
- I began meeting people from my own country and hanging around with them in my free time.

4. 解答 (B)

会話の一部をもう一度聞きなさい。それから、質問に答えなさい。

女性がこのように言うことで、アジアの外国人について何が推測できるか。

(A) アジアには外国人があまりいない。

(B) アジアでは外国人であることが簡単にわかる。

(C) アジアで外国人を見かけることはそれほど珍しくない。

(D) アジアでは簡単に外国人を避けられる。

解説 トランスクリプトの下線部参照。ここでいう foreigners とは、アジアで出会う外国人のこと。アジア人とは顔形の違う、例えば英語を母語とする人たちのことである。

🎧 Student B: Me? But I'm the foreigner. In my country, people go out of their way to speak to foreigners.

Student A: **Yeah, because you're from Asia and in Asia it's obvious when a person is a foreigner. Here, there are so many foreigners that it's not such a big thing.**

5. 解答 (B)

会話の一部をもう一度聞きなさい。それから、質問に答えなさい。

女性はなぜこのように言っているのか。

(A) 彼女は男性の不平を聞くことにうんざりしている。

(B) 彼女は男性の態度を批判している。

(C) 彼女は男性にアドバイスを求めている。

(D) 彼女は男性に同情している。

解説 トランスクリプトの下線部参照。ここでの have to は、聞き手を批判するときの用法。「そんなふうに考えるのはやめたほうがいいんじゃないの」と言って批判している。

🎧 Student B: But I'm kind of afraid they may not understand me. I'm a little nervous about that.

Student A: It's normal to feel that way, but your English is fine. **Unless you want to waste your time in the U.S., you have to stop thinking like that. It's all up to you.**

Questions 6-11

トランスクリプト

So to review what I talked about last time, Van Gogh painted in a way that conflicted too much with what the public considered "good art." Sure, now we see what he painted as being particularly expressive, despite the technique. Because at that time, his technique was not considered worthy of serious artistic attention. In fact, Van Gogh fits in perfectly with the popular stereotype of the artist as a person struggling for recognition in a world that doesn't appreciate him or her. Indeed, in this popular stereotype, the artist lives in poverty and eventually dies unknown to the world. Well, Van Gogh certainly exemplifies this stereotype (Q6), since he only sold one painting during his lifetime — and that to his own brother. Yet, this stereotype doesn't always hold true. Other artists have achieved significant recognition during their lifetimes and have even become famous. And I can't think of anyone who probably achieved more recognition in his lifetime than Pablo Picasso (Q6). So what was it that Picasso had, and Van Gogh did not?

Well first of all, Picasso was recognized as a gifted artist as early as age 15, and make no mistake about it, this was extremely important (下線 Q7：太字と下線 Q8). From then on he was taken seriously no matter how abstract he became in his art. His transition through many varieties of styles was always looked upon with interest, and he eventually became the only living artist to have his work exhibited in Paris' Louvre Museum. Another stereotype is that the artist is a person who dies young. Van Gogh died at 37. Here again, Picasso goes against the stereotype, as he lived for 93 years (Q7). This fact alone may have helped him realize the great degree of fame he saw in his lifetime. And there is no doubt that Picasso understood this fame and used it to his advantage (Q10).

Along these lines, let me just tell you an anecdote (Q10) I once heard that will show you just how aware Picasso was of his fame. According to the story, one night Picasso decided to take a large group of his friends to dinner at an exclusive Paris restaurant. They ordered all the finest foods and drank the finest wines and champagne and all that. But as he was eating, one of his friends noticed that Picasso had ordered fish, and that he was carefully removing the skeleton from the fish (Q9-1). He then placed the skeleton beside his plate. At first this friend didn't think a lot about this. Maybe Picasso was just a very careful person. But then he noticed that Picasso spent a long time cleaning the skeleton with his napkin. Well, he was a little confused but decided to keep an eye on Picasso throughout the evening.

And everyone went on eating and drinking and all, when towards the end of the meal, Picasso took out a sheet of paper (Q9-2) and put it on the table. He then took the skeleton of the fish and placed it on the paper, took a red pencil and began carefully tracing the outline of the skeleton on the paper (Q9-3). When he was done, he traced the skeleton again with a yellow pencil (Q9-4). His friend, the one who told the story, just thought it was a moment of artistic inspiration.

But as the party was ending, the waiter came to Picasso and politely asked him about paying the check. Picasso took the paper with the drawing of the fish skeleton, signed his name under it and gave it to the waiter saying something like, "This should take care of it." The waiter took the picture, bowed and left, apparently happy with the payment. **Now, how famous must you think you are to do something like that?** (Q10)

OK, so Picasso was not only famous in his own lifetime, he was also well aware of it. This gave him a certain freedom that other artists could only hope for. He had the freedom to produce any style of art he wanted (Q11) and was assured of receiving critical acclaim. So, let's look at the stages Picasso went through and see how his ideas were received (Q11).

訳例

　前回お話ししたことを復習しますと、ヴァン・ゴッホは大衆が「よい芸術作品」であると考えていたものとはかなり違った方法で絵を描いていました。もちろん、現在では私たちは彼が描いたものを、その技術にもかかわらず、大変表現力に富むものだと考えていますが、当時は彼の技術は、本格的な芸術的関心を寄せるに値するとは考えられていませんでした。事実、ヴァン・ゴッホは、個人の価値を認めない世間の中で、評価を求めて葛藤した芸術家というよくあるステレオタイプに完全に当てはまっています。実際には、このよくあるステレオタイプにおいては、芸術家は貧困の中に暮らし、最終的には世間に知られないまま死んでいくのです。ヴァン・ゴッホは、彼の人生において自分の兄弟にたったひとつの作品を売っただけなので、間違いなくこのステレオタイプの好例となっています。しかし、このステレオタイプが常に真実というわけではありません。ほかの芸術家たちは、生きている間に大きな評価を得て、有名になることさえありました。そして、おそらく、生きている間にパブロ・

ピカソより高い評価を得た人はいないでしょう。では、ピカソが持っていて、ヴァン・ゴッホが持っていなかったものとは何だったのでしょう。

　まずいえるのは、ピカソは15歳のときに早くも天才芸術家として認められており、これは、間違いなく非常に重要なことでした。それ以来、彼の芸術はどれほど抽象的になっても真剣に受け取られました。多くの種類のスタイルを経た彼の変遷は常に興味のあるものと見なされ、彼はついに生きている間にパリのルーブル美術館に作品が飾られた唯一の芸術家となったのです。また別のステレオタイプには、芸術家とは「若くして死んでしまう人物」だという概念もあります。ヴァン・ゴッホは37歳で亡くなりました。ここでも再び、ピカソはステレオタイプと異なり、93歳まで生きました。この事実だけでも、彼が生きている間に偉大な名声を実現した助けになったであろうことがわかります。そして、ピカソが自分の名声について認識しており、これを自分のために有利に使ったのは確かなことです。

　では、これらのことに関して、私がかつて聞いたことがある逸話をお話しさせてください。ピカソがどれほど自分の名声について意識していたかを明らかにするものです。その話によると、ある夜、ピカソはパリの高級レストランに大勢の友人を夕食に連れて行くことに決めました。彼らは最高の料理のすべてを注文し、最高のワインやシャンパンを飲んだりしたのです。しかし、食事をしていた彼の友人のひとりが、ピカソが魚を注文して、注意深く魚から骨を取っているのに気づいたのです。そして彼はその骨を皿の横に置きました。最初、この友人はこのことについて多くを考えませんでした。おそらく、ピカソはとても注意深い人であるだけなのかもしれませんから。しかし、その後ピカソが長い時間をかけて自分のナプキンでその骨をふいていることに気づいたのです。彼は少し混乱したのですが、その夜はピカソから目を離さないことに決めました。

　そして皆が食べたり飲んだりを続け、食事が終わりに近づいたとき、ピカソは1枚の紙を取り出してテーブルに置きました。そして彼は魚の骨を出して紙の上に置き、赤の色鉛筆を取り出して注意深く骨の輪郭を紙に写し始めました。それが終わると、彼は黄色の色鉛筆で再び輪郭を写しました。その友人は、この話をしてくれた人ですが、それはまさに芸術的ひらめきの瞬間であったと思ったそうです。

　しかし、パーティーが終わりに近づくにつれて、ウェイターがピカソのところに来て丁寧に支払いを頼みました。ピカソは魚の骨の絵が描かれた紙を取り、彼の名前を下にサインして、「これで支払いができるでしょう」というようなことを言ってウェイターに渡しました。ウェイターは絵を受け取り、頭を下げると、その支払いに明らかに満足した様子で立ち去ったのです。このようなことをするには、どれほど有名でなければいけないと思いますか。

　つまり、ピカソは生きている間に有名になっただけでなく、そのことをはっきりと意識していたのです。この事実は、ほかの芸術家にとっては、そうありたいと思っていたある種の自由を彼に与えたのです。ピカソには、自分が好きなどんなスタイルの芸術でも制作する自由があり、批評家の称賛を受けることにも自信がありました。では、ピカソがどのような段階を踏んでいったのか、彼の（このような）考え方がどのように受け止められたのかを見てみましょう。

6. 解答 (C)

教授は講義の中でどのような主題について話しているか。

(A) ピカソの人生

(B) ヴァン・ゴッホとピカソの芸術的スタイルの違い

(C) 誤解を招きがちな芸術家についての固定観念

(D) 芸術的なひらめき

解説 トランスクリプトの下線部参照。

- Indeed, in this popular stereotype, the artist lives in poverty and eventually dies unknown to the world. Well, Van Gogh certainly exemplifies this stereotype, ...

- Yet, this stereotype doesn't always hold true. Other artists have achieved significant recognition during their lifetimes and have even become famous. And I can't think of anyone who probably achieved more recognition in his lifetime than Pablo Picasso.

7. 解答 (A)、(D)

ピカソが名声を得た主要な2つの理由は何か。

解答を2つ選びなさい。

(A) 彼はわずか15歳で、才能のある芸術家として扱われていた。

(B) 彼の技術が大衆に訴求した。

(C) 彼は何度もスタイルを変えた。

(D) 彼は93歳まで生きた。

解説 トランスクリプトの下線部参照。

- Picasso was recognized as a gifted artist as early as age 15, and make no mistake about it, this was extremely important.

- Picasso goes against the stereotype, as he lived for 93 years.

8. 解答 (A)

講義の一部をもう一度聞きなさい。それから、質問に答えなさい。

教授はこのように言うことで何をほのめかしているのか。

(A) 彼は、より若いうちに芸術家として真剣に扱われるほど、有名になる可能性が高まるとほのめかしている。

(B) 彼は、若いうちに才能を見せつけなければ、誰も後になって注目してはくれないと述べている。

(C) 彼は、人は生まれつき芸術的才能があるか、そうでないかのどちらかだとほのめかしている。

(D) 彼は、たとえ15歳で見いだされていなかったとしても、ピカソは有名になっていただろうと述べている。

解説 トランスクリプトの下線部参照。下線部の Picasso was recognized as a gifted artist as early as age 15 と this was extremely important. から、正解は (A) とわかる。

🎧 **Well first of all, Picasso was recognized as a gifted artist as early as age 15, and make no mistake about it, this was extremely important.** From then on he was taken seriously no matter how abstract he became in his art.

9. 解答 （下の表を参照）

1. He prepared the fish skeleton.
2. He took out a sheet of paper.
3. He traced the bones in red pencil.
4. He used a yellow pencil.

教授はピカソの創造過程についての逸話を披露している。出来事を順番に並べ、この過程を要約しなさい。

- 骨を赤鉛筆でなぞった。
- 魚の骨を準備した。
- 紙を 1 枚取り出した。
- 黄色の鉛筆を使った。

解説 トランスクリプトの下線部参照。

- Picasso had ordered fish, and that he was carefully removing the skeleton from the fish. (1)
- Picasso took out a sheet of paper (2)
- took a red pencil and began carefully tracing the outline of the skeleton on the paper. (3)
- he traced the skeleton again with a yellow pencil. (4)

10. 解答 (B)

講義の一部をもう一度聞きなさい。それから質問に答えなさい。

教授はなぜこのようなことを言うのか。

(A) 彼は学生に意見を述べてほしいと思っている。

(B) 彼はピカソの自分の名声に関する理解を強調している。

(C) 彼は学生たちが名声の重要性について議論することを望んでいる。

(D) 彼はピカソの行動を批判している。

解説 トランスクリプトの下線部参照。太字にある ... something like that は、第2パラグラフ最後の Picasso understood this fame and used it to his advantage. の例題として挙げられた逸話 (an anecdote) のようなことを指す。従って、正解は (B) とわかる。

- Picasso understood this fame and used it to his advantage.
- an anecdote
- 🎧 The waiter took the picture, bowed and left, apparently happy with the payment. **Now, how famous must you think you are to do something like that?**

11. 解答 (C)

講義の次の話題は何だと考えられるか。

(A) ピカソの芸術界への影響

(B) ピカソの作品への批判

(C) ピカソの芸術スタイルの歴史

(D) ピカソが若くして名声を得たことへの批評家たちの反応

解説 トランスクリプトの下線部参照。

- He had the freedom to produce any style of art he wanted
- So, let's look at the stages Picasso went through and see how his ideas were received.

トランスクリプト

Woman: Can I help you?

Student: Yes, I'm wondering if you've got anything available. I know it's a little late but I haven't been able to find anything off campus (Q12).

Woman: Yeah, a lot of students are having trouble with housing this year. We've got a few places left. What kind of place are you looking for?

Student: Well, to tell you the truth, I need something that's not too expensive. I don't really care how elegant it is. Anything will do (Q13).

Woman: We have some apartments in the new dorm, but they're pretty expensive. Much more than what you would pay off campus, to be honest with you.

Student: Yeah, I think I'll forget about those.

Woman: Look, if you really need something cheap, you might think about a sleeping room (Q13).

Student: What's that?

Woman: Well, it's just one room with a bed, a desk, a closet and a bureau. Oh, yeah, and there's a sink but you have to share the bathroom and showers with the other tenants. There's also a TV room that everyone can use.

Student: Is there a kitchen on the floor? (Q14)

Woman: Well, that's the problem. It's up to you to take care of your food (Q14).

Student: So can I buy something like a hot plate or something to cook on? (Q14)

Woman: Actually, no (Q14). It's against the fire code to cook anything in your room. I should also mention that if you get caught cooking anything you'll be evicted.

Student: Sounds pretty strict.

Woman: Yeah, but a couple of years ago, someone left a pan of food on a hot plate, forgot about it, and went to class. By the time he came back, the fire department was there and much of his room was destroyed. It could have been much worse. Ever since then the rule against hot plates has been strictly enforced.

Student: But I'm curious about what the guys who live there eat.

Woman: Well, off the record I think a lot of them eat things like sandwiches and instant noodles, soups, you know, simple things like that.

Student: So they must get hot water from somewhere.

Woman: That's what I'm not sure about. **Maybe it's OK to have an electric teapot for hot water. I'm not really sure where they draw the line. I'd have to talk with the building manager to find out for sure** (Q15). Of course you could talk with some of the people who live there.

Student: Have you seen these rooms personally?

Woman: **Yeah, and they're not so bad. The whole place was recently remodeled. There are about five showers in each of the bathrooms and even an iron and ironing board. It's all quite modern and clean,** even though they're in one of the oldest **buildings on campus** (Q16). The good news is they are right near the center of campus, across from the library.

Student: Oh, yeah, I think I know which building you mean. Do you think I could go see one of these apartments?

Woman: I could give them a call right now if you'd like.

Student: Great, I'd appreciate that. It may be just what I'm looking for.

訳例

女性：どうなさいましたか。

学生：はい、入居できる部屋があるかと思いまして。少し遅いのはわかっているのですが、キャンパス外では部屋を見つけられずにいます。

女性：ええ、今年は多くの学生が住居を見つけるのに苦労しているんですよ。いくつかの部屋は残っていますよ。どんな所を探していますか。

学生：はい、正直に言うと、あまり高過ぎない所がいいんですが。それがきれいかどうかはあまり気にしません。何でもいいんです。

女性：新しい寮にいくつか部屋がありますが、かなり高いですよ。あなたがキャンパス外で払うかもしれない家賃より高いでしょうね、正直に言って。

学生：そうですか、それは無理だと思います。

女性：もし本当に安い部屋を探しているなら、スリーピング・ルームはどうでしょう。

学生：何ですか、それは？

女性：ベッド、机、クローゼットと整理だんすが備えつけられているワンルームのことです。ああそうだ、流し台もありますが、バスルームとシャワー器具はほかの住人と共有しなければなりません。誰でも使えるテレビ部屋もありますよ。

学生：その階には台所はありますか。

女性：それが問題なんです。食事のことは自分自身で何とかしなければなりません。

学生：じゃあ、ホットプレートのようなものか、調理できる何かを買ってもよいのでしょうか。

女性：実際のところ、駄目なんです。自分の部屋で何かを調理することは消防規則に反します。それに、何かを調理しているところを見つかったら強制退去させられることもお伝えしておかなければ。

学生：かなり厳しそうですね。

女性：ええ、でも数年前に誰かが食べ物が入ったフライパンをホットプレートに置いたままそのことを忘れてしまって、授業に出掛けたのです。彼が帰って来たときには消防隊が来ていて、彼の部屋の大部分は燃えてしまいました。もっと悪いことになったかもしれないのです。それ以来、ホットプレートに関する規則が厳しく施行されています。

学生：でも、そこに住んでいる人たちが何を食べているのか興味がありますね。

女性：ええ、ここだけの話ですが、多くの人はサンドイッチ、インスタントラーメンやスープなどの簡単なものを食べていると思いますよ。

学生：だったらお湯をどこかから手に入れているはずですよね。

女性：それについてはわかりません。お湯を沸かすための電気ポットは持てるのかもしれませんね。どこで線引きがされているのかよくわからないのです。確かめるにはビルの管理人と話さないと。もちろんそこに住んでいる人と話すこともできますけど。

学生：その部屋を直接ご覧になったことはありますか。

女性：ええ、そんなに悪くはないですよ。全館が最近改築されたんです。それぞれのバスルーム（トイレ兼浴室）にはだいたいシャワーが5つあるし、アイロンとアイロン台まであありますよ。キャンパスの中では最も古い建物のひとつの中にある部屋ですが、とても近代的で清潔です。いい点といえば、キャンパスの中心のすぐそばにあることです。図書館の向かいですね。

学生：ああ、なるほど、どの建物のことかわかります。部屋を見に行くことができますか。

女性：よろしければ、今すぐに電話してみますが。

学生：よかった、ありがとうございます。探している物件にぴったりかもしれません。

12. 解答 (D)

男性はなぜ女性を訪ねているのか。

(A) 彼はもっと良いアパートを探している。

(B) 彼は新しい寮に住みたがっている。

(C) 彼はスリーピング・ルームを見つけたがっている。

(D) 彼は住む場所が見つからない。

解説 ▶ トランスクリプトの下線部参照。

• I'm wondering if you've got anything available. I know it's a little late but I haven't been able to find anything off campus.

13. 解答 (A)

なぜ女性はスリーピング・ルームに言及しているのか。

(A) 彼女は彼にほとんどお金がないことを知っている。

(B) 彼女には他に紹介できる住居がない。

(C) それらはキャンパス外にある。

(D) それらは最近改築された。

解説 トランスクリプトの下線部参照。

- I need something that's not too expensive. I don't really care how elegant it is. Anything will do.
- Look, if you really need something cheap, you might think about a sleeping room.

14. 解答 (D)

スリーピング・ルームに住むことの最大の問題は何か。

(A) 学生たちはバスルームを共有しなければならない。

(B) 部屋にテレビがない。

(C) 学生たちは室内での飲食が許されない。

(D) 調理が許されない。

解説 トランスクリプトの下線部参照。

- Is there a kitchen on the floor?
- Well, that's the problem. It's up to you to take care of your food.
- So can I buy something like a hot plate or something to cook on?
- Actually, no.

15. 解答 (B)

会話の一部をもう一度聞きなさい。それから質問に答えなさい。

彼女は次のように発言することで、何を言おうとしているのか。

(A) 彼女は学生たちが調理できるかどうかに確信を持てない。

(B) 彼女は学生たちが何を自室に持ち込めるかについての詳細を知らない。

(C) 彼女は部屋で湯を出せるかどうか確信がない。

(D) 建物の管理人に空き物件があるか聞いてみなければならない。

解説 トランスクリプトの下線部参照。

🎧 Student: So they must get hot water from somewhere.

Woman: That's what I'm not sure about. **Maybe it's OK to have an electric teapot for hot water. I'm not really sure where they draw the line. I'd have to talk with the building manager to find out for sure.** Of course you could talk with some of the people who live there.

16. 解答 (B)

会話の一部をもう一度聞きなさい。それから質問に答えなさい。

次の発言から何が推測できるか。

(A) 女性はスリーピング・ルームについてあまり乗り気ではない。

(B) スリーピング・ルームは人が思うよりも良いかもしれない。

(C) 女性は、男性が他の場所に住むことを本気で考えるべきだとほのめかしている。

(D) 建物がかなり古いので、男性は部屋にあまり期待すべきではない。

解説 トランスクリプトの下線部参照。ここでは、sleeping rooms も含めた全館が最近改築され（recently remodeled）、バスルームにはアイロンやアイロン台まであると言っている。つまり、考えているよりずっといい所だと言っている。

🎧 Student: Have you seen these rooms personally?

Woman: **Yeah, and they're not so bad. The whole place was recently remodeled. There are about five showers in each of the bathrooms and even an iron and ironing board. It's all quite modern and clean,** even though they're in one of the oldest buildings on campus. The good news is they are right near the center of campus across from the library.

Questions **17-22**

トランスクリプト

I think we had better get something straight from the start. Psychology is not a science. Now some of you may disagree with this, and you will probably find in your textbook that psychology is defined as the "science of behavior," but this is really a misnomer. It is a science in the same way that any social science is a science, which means that it doesn't follow any hard and fast scientific laws such as, say, chemistry and physics (Q18-e). No social science or any study which depends on the behavior of humans can be one hundred percent predictable. That's just the way it is.

So why have a discipline called psychology at all if we can never learn the facts of human behavior? Well, we may not be able to get scientific facts, but we can get statistical probabilities that are accurate a large amount of the time (Q18-a). And in the end, psychologists exist to help people with a particular kind of problem, and even if we can only help them 60 or 70 percent of the time, it's better than not being able to help them at all. Besides, I think psychology is becoming more and more scientific, in the real sense, all the time. For example, the more we understand about the chemistry of the human brain and the more we can use its influence on behavior to help us (Q18-c), the more predictable our treatments become.

It should come as no surprise that chemicals have been used to treat psychological problems since mankind began to have psychological problems (Q17). Some of these first chemical treatments are still in use today. I'm thinking of one that some of you may be familiar with: alcohol. Yes, that's right. If you use alcohol to alter your behavior because you don't like the way it is, or to forget something that makes you depressed, you are, in fact, prescribing a drug for yourself to relieve your problem. It may sound funny to think of alcohol as a psychological drug, but it is for many (Q19) even though it is unlikely your psychiatrist will ever recommend it to you (Q18-d).

I'm only half joking here because alcohol, like all drugs to alter behavior, can alter behavior for only as long as you take the drug. You stop taking it, and you are back to your old self again. And here is where

psychology or psychiatry comes in (Q20). They try to offer drug-free improvement which is long lasting (Q18-b). A noble goal to be sure, but one that people with problems are really looking for.

But to return to the topic of understanding brain chemistry and the subsequent use of drug therapy for helping with psychological problems, I'd like to look at a drug (Q17) that is often prescribed and that all of you have probably heard of. I would then like to give you some scientific reasons as to why it seems to work. The drug I am talking about is lithium.

Lithium is a drug commonly used in the treatment of bipolar disorder, or manic depression. People who experience this disorder often have emotional swings from being severely depressed to being extremely elated or manic (Q21). Now you may think that only the depression is a problem, but if your emotional state doesn't really match the circumstances, you may be extremely happy, all right, but others would only see you as extremely strange. I mean, if you started joking and laughing at a funeral, for example, your behavior would probably be considered irrational and may even signal deeper psychological problems. When, however, such people are given lithium treatments, they are helped from 70 to 80 percent of the time.

So what is the science behind this psychological remedy? Well, apparently, lithium changes the strength of chemicals like serotonin in the brain (Q21). These chemicals help to transmit signals but if there's too much or too little of these chemicals, extreme changes in a person's mood may take place. It seems that lithium somehow substitutes for these chemicals and balances the brain's chemistry (Q21). So, in other words, here is a clear example of science applied to treat problems in behavior that were once thought of as being outside the range of science.

So let me once again highlight what I've been trying to say here (Q22). Psychology may not be a science, but it is clearly taking steps to make itself so. Lithium is but one example of a drug that can be used to alter behavior in a positive manner. Many more new drugs are appearing on the market that will hope to influence a person's personality. But drugs alone aren't often enough. Next time, I'd like to talk about the role of the psychiatrist in all of this.

訳例

　初めにはっきりさせておいたほうがいいと思います。心理学は科学ではありません。皆さんの何人かはこれに同意しないかもしれませんし、皆さんの教科書に心理学が「行動の科学」と定義されているのを見つけるかもしれません。でも、それは本当は誤った名称です。もちろん、心理学は、ほかのすべての社会科学が科学であるというのと同じ意味では科学です。つまり、化学や物理学のように厳格な科学の法則には従わないという意味です。人間の行動に依存するものは、どのような社会科学や研究でも、100 パーセント予測可能ではないのです。人間の行動とはそういうものなのです。

　もし、人間の行動に関する事実を決して学ぶことができないのであれば、なぜ心理学と呼ばれる学問があるのでしょうか。私たちは、科学的事実は得られないかもしれませんが、大抵の場合には、正確な統計学上の確率を得ることができます。最終的には心理学者たちはなんらかの問題を抱えている人々を助けるためにいるのです。60 パーセントか 70 パーセントの確率でしか彼らを助けられないとしても、まったく助けられないよりはましなのです。それに、心理学は常にますます、本当の意味で科学的になってきていると思います。例えば、私たちが人間の脳の作用について理解すればするほど、そして脳が行動に与える影響を、人々の持つ問題を解決する際に利用できるようになればなるほど、私たちの治療はより予測可能になっていくのです。

　人類が精神的問題を抱えるようになって以来、薬物が精神上の問題を治療するために使われていることは驚くことではありません。これら初期の薬物治療のいくつかは現在でも使われています。皆さんの中の何人かにはなじみのあることをお話ししているのですが……。そうです、アルコールです。もし今の自分が嫌だからと自分の行動を変化させるために、または自分自身を落ち込ませる何かを忘れるためにアルコールを使うとすれば、実際には自分の問題を軽減するために自分自身に薬を処方しているのです。精神上の薬物としてアルコールをとらえるのはおかしなことに思えるかもしれませんし、精神科医がそれを推薦することはないかもしれませんが、多くの人にとってそれは薬なのです。

　行動を変化させるすべての薬物と同じように、アルコールはそれを摂取しているときに限り、人の行動を変化させることができるので、私はここで真剣にお話ししているわけではないのです。人がそれを摂取するのをやめれば、以前のその人に戻ります。そして、ここが心理学または精神医学が役立つところなのです。それら（心理学と精神医学）は、長く続く、薬物の必要のない改善を提供しようとしているのです。確かに高潔な目標ですが、問題を抱えている人たちが本当に求めているものなのです。

　それでは、脳の作用の理解と、それに続く精神上の問題を解決するための薬物療法というトピックに戻って、しばしば処方され、皆さんのすべてがおそらく聞いたことのある薬に注目したいと思います。そして、なぜこの薬に効果があると思われるのかについての科学的理由について皆さんにお話ししたいと思います。私が話している薬とは、リチウムのことです。

　リチウムは双極性障害、いわゆるそううつ病の治療に一般的に使用される薬です。この障害を持っている人は、激しく落ち込んでいる状態から極端に高揚したりそう状態になったりという感情的な揺れをしばしば経験します。皆さんは、うつ状態だけが問題だと思うかもしれませんが、もし自分の感情が周囲の状況に実際には合っていないとすれば、自分自身はとても幸せで、正常だと思うかもしれませんが、ほかの人にしてみればものすごく奇妙な人だと思うでしょう。つまり、例えば、葬式でジョークを言い始めたり、笑い始めたりしたら、そんな人の行為はおそらく分別のないものだと考えられるでしょうし、それどころか、より深刻な精神上の問題があるという兆候になるかもしれないのです。しかし、こういう人もリチウムを与えられると、70 パーセントから 80 パーセントの確率で助けられるのです。

この心理学的治療の裏にある科学とは何でしょうか。どうやらリチウムは脳の中のセロトニンのような化学物質の強度を変化させるようです。これらの化学物質は信号の伝達を助けるのですが、これらの化学物質が多過ぎたり少な過ぎたりすると、人の心的状態に極端な変化を引き起こすかもしれないのです。リチウムはなんらかの形でこれらの化学物質の代わりをしたり、脳内の化学反応を調整したりするようです。つまり、別の言い方をすれば、これは科学が以前は科学の領域外だと考えられていた行動における問題の治療に応用されたというはっきりとした例なのです。

　それでは、ここで私がお伝えしようとしていることをもう一度強調させてください。心理学は科学ではないかもしれませんが、そうなるための手段を明らかに講じています。リチウムは、よい意味で行動を変化させるために使うことのできる薬物のひとつの例でしかありません。ほかにも、人間の性格に影響を与えると考えられている多くの新しい薬物が市場に出てきています。しかし、薬物だけでは十分ではないことが多いのです。次回は、これらのすべての状況における精神科医の役割についてお話ししたいと思います。

17. 解答 (C)

この講義の主題は何か。

(A) 心理学は科学か否か

(B) いつ精神的問題に対して薬物を処方するか

(C) 心理学における薬物の使用

(D) 脳化学

解説 トランスクリプトの下線部参照。講義ではまず、ここで使われている専門用語である psychology について定義をして、それから薬物が精神上の問題を治療するために使われているというトピックに移る。そして、「〜というトピックに戻って」という下線部で具体例を挙げていることより、正解は (C) であるとわかる。

- chemicals have been used to treat psychological problems since mankind began to have psychological problems.
- But to return to the topic of understanding brain chemistry and the subsequent use of drug therapy for helping with psychological problems, I'd like to look at a drug...

18. 解答 （下の表を参照）

		Yes	No
a	Depends on statistical analysis	○	
b	Aims for psychological changes that are long lasting and drug-free	○	
c	Needs to understand brain chemistry	○	
d	Sometimes prescribes alcohol as a psychological drug		○
e	Is closer to a social science than a science	○	

講義の中で、教授は心理学の要素について情報を提供している。次の各文がそれらの要素の一つかどうかを示しなさい。

統計分析によって決まる

長期的で薬物を使わない心理的変化を目指す

脳化学を理解する必要がある

ときに精神薬としてアルコールを処方することがある

科学というよりも社会科学に近い

解説　トランスクリプトの下線部参照。

- It is a science in the same way that any social science is a science, which means that it doesn't follow any hard and fast scientific laws such as, say, chemistry and physics. (e)

- we can get statistical probabilities that are accurate a large amount of the time. (a)

- the more we understand about the chemistry of the human brain and the more we can use its influence on behavior to help us (c)

- it is unlikely your psychiatrist will ever recommend it to you. (d)

- They try to offer drug-free improvement which is long lasting. (b)

19. 解答 (B)

なぜ教授はアルコールに言及しているのか。

(A) 彼女は授業で冗談を言いたがっている。

(B) 彼女はアルコールが精神の薬物と見なされ得ることを示したがっている。

(C) 彼女は学生たちに、アルコールがいかに彼らの脳に悪影響を与えるかを示したがっている。

(D) 彼女はアルコールとセロトニンを比較したがっている。

解説 トランスクリプトの下線部参照。

- It may sound funny to think of alcohol as a psychological drug, but it is for many ...

20. 解答 (A)

講義の一部をもう一度聞きなさい。それから質問に答えなさい。

教授はこのように発言することで、何を言おうとしているのか。

(A) 性格を変える目的で使われる薬物に長期的な効果はない。

(B) アルコールの摂取を冗談だと見なすべきではない。

(C) 薬物は行動を変えるのに役立つ。

(D) 心理学や精神医学では、人々を昔の自分に戻らせるために薬物を使用する。

解説 トランスクリプトの下線部参照。

🎧 I'm only half joking here because alcohol, like all drugs to alter behavior, can alter behavior for only as long as you take the drug. You stop taking it, and you are back to your old self again. And here is where psychology or psychiatry comes in. They try to offer drug free improvement which is long lasting.

21. 解答 (B)、(D)

教授によると、リチウムを使用した結果はどのようなものか。

解答を 2 つ選びなさい。

(A) 人がより幸福になる。

(B) 人の性格が安定する。

(C) セロトニンが脳内で生成される。

(D) 化学的な均衡が脳内で生じる。

解説 トランスクリプトの下線部参照。

- Lithium is a drug commonly used in the treatment of bipolar disorder, or manic depression. People who experience this disorder often have emotional swings from being severely depressed to being extremely elated or manic.
- lithium changes the strength of chemicals like serotonin in the brain.
- It seems that lithium somehow substitutes for these chemicals and balances the brain's chemistry.

22. 解答 (A)

講義の一部をもう一度聞きなさい。それから質問に答えなさい。

教授はなぜこのようなことを言うのか。

(A) 講義の要旨を紹介するために

(B) 要点を強調するために

(C) 要点を明確にするために

(D) この話題が議論するにはどれほど難しいかを説明するために

解説 トランスクリプトの下線部参照。文脈の中で考えると、太字の下線部 highlight what I've been trying to say here. から、要約をするのだとわかる。また、この後に続く内容からも、要約をするための発言であるとわかる。

🎧 So let me once again **highlight what I've been trying to say here.** Psychology may not be a science, but it is clearly taking steps to make itself so. Lithium is but one example of a drug that can be used to alter behavior in a positive manner.

トランスクリプト

Professor: When we talk about evolution, what we are really talking about is adaptation. What I mean is how an organism, whether it's a plant or animal, manages to survive within the extremes of the environment it finds itself in. Today I want to talk a little more about adaptation and break it into what's generally considered its three main parts (Q23). These are amplitude, efficiency and duration (Q24).

OK, let's begin. Amplitude. Do you know in general what the word means?

Student A: Yeah, but not in terms of evolution. If you're talking about sound, it means something like the changes in volume.

Professor: It's not so different. Think of amplitude in adaptation as the ability to survive in high or low "volumes" or intensities of elements in the environment — in other words, the extremes of environment that an organism finds itself in. This could be something like yearly changes in temperature or precipitation. A low amplitude organism would have a more narrow range in which it could survive, while a high amplitude organism would survive in a wide range of conditions. The cockroach would be an example of a high amplitude organism (Q25 : Q26) because it seems to tolerate a range of conditions throughout the world (Q25 : Q26), whereas corals are much lower in amplitude (Q26). Their environment must be more stable if they are to survive.

Student B: So humans would be high amplitude organisms.

Professor: Right. They have a wide geographical distribution and they can survive in a wide variety of conditions.

Student A: I'm not sure if this question will make any sense, but is it possible for an animal to have a high amplitude but not be very widespread? Because from what you've said, it seems like this "amplitude" is enough to make it a successful organism if we measure success by how many members of a species there are around the world.

Professor: That's true for many organisms, but it's possible for an organism to have high amplitude but not be so widespread. I guess this could lead into the next idea, and that is efficiency. **Animals or plants might be able to adapt to extremes in the environment but may only be able to reproduce within a narrow range. So that means you may be able to find them in a lot of places but not in any great amounts. You got the idea?** (Q28)

Student A: Can you give us an example?

Professor: Yeah, well, some plants can be found in a lot of places. Think of trees (Q26) that grow on mountains up to the tree line. Often these are evergreens, and though they can grow at high altitudes where other trees can't, they are often small, dwarfish trees that aren't going to reproduce very efficiently (Q27). They're simply hanging on in a rough environment. They may exist farther down the mountains in large forests, but often these forests occupy a rather narrow zone in their total distribution. So such trees can exist in many extreme conditions within a narrow environment, in this case, a limited zone on a mountain. They have high amplitude but low efficiency (Q26).

Student A: So a very efficient organism would be able to reproduce in a wide range of environments, right?

Professor: Yes, but sometimes they have to change their characteristics in order to do so. In some places, such plants or animals actually form different races in the process of adaptation to different environments.

Student B: You mean they form a new species?

Professor: No, not at first. First they form races but if they persist and differentiate enough, they could eventually form species, yes.

But let me continue on with the third part of adaptation, which is duration. Even though some organisms may be widespread or have a high efficiency, many seem to be more or less dependent on specific types of environments at specific times of the year. Like for example, toads (Q26). Now, they can wander around in the hot sun and even in deserts, being quite adaptable, I mean, they can be high amplitude creatures (Q26). They are also found all over the world so they have pretty high efficiency. But when it comes time to reproduce, well, they still need water to lay their eggs in. And their tadpoles are not going to quickly adapt if the water dries up. We can say that toads, therefore, have low duration (Q26). Tough, yes, widespread, yes, but limited during certain times of the year. Other animals are not so dependent on specific environmental features during specific stages of their life cycle and therefore are, in effect, more adaptable. That is, they have higher duration.

訳例

教　授：進化論について語るとき、私たちが本当に話しているのは適応についてです。つまり、ある生物が、それが植物であろうと動物であろうと、どのようにそれが置かれた危機的環境の中で生き延びるかということです。今日は、適応についてもう少しお話しし、適応を、一般的に3つあると考えられている主要な部分に分けたいと思っています。これらは振幅、効率、そして存続時間です。
　　　　それでは始めましょう。振幅。この言葉の一般的な意味が何か知っていますか。

学生Ａ：ええ、でも進化論においてどういう意味かは知りません。もし先生が音について話されているのであれば、それは音量の変化のようなものを意味します。

教　授：（進化論においても）そんなに違うものではありません。適応における振幅とは、環境におけるある成分の「音量」または「強度」が高かったり低かったりする場合の、別の言い方をすると、ある生物が置かれている危機的環境においての、生き残る能力であると考えてください。これは、毎年の気温や降水量の変化のようなものです。振幅が低い生物は、生き残ることのできる範囲が狭いのに対し、振幅が高い生物は広い範囲の条件の下で生き残ります。ゴキブリは、世界中のさまざまな条件の下で生き残るようなので、振幅の高い生物の例だといえるでしょう。それに対し、サンゴの振幅はずっと低いです。サンゴが生き残るためには、その環境はより安定したものでなければなりません。

学生Ｂ：そうすると、人間は高い振幅を持つ生物ですね。

教　授：そうですね。人間は広い地理的分布を持っており、さまざまな条件の下で生き残ることができます。

学生Ａ：この質問が適切かどうかわかりませんが、高い振幅を持つ動物なのにあまり広く分布していないということはあり得ますか。先生がおっしゃったことからすると、もし私たちがある種の生物の繁栄を、世界にその種の構成員がどれだけ存在するかによって決めるとすれば、「振幅」があるだけで十分に成功した生物だといえると思うのですが。

教　授：多くの生物にとっては、それは正しいです。しかし、高い振幅を持つ生物が、それほど広く分布しないこともあり得ます。これは効率という次の考えに結びつくようですが。動物や植物は危機的環境に適応することはできるかもしれませんが、限られた状況の中でしか繁殖できないかもしれません。つまり、多くの場所で見ることができる生物でも、量を考えてみると、大したことがないということです。わかりますか。

学生Ａ：例を挙げていただけませんか。

教　授：はい、そうですね、ある植物は多くの場所で見られます。山の上の樹木限界線の辺りで育

つ木々について考えてください。それらは、しばしば常緑樹で、ほかの木々は育たない高い高度でも育つのですが、大抵は小さく、あまり効率よく繁殖しないだろうと思われる小さな木々です。それらはただ、厳しい環境にしがみついているだけです。それらの木々は山のずっと下の大きな森でも見られるかもしれませんが、分布の総計では狭い地域を占拠しているだけのことがほとんどです。つまり、それらの木々は限られた環境においては、さまざまな厳しい状況の中で生き残っています。ここでは、山の中の限られた地域においてです。それらは高い振幅を持っていますが、効率が悪いのです。

学生Ａ： すると、効率のとてもよい生物はさまざまな環境において繁殖することができるのですね？

教　授： はい、でもそのために、ときどき自らの特質を変化させなければなりません。ある場所では、このような植物や動物は異なった環境に適応する過程において実際に別の種を形成するのです。

学生Ｂ： 新しい種を形成するということですか。

教　授： いえ、最初は違います。最初は亜種を形成するのですが、もしそれらの亜種が生き残り、十分に差別化されれば、最終的には種を形成するかもしれません、はい。

　　では、適応の3番目の部分である存続時間へと話を続けさせてください。いくつかの生物が広く分布したり、効率がよかったりしても、その多くは、多かれ少なかれ1年のうちの特定の時期は特定の種類の環境に依存しているように見えます。例えば、ヒキガエルです。ヒキガエルは熱い太陽の下や砂漠でさえも動き回ることができて、適応力が高い。つまり、ヒキガエルは高い振幅の動物なのです。それに、ヒキガエルは世界中どこでも見ることができますから、効率もかなりよいのです。しかし、繁殖の時期が来ると、産卵のためには水が必要となります。それに、オタマジャクシは、もし水が干上がってしまったとしたら、急に適応はできないでしょう。従って、ヒキガエルの存続時間は短いといえます。丈夫で、広く分布していても、1年のある時期には限られた数しかいないのです。ほかの動物はそのライフサイクルの特定の段階で、これほど特定の環境特性に依存していないので、実質的にはより適応力があるのです。つまり、存続期間が長いということです。

23. 解答 (B)

この講義の主題は何か。

(A) 成功した生物

(B) 適応の要素

(C) 極端な環境への適応

(D) 自然の多様性

解説 トランスクリプトの下線部参照。

• Today I want to talk a little more about adaptation and break it into what's generally considered its three main parts.

24. 解答 (A)

適応の 3 つの主要な要素は何か。

(A) 振幅、存続時間、効率

(B) 繁殖、効率、分配

(C) 分配、繁殖、振幅

(D) 存続時間、繁殖、効率

解説 トランスクリプトの下線部参照。

- These are amplitude, efficiency and duration.

25. 解答 (A)、(D)

なぜ教授はゴキブリに言及しているのか。

解答を 2 つ選びなさい。

(A) それは幅広く生存する生物の一例である。

(B) それは上手に繁殖できる生物の一例である。

(C) それは効率の一例である。

(D) それは多くの環境に耐える生物の一例である。

解説 トランスクリプトの下線部参照。

- while a high amplitude organism would survive in a wide range of conditions. The cockroach would be an example of a high amplitude organism

- it seems to tolerate a range of conditions throughout the world.

26. 解答 （下の表を参照）

	Alpine Trees	*Toad*	*Cockroach*	*Coral*
High amplitude, high efficiency			○	
High amplitude, low efficiency	○			
High amplitude, low duration		○		
Low amplitude				○

教授はさまざまな生物の適応の特性について説明している。これらの特性を生物と結び付けなさい。

アルプスの樹木　ヒキガエル　ゴキブリ　サンゴ

高い振幅、高い効率

高い振幅、低い効率

高い振幅、短い存続時間

低い振幅

解説　トランスクリプトの下線部参照。

《Alpine Trees の根拠》

- Think of trees (Alpine Trees)
- So such trees can exist in many extreme conditions within a narrow environment, in this case, a limited zone on a mountain. They have high amplitude but low efficiency.

《Toad の根拠》

- Like for example, toads.
- they can be high amplitude creatures.
- But when it comes time to reproduce, well, they still need water to lay their eggs in. And their tadpoles are not going to quickly adapt if the water dries up. We can say that toads, therefore, have low duration.

《Cockroach の根拠》

- while a high amplitude organism would survive in a wide range of conditions. The cockroach would be an example of a high amplitude organism
- it seems to tolerate a range of conditions throughout the world

《Coral の根拠》

- corals are much lower in amplitude.

27. 解答 (C)

教授は、過酷な環境下だけに生育するアルプスの樹木についてどのように述べているか。

(A) それらは繁殖の成功を示している。

(B) それらは極端な環境によって制限を受けている。

(C) それらは丈夫だが、効率的に繁殖できない。

(D) それらは狭い範囲に限定されていない。

解説 トランスクリプトの下線部参照。

- though they can grow at high altitudes where other trees can't, they are often small, dwarfish trees that aren't going to reproduce very efficiently.

28. 解答 (B)

講義の一部をもう一度聞きなさい。それから、質問に答えなさい。

教授はなぜこのようなことを言うのか。

(A) 学生たちが理解していると確信したことを強調するために

(B) 学生たちの理解度を確認するために

(C) 学生たちに質問するよう促すために

(D) 学生たちの誤解を指摘するために

解説 トランスクリプトの下線部参照。"You got the idea?" という表現は、学生の理解を確認するときに、使われる。

- I guess this could lead into the next idea, and that is efficiency. **Animals or plants might be able to adapt to extremes in the environment but may only be able to reproduce within a narrow range. So that means you may be able to find them in a lot of places but not in any great amounts. You got the idea?**

Speaking Section　解答・解説

1. 比較選択に関する問題
[15秒で準備して、45秒話す]

質問の訳
次の意見に賛成するか反対するか。テレビを見ることは子どもたちに悪影響を及ぼし得る。具体例を挙げて答えを裏付けなさい。

模範解答 （一例）

mp3
45

　I guess it depends on what they watch and how much TV they watch. Generally, no, I don't think it's bad. Sure, a lot of programs may be useless like, say, cartoons or soap operas or bad action movies. But there is a lot of good stuff on TV, too. They can learn about science, current events, history and many other things in a more interesting way than they would in some classrooms. It's not the TV that's the problem. It's how they use it. I think this is largely the responsibility of parents. I remember when I was a kid, I started watching some nature series on dinosaurs. I was really fascinated and it led me to go to the library to check out some books on dinosaurs. So I think in many ways a child's curiosity and imagination can be stimulated by what they see on TV.

訳例
　子どもたちが何を見るか、どのくらいテレビを見るかによって違うでしょう。全体としては、いいえです、つまりテレビが悪いとは思いません。確かに、多くの番組が役に立たないかもしれません。例えば、漫画もメロドラマも、良からぬアクション映画もしかり、です。でも、良い番組もたくさんテレビで放映されています。子どもたちは、科学や時事問題、歴史をはじめ、さまざまなことを学べます。それも、下手な学校の授業よりも面白い方法で。テレビ自体が問題なのではありません。どう使うかなのです。これには親の責任が大きいと思います。思い返すと、私は子どもの頃、恐竜をテーマに据えた自然に関するシリーズ番組を見始めました。私はすっかり夢中になり、その後、図書館に行って恐竜の本を何冊か借り出したほどです。ですから、いろいろな形で、子どもたちの好奇心や想像力が視聴するテレビ番組によって刺激されるのだと思います。

ポイント

　本問は「テレビを見ることは子どもにとって悪いことだという考えに賛成か反対かを述べよ」という問題である。まず設問に対して率直に自分の考えを述べ、それをサポートする理由をつけていく。具体例を挙げるに当たっての理論展開は、解答例にあるようにテレビの短所を出してから、長所を挙げてそれに反論し、自己の見解をサポートしていく方法もある。時間が許せば、そのほかの理由を挙げ、さらに自己の意見をサポートするとよい。最後に結論を述べて締めくくる。重要な役割をするつなぎ言葉として、解答例では *I guess*、*Generally*、*Sure*、*But*、*I think*、*I remember when*、*So* などが使われている。

45 秒の構成

　　　短い一般論
　　　設問に対する解答（自己意見）
　　　自己の意見をサポートする理論展開（理由）
　　　　● テレビの短所
　　　　● 短所の具体例
　　　　● テレビの長所（反論）
　　　　● 長所の具体例
　　　自己の意見をサポートするほかの理由
　　　ほかの理由をサポートする具体例
　　　まとめ

話の組み立て方

　まず考えることは、いちばん大きな概念である（設問に対する解答：テレビを見るのは子どもにとってよくないという考えに賛成か反対かを決める）。

① **短い一般論：**

I guess it depends on what they watch and how much TV they watch.

② **自己意見（解答）：**

Generally, no, I don't think it's bad.

③ **自己意見をサポートする理由：**

テレビの短所　▶ Sure, a lot of programs may be useless

短所の具体例　▶ like, say, cartoons or soap operas or bad action movies.

長所を使って短所に反論　▶ But there is a lot of good stuff on TV, too.

長所の具体例　▶ They can learn about science, current events, history and many other things in a more interesting way than they would in some classrooms.

④ 自己の意見をサポートするほかの理由：

It's not the TV that's the problem. It's how they use it. I think this is largely the responsibility of parents.

⑤ ほかの理由をサポートする具体例：

I remember when I was a kid, I started watching some nature series on dinosaurs. I was really fascinated and it led me to go to the library to check out some books on dinosaurs.

⑥ まとめ：

So I think in many ways a child's curiosity and imagination can be stimulated by what they see on TV.

2. 読む・聴く・話す問題
──大学要覧の情報
[30秒で準備して、60秒話す]

質問：
女性は自分が観察期間に置かれている理由を述べている。彼女が話した理由を述べ、彼女が次に起こると予想している事柄について話しなさい。

模範解答（一例）

mp3
46

The woman gives two reasons why she thinks she is on probation. First of all, she was told to take too many difficult classes by her adviser. She was a freshman so she didn't know how difficult it would be. Anyway, she had a hard time all term. The second reason she's on probation is simply because of bad luck. She planned to study really hard for her physics exam but accidentally fell asleep and woke up just before the exam the next morning. She tried to get out of taking the exam but in the end she took it, and she failed. She really needed to pass this exam to pass the course. So, because she failed the exam, her GPA fell below 2.0 and she was put on probation. But, she's pretty sure she will pass this term and she thinks this whole experience at least taught her a good lesson.

訳例

　女性は、自分が観察期間に置かれていると考える理由を2つ挙げています。まず、指導教官からあまりにも多くの難しい科目を履修するように言われました。彼女は新入生だったので、それがどれほど大変なことかわかりませんでした。とにかく、彼女は学期を通じて苦労しました。彼女が観察期間に置かれている2つ目の理由は、単に不運だったことです。物理学の試験に向けて一生懸命勉強する予定だったのに、うっかり眠ってしまい、目が覚めたのは翌朝の試験直前でした。試験を受けるのをやめようとしましたが、結局受験し、うまくいきませんでした。この科目で単位を取るには、この試験でどうしても合格点を挙げる必要がありましたが、試験で失敗したのでGPAが2.0を下回り、観察期間に置かれてしまったのです。でも、彼女は今学期には単位を取れると確信しており、今回の一連の経験は少なくとも自分にとって良い教訓になったと思っています。

ポイント

　設問に的確に答えていく。女性はprobationの理由を2つ挙げているので、ま

ず2つあることを述べてから（一般的なことから具体的例題へという話の枠組みをつくる）、次に state her reasons の解として2つの理由とは何かを述べる。最後に、tell what she expects to happen の解となる、この件に対する彼女の期待するところを述べる。

話の組み立て方

① トピックの提起：

The woman gives two reasons why she thinks she is on probation.

② その理由：

最初の理由　▶ First of all, she was told to take too many difficult classes by her advisor. She was a freshman so she didn't know how difficult it would be. Anyway, she had a hard time all term.

2つ目の理由（一言でまとめること）　▶ The second reason she's on probation is simply because of bad luck.

2つ目の理由（詳細）　▶ She planned to study really hard for her physics exam but accidentally fell asleep and woke up just before the exam the next morning. She tried to get out of taking the exam but in the end she took it, and she failed. She really needed to pass this exam to pass the course.

2つ目の理由（まとめ）　▶ So, because she failed the exam, her GPA fell below 2.0 and she was put on probation.

③ 本人の期待：

But, she's pretty sure she will pass this term and she thinks this whole experience at least taught her a good lesson.

読むテクスト

Probation

Students who fail a course or who earn a cumulative grade point average below 2.0 are automatically placed on probation（本問での中心事項）. A student who is on probation will have one term in which to show that he or she is capable of doing university level work. In general, this is shown by either retaking and passing the failed course or by finishing the semester with a grade point average above 2.0, whichever is appropriate.

In general, students on probation are expected to earn a grade point average of at least 2.0 while taking at least 12 credit hours of courses during the semester following imposition of probationary status. Any student who fails to meet all of these conditions may be suspended or dismissed at the end of the following semester. Students have the right to appeal any such decisions. Please note that no notation of academic probation is made on the student's transcript.

mp3
40

聴くテクスト

Student A: Well, how did your grades turn out last term?

Student B: Don't even ask. It was a disaster.

Student A: Why, what happened?

Student B: Well, if you must know I'm on probation this term.

Student A: You? Come on. You're joking. You've been working hard.

Student B: I was working hard because I got in over my head. My adviser told me it might be a good idea to take all my required courses at once. What did I know? I'm only a freshman. Anyway, I believed him and took physics, calculus, chemistry and American history (解答では *First of all, she was told to take too many difficult classes by her adviser. She was a freshman so she didn't know how difficult it would be*).

Student A: That's a big load.

Student B: Yeah, too big as it turned out. I was struggling all term in physics and calculus but I was on the borderline and just needed to pass the finals to pass both courses. I planned to stay up all night studying for the physics exam but decided to lie down after supper for a short rest before I began to study. The next thing I knew, I was awake and saw it was light outside. Yeah, I slept the whole night and didn't study at all（解答では*The second reason she's on probation is simply because of bad luck. She planned to study really hard for her physics exam but accidentally fell asleep and woke up just before the exam the next morning*）.

Student A: Geez, what did you do?

Student B: Well, I mean, I panicked. I tried calling the physics office to say that I was sick but the secretary said I had to come to the exam or I would fail. So I went（解答では *She tried to get out of taking the exam but in the end she took it, ...*）.

Student A: And you failed the course?（ここで言う failed とは、試験のことではなくてコースのことである。つまりそのコースの単位を落とすこと）

Student B: No, I got a D,（ここでは、試験に失敗したので全体としてのコース成績が D になってしまったということである）but it brought my grade point average to just below two and just enough to earn probation（解答では *So, because she failed the exam, her GPA fell below 2.0 and she was put on probation*）.

Student A: Hey, come on, that's not so bad. Just pass all your courses this term and everything will be fine.

Student B: Yeah, I know, and I'm sure I will. Anyway, at least I learned a good lesson（解答では *But, she's pretty sure she will pass this term and she thinks this whole experience at least taught her a good lesson*）.

訳例

学生 A： 先学期の成績はどうだった？

学生 B： 聞かないで。悲惨だったの。

学生 A： どうして、何があったの？

学生 B： 言うしかないわね。今学期、観察期間なの。

学生 A： 君が？　まさか。冗談だろう。一生懸命勉強していたじゃないか。

学生 B： 完全にお手上げだったから一生懸命勉強していたのよ。指導教官が、一度にすべての必修科目を取るのがいいかもしれないって言ったの。で、何も知らなかったってわけなの、まだ 1 年生だったから。とにかく、指導教官を信じて、物理、微積分学、化学、それにアメリカ史を取ったのよ。

学生 A： それってすごい勉強量になるよね。

学生 B： ええ、結局、大変過ぎたのよ。物理と微積分学は、学期中ずっと苦労していたんだけど、ぎりぎりのところで、期末試験に合格すれば両方の授業に合格できたの。それで、物理の試験勉強のために徹夜するつもりだったんだけど、夕食の後にちょっと休もうと思って勉強を始める前に横になることにしたの。次に覚えているのは、目を覚ましたときには外が明るかったってこと。ひと晩中眠ってしまって、まったく勉強できなかったのよ。

学生 A： わあ、それでどうしたの？

学生 B： パニックになったわ。物理学の事務所に電話をして病気になったと言ったんだけど、秘書は試験に来なければ落第するって言ったの。だから行ったわ。

学生 A： それで落第したの？

学生 B： そうじゃなくて、D を取っちゃったのよ。それで成績平均点が 2 よりちょっと低くなって、観察期間になってしまったの。

学生 A： なんだ、そうだったの。そんなに悪くもないよ。今学期全部の授業に合格すれば、すべて解決するよ。

学生 B： わかってる、確実に合格するわ。少なくともいい教訓になったわ。

重要語句

- □ appeal 抗議する、訴える、懇願する
- □ borderline 境界線
- □ calculus 微積分学
- □ college catalog 大学要覧
- □ credit hour 履修単位時間
- □ cumulative 累積の、累積した
- □ disaster 災難、災害、大失敗、悲惨なこと
- □ dismiss 追放する、解雇する、退学にする
- □ got in over one's head 深みに入る、収拾がつかなくなる
- □ grade point average (GPA) 成績評価平均制度
- □ grade point 成績評価点
- □ imposition 課すこと、賦課、強制
- □ lie down 横になる、横たわる
- □ load 負担、負荷
- □ notation 覚書、注釈
- □ physics 物理学
- □ probation 保護観察、執行猶予、仮採用
- □ required course 必須科目
- □ secretary 秘書
- □ semester 学期
- □ status 地位、身分、情勢
- □ stay up all night 徹夜する
- □ struggle もがく、奮闘する
- □ supper 夕食、夜食
- □ suspend 停学を命じる
- □ transcript 成績証明書
- □ turn out 結局〜になる

3. 読む・聴く・話す問題
——経済学（景気循環）

［30 秒で準備して、60 秒話す］

質問の訳

質問：

経済循環の 4 つの周期と、実際にそれらを特定するのが多くの場合、難しい理由を説明しなさい。

模範解答（一例）

mp3 **47**

　　The four stages of the economic cycle are prosperity, liquidation, which we now call recession, depression and recovery. Prosperity is when things are going well for businesses. They can invest money and expand. People are rich so they can buy a lot of things. But if prices are too high, people stop buying. If they do, then the companies or businesses don't get enough money and they can't invest. They may have to lay off workers. This could lead to a recession and if it gets worse it could be called a depression. Recovery occurs when people start buying again, and businesses get enough money to hire workers and expand their businesses. There's no clear line between these different stages, and sometimes the cycle seems not to work at all. I mean sometimes a recovery is only temporary and everything returns to recession again. Economists seem to have a hard time defining exactly what each stage is and when it occurs.

訳例

　　経済循環の 4 つの周期は、拡張、後退——これは現在、不況と呼ばれますが、そして収縮、回復です。拡張とは物事が事業者にとって順調に進んでいる状況のことです。事業者は資金を投じて拡張できます。人々はお金を持っているので、たくさんのものを買えます。しかし、物価が高すぎると人々は購買をやめてしまいます。そうなると、企業や事業者は十分な資金を得られず投資に回せなくなります。企業や事業者は労働者を解雇しなければならなくなるかもしれません。これが不況につながる可能性があり、さらに悪化するといわゆる恐慌になり得るのです。回復が起こるのは、人々が再び購買を始め、事業者が十分な資金を得て労働者を雇用し、事業を拡大する場合です。この各周期の間に明確な境界線はなく、時には循環がまったく機能していないように見えることもあります。つまり、場合によっては回復が一時的なものにすぎず、全てが再び不況に逆戻りしてしまうのです。経済学者たちは、各周期がどういうもので、いつ起こるのかを正確に定義するのに苦心しているように思えます。

　本問では、まず経済循環の4つの周期（the four stages in the economic cycle）とは何かを述べてから（一般的なことからそれぞれの詳細へという話の枠組みをつくる）、explain the four stages in the economic cycle の解としてそれぞれの周期の詳細を述べる。そして、why they are often difficult to identify in practice の解として、なぜ実際にはそれぞれの段階の線引きが難しいのかを述べる。

- **Explain the four stages in the economic cycle（経済循環の4つの周期）：**
  The four stages of the economic cycle are prosperity, liquidation, which we now call recession, depression and recovery.

  周期のひとつ　▶ Prosperity is when things are going well for businesses. They can invest money and expand. People are rich so they can buy a lot of things.

  次に起こるのが　▶ But if prices are too high, people stop buying. If they do, then the companies or businesses don't get enough money and they can't invest. They may have to lay off workers. This could lead to a recession

  その次に起こるのが　▶ and if it gets worse it could be called a depression.

  最後の段階が　▶ Recovery occurs when people start buying again, and businesses get enough money to hire workers and expand their businesses.

- **Why they are often difficult to identify in practice：**
  There's no clear line between these different stages, and sometimes the cycle seems not to work at all. I mean sometimes a recovery is only temporary and everything returns to recession again. Economists seem to have a hard time defining exactly what each stage is and when it occurs.

　Business activity and the economy in general seem to follow distinct four-part cycles. The four parts are known among economists as prosperity, liquidation, depression and recovery（本問での中心事項：経済循環の4つの周期）（解答では *The four stages of the economic cycle are prosperity, liquidation, which we now call recession, depression and recovery*）. During prosperity, there is a rise in productivity, employment and wages（解答では*Prosperity is when things are going well for businesses*）. Optimism runs high and investment, in order to expand productivity, is common. Unfortunately, the natural outgrowth of such high productivity is an increase in prices, which at some point inhibits consumer spending. As demand declines, so does productivity and then employment. The result is a pessimistic period known as liquidation, when little investment occurs（解答では*But if prices are too high, people stop buying. If they do, then the companies or businesses don't get enough money and they can't invest. They may have to lay off workers. This could lead to a recession*）. If liquidation worsens, unemployment will grow, demand for products — even at lower prices — decreases and factories are forced to shut down. Such severe economic times are referred to as depressions（解答では *[and] if it gets worse it could be called a depression*）. The fourth stage of the cycle, recovery, may take some time, and it is not clear what factors may most influence it.

訳例

　事業活動と経済は一般に、4つの異なる周期に従っているようである。それらの4つの周期は経済学者には、拡張（好況）局面、後退（流動）局面、収縮（不況）局面、そして回復局面として知られている。拡張（好況）期には生産性、雇用、それに賃金が上がる。楽観主義が広がり、生産性を向上させるための投資が普及する。残念なことに、このような高い生産性の当然の結果は物価上昇であり、ある時点でこれが個人消費を抑制することとなる。需要が低下するにつれ、生産性が落ち、それから雇用率が下がる。その結果が、投資がほとんど行われない後退期として知られる悲観主義の期間である。後退期が悪化すると、失業率が高くなり、製品の需要はそれが低価格であってさえ低くなり、工場は閉鎖に追い込まれる。このように経済的に厳しい期間を不況期と呼ぶ。周期の4番目の段階である回復期に至るには時間がかかる可能性があり、またどのような要因が最も大きな影響力となるのかは明らかでない。

聴くテクスト

mp3 **42**

　Well, I'd like to begin today by giving you the name of an economist you have probably never heard of but who was very influential in the study of economics. His name was Wesley Mitchell. Basically, he was a man who dedicated his life to the study of business cycles. In fact, many of the terms he coined are still in use today. He divided business cycles into four parts: prosperity, liquidation, depression and recovery. Well, actually, we don't use the term liquidation any more, but I think you've all heard of recession which means the same thing（解答では*The four stages of the economic cycle are prosperity, liquidation, which we now call recession, depression and recovery*）.

But I think the main question we should ask is: Is it true? And if it is true, why can't we do something to stop it, or at least stop the bad parts of the cycle? Well, in answer to the first question, yeah, the cycles seem to be true in a general way, but they are not always so easy to find. During the Great Depression, for example, a recovery finally started. But then, just as it seemed everything would be wonderful, another recession occurred in the late 30s, which kind of ruined the cycle idea (解答では*There's no clear line between these different stages, and sometimes the cycle seems not to work at all. I mean sometimes a recovery is only temporary and everything returns to recession again*).

And then there's timing. Some so-called cycles are longer and some are shorter. Sometimes it's hard to tell one part of a cycle from another. I mean, one economist's depression may be another's recession. And how do you really know when recovery has reached prosperity? (解答では*There's no clear line between these different stages, ...*) These are not things so easy to measure, although many economists have tried to quantify them in terms of consumption, unemployment or investment (解答では*Economists seem to have a hard time defining exactly what each stage is and when it occurs*).

訳例

さて、今日は、皆さんがおそらく聞いたことがない、しかし経済学に大きな影響を与えた経済学者の名前をお伝えすることから始めたいと思います。彼の名はウェスリー・ミッチェルといいます。基本的には、彼は自身の人生を景気循環の研究にささげた人です。事実、彼がつくった専門用語の多くは今日でもまだ使われています。彼は景気循環を4つの局面、拡張（好況）局面、後退（流動）局面、収縮（不況）局面、そして回復局面に分割しました。実際には liquidation（流動期）という用語はもう使われていませんが、皆さんはこれと同じことを意味する recession（景気後退）という用語を聞いたことがあると思います。

いずれにしても、私たちが問うべき主な問題は、「それは本当か」ということだと思います。そして、もしそれが本当であれば、なぜ私たちはそれを止めるために何かができないのか、もしくは少なくともこの循環の悪い部分だけでも止めることができないのか、ということです。最初の疑問に対する答えですが、一般的にはこの循環は正しいようですが、いつも簡単に見分けられるわけではありません。例えば、世界大恐慌のとき、ついに回復期が始まり、すべてがうまくいくだろうと思われたそのとき、循環という考え方をある意味崩壊させた別の景気後退が30年代後半に起こったのです。

タイミングの問題もあります。周期と呼ばれているもののいくつかは、ほかよりも長く、またあるものはほかよりも短いのです。ときどき、循環の一局面をほかの局面から見分けるのが難しいことがあります。つまり、ある経済学者が不況期と呼んでいるものは、ほかの経済学者にとっては景気後退であるかもしれません。そして、いつ回復期が拡張（好況）期に本当に到達したといえるのでしょうか。多くの経済学者は消費、失業率または投資の点から

これらのことを数値化しようとしていますが、そう簡単に測れるものではないのです。

重要語句

- □ business cycles 景気循環
- □ coin（新しい言葉）をつくる
- □ common 共通の、一般の、普及している
- □ consumer spending 個人消費
- □ consumption 消費
- □ decline 下降する、衰える
- □ dedicate 専念する、打ち込む
- □ demand 需要
- □ depression 下降、不況、不振
- □ distinct 異なった、目立つ、明確な
- □ employment 雇用
- □ Great Depression 世界大恐慌
- □ in a general way 一般に
- □ in terms of ... ～の点から見て、～に関して
- □ influential 影響力の大きい、有力な
- □ inhibit 抑制する、妨げる
- □ investment 投資、投下資本
- □ liquidation 清算、整理、流動化（後退）
- □ optimism 楽観、楽観主義
- □ outgrowth 伸び出ること
- □ pessimistic 悲観的な、悲観主義の
- □ productivity 生産性
- □ prosperity 繁栄、成功、好況
- □ quantify 定量化する
- □ recovery 回復、復興
- □ ruin 破壊する、ぶち壊す、崩壊する
- □ shut down 活動を停止する、閉鎖する
- □ term 言葉、用語、表現
- □ unemployment 失業
- □ wage 賃金、給与

4. 聴く・話す問題
——歴史学（1900年代初期のアルコール）
［20秒で準備して、60秒話す］

mp3
48

質問の訳

質問：

20世紀初頭のアメリカでの禁酒法の歴史を要約しなさい。

模範解答（一例）

There was a growing reaction against alcohol in the early 1900s. People thought that much of the crime at the time could be traced to alcohol abuse. There were also a lot of health problems connected to alcohol. They thought that it would be a good idea if the production and use of alcohol were prohibited. Finally, the U.S. Congress passed an amendment that prohibited the sale and use of alcohol for the entire country.

At first it seemed that this prohibition helped, but soon people tried to get around the law. They could do this because the law was not enforced very strictly. They opened secret bars called "speakeasies," and organized crime began to control the secret production and smuggling of alcohol. In fact, the use of alcohol actually increased during the 1920s. Crime also increased, probably because of alcohol's connection to organized crime. The Roaring Twenties was the name given to the decade of Prohibition.

In the end, it had to be admitted that Prohibition didn't work. Because of this Congress ended Prohibition in 1933.

注：Summaryを書くときに留意しておきたい点は以下のとおり：
(1) 書き手が言いたいことは何か。
(2) 全体の流れにおける大切な点を考える。
(3) 談話レベルでの文のつながりを考える。

訳例

1900年代初頭に、アルコール反対の機運が高まりました。人々は、当時の犯罪の多くがアルコールの乱用に起因すると考えていました。アルコールに絡む健康上の問題もたくさんありました。人々は、アルコールの製造や消費が禁止されるなら、それは好ましいと考えました。ついにアメリカ議会は、全米でアルコールの販売と消費を禁じる修正法案を可決しました。

当初、この禁止法は効果があるように見えましたが、すぐに人々は法の目をくぐろうとす

るようになりました。これが可能だったのは、法律が厳格に施行されていなかったからです。「酒類密売店」と呼ばれる潜りのバーを開き、犯罪組織がアルコールの密造や密輸を管理し始めました。事実、アルコールの消費が 1920 年代を通じて実際には増加したのです。犯罪も増えました。これはおそらく、アルコールと犯罪組織のつながりが原因だったのでしょう。「狂騒の '20 年代」が、禁酒法が施行された 10 年間に付けられた名称です。

　結局のところ、禁酒法はうまくいかなかったと認めざるを得なくなり、議会は 1933 年に禁酒法を廃止したのです。

ポイント

　要約をすることで設問に答えていく。まずトピックを提起し、それをサポートする理由を述べていくのが英語式の話の展開方法である。また、聴いたままを伝えるのではなく、自分の言葉で言い換えることがポイントだ。本問では設問の性質上、時間の流れに沿って、禁酒熱が高まった時点から、禁酒法制定とその後の成り行き、そして禁酒法廃止に至るまでを要約をしていくことになるが、ここでもやはり、まずトピックを提起してそれをサポートする具体例をつけていく方法で話を展開させていくことが大切。

話の組み立て方

① トピックの提起（禁酒熱が高まる）：

There was a growing reaction against alcohol in the early 1900s.

② サポートする理由：

People thought that much of the crime at the time could be traced to alcohol abuse.

2 番目の理由 ▶ There were also a lot of health problems connected to alcohol.

③ 禁酒法制定の動機（connecting information）：

They thought that it would be a good idea if the production and use of alcohol were prohibited.

④ 禁酒法時代の始まり

Finally, the U.S. Congress passed an amendment that prohibited the sale and use of alcohol for the entire country.

⑤ その後の成り行き（時間的経過に沿って）：

At first it seemed that this prohibition helped, but soon people tried to get around the law.

345

⑥ ⑤をサポートする理由：

They could do this because the law was not enforced very strictly.

⑦ ⑥をサポートする具体例：

They opened secret bars called "speakeasies," and organized crime began to control the secret production and smuggling of alcohol.

⑧ 禁酒法制定により、行きついた結果と、考え得る原因：

In fact, the use of alcohol actually increased during the 1920s. Crime also increased, probably because of alcohol's connection to organized crime. The Roaring Twenties was the name given to the decade of Prohibition.

⑨ 締めくくり（禁酒法廃止）：

In the end, it had to be admitted that Prohibition didn't work. Because of this Congress ended Prohibition in 1933.

聴くテクスト

mp3
43

Now, throughout the early 1900s, there was a growing sentiment against alcohol (解答では *There was a growing reaction against alcohol in the early 1900s*). Alcohol was seen as the source of numerous social problems. Families were destroyed by it, life expectancy was lowered by it, and it tended to be behind many types of crimes. By 1920, most states had passed prohibition laws, which were laws against the sale and consumption of alcohol.

（ここまでを要約すると *People thought that much of the crime at the time could be traced to alcohol abuse. There were also a lot of health problems connected to alcohol. They thought that it would be a good idea if the production and use of alcohol were prohibited.*）

So it really wasn't too surprising when a new amendment was added to the U.S. Constitution that did the same thing. In the context of the times, it seemed like a reasonable thing to do.

（禁酒法時代の始まりの部分を要約すると *Finally, the U.S. Congress passed an amendment that prohibited the sale and use of alcohol for the entire country.*）

Well, at first Prohibition seemed to work. But as people realized that no one was too interested in enforcing this law, they began to work around it.

（解答では *At first it seemed that this prohibition helped, but soon people tried to get around the law. They could do this because the law was not enforced very strictly.*)

Secret bars called "speakeasies" were opened in almost every town. Some historians say that there were more speakeasies in some cities after Prohibition than there were bars before it. Then people started to make their own alcohol or to have alcohol smuggled into the country from places such as Canada. It wasn't long before organized crime realized that they could make a lot of money by taking over the production and smuggling of illegal alcohol. And as you could probably guess, there were a lot of gang-related crimes which helped to actually increase, rather than lower the crime rate.

（ここまでを要約すると *They opened secret bars called "speakeasies," and organized crime began to control the secret production and smuggling of alcohol.*）

In the end, it seemed that prohibition had almost the opposite effect from what had been anticipated. Not only did crime increase, but alcohol consumption increased. This whole era of Prohibition began to be referred to as the Roaring Twenties which was almost synonymous with wild parties featuring illegal alcohol.

（ここまでを要約すると *In fact, the use of alcohol actually increased during the 1920s. Crime also increased, probably because of alcohol's connection to organized crime. The Roaring Twenties was the name given to the decade of Prohibition.*）

In the end, it had to be agreed that Prohibition was a failure, and in 1933, Congress repealed the prohibition.

（最後の部分を要約すると *In the end, it had to be admitted that Prohibition didn't work. Because of this Congress ended prohibition in 1933.*）

訳例

　さて、1900年代初期を通じて、アルコールに反対する感情が高まりました。アルコールは多くの社会問題の源であると考えられていたのです。アルコールは家庭を破壊し、平均寿命を短くしました。アルコールはまたさまざまな種類の犯罪を引き起こす傾向を持っていたのです。1920年までに、ほとんどの州では、アルコールの販売や消費に反対する法律である禁酒法が可決されました。従って、同様の内容を規定する新たな修正案が合衆国憲法に加えられたのも、それほど驚くようなことではなかったのです。当時の状況では、それは道理にかなったことのようでした。

　禁酒法は、最初は効果があったようですが、人々は、誰もこの法律を強制することに関心がないことに気づくにつれ、抜け道を見つけ始めたのです。ほとんどすべての町で「酒類密

売店」と呼ばれる秘密のバーが開かれました。一部の歴史家は、ある都市では禁酒法以前にあったバーの数より多くの酒類密売店が禁酒法施行後にできたと言っています。その後、人々は自分でアルコールを造ったり、カナダのような所からアメリカにアルコールを密輸し始めました。犯罪組織が、違法アルコールを製造したり密輸したりすることによって多額のお金を稼ぐことができることを認識するまで、それほど時間はかかりませんでした。そして、たぶん皆さんも推測できると思いますが、犯罪率を低下させるどころか増加させる助けになり、ギャングたちによる犯罪が多く存在したのです。

　結局、禁酒法は期待されていたのとはほぼ反対の効果をもたらしました。つまり、犯罪が増加しただけでなく、アルコールの消費も増えたのです。禁酒法が施行されていたこの時代全体は、違法アルコールを呼び物とする熱狂的なパーティーとほぼ同義語である狂騒の 1920 年代と呼ばれ始めました。ついに、禁酒法は失敗であったという合意に至り、1933 年には議会は禁酒法を廃止しました。

重要語句	
□ amendment 修正案、訂正	□ numerous 多数の、非常に多くの
□ by ... 〜までに	□ prohibition law 禁酒法
□ consumption 消費	□ sentiment 気持ち、感情
□ crime 罪、犯罪	□ throughout ... 〜の間中
□ life expectancy 平均寿命	

Writing Section　解答・解説

1. 読む・聴く・書く問題（20 分で書き上げるエッセイ）
——言語学の講義（ピジン語）

指示文・質問の訳

指示文：

このタスクでは、3 分間でパッセージを読みます。その後、読み終えた文章の話題に関する講義の一部を聞きます。講義の後、20 分間で解答を考え、作成します。理想的な解答は 150 から 225 語です。

次のパッセージを読みなさい。

リスニング：

では、読み終えたピジン語という話題に関する講義の一部を聞きなさい。講義を聞きながらメモを取ることができます。

では、質問に答えなさい。メモを使って解答できます。

質問：

ピジン語の発展と形成に関する主要なポイントを要約しなさい。教授のコミュニケーションについての考えと、文章中に示された考えはどのように対照的なのかを説明しなさい。

模範解答（一例）

　　A pidgin is a language that forms when two groups of people who have different languages need to communicate with each other. Sometimes this communication is needed so that they can trade with each other, but at other times it may be for other needs. The important factor, however, is this need to communicate, because if this does not exist, the two groups will remain isolated even if they live next to each other.

It is also important that the two groups do not share a third language. If this is the case, and they want to communicate, then they will most likely use this third language, and a pidgin will probably not develop.

A pidgin is a simple language. It often has a simple form and relies on vocabulary more than grammar to communicate. This is good in some ways, because one of the main goals of having a language is for people to communicate. The professor, however, points out that relying too much on simple communication may cause problems. Although basic or main ideas may be communicated, there may be problems communicating fine points. Therefore, where serious negotiations are concerned, groups are most likely to depend on a third language, such as English, to attain full understanding of one another.

訳例

ピジン語は、異なる言語を話す2つの集団が互いにコミュニケーションを取る必要がある状況下で形成される言語だ。ここで言うコミュニケーションは、相互の取引で必要になることもあれば、他の理由で必要になることもある。とはいえ、重要な要素はコミュニケーションの必要性である。それがなければ2つの集団は、たとえ隣り合って暮らしていたとしても分離されたままでいるからだ。

他にも重要なのは、この2つの集団が第3の言語を共有していないことだ。もしもこの共通言語があると、コミュニケーションを図りたいとき、彼らは十中八九、その第3言語を使い、ピジン語はおそらく発展しないだろう。

ピジン語は単純な言語である。たいていは単純な言語形態を備え、コミュニケーションでは文法よりも語彙に頼る。これはある意味、いいことだ。人が言語を身につける主たる目的の一つはコミュニケーションを取ることだからだ。しかし教授は、単純なコミュニケーションに頼りすぎると問題を引き起こす可能性があると指摘する。基本的な、あるいは主要な考えは伝わるかもしれないが、細かい点を伝える上では問題があるかもしれないのだ。そのため、重要な交渉においては、集団同士、ほとんどの場合で英語のような第3言語に依存し、互いに完璧に理解し合おうとするのである。

ポイント

20分で構想をまとめ、読んだことと聞いたことに基づいて解答を書き上げる問題。聞かれていることに答えるという形で解答の組み立てを考えていく。さらにここで大切なのは、アカデミック・ライティングの基本に沿って解答を書くということだ。本問では、まず要約をするわけなので、最初のパラグラフでは一般的概念を書いてから、connecting information（一般的概念と主題をつなぐ情報）を書き、要約の主題を書く。続くそれぞれのパラグラフには、トピック・センテンスを書き、それをサポートする具体例などを書くことによって設問に答えていく。ここで大切なのは、読んだこ

とや聴いたことを、まったくそのままの文章を使うのではなく、違う表現に言い換えて（paraphrasing）書くことだ。具体的には、まず最初の設問 Summarize the main points concerning the <u>development</u>. に答えてから、Summarize the main points concerning <u>form of pidgins</u>. に答える。続いて教授の反論とそれをサポートする理由を書き、2 つ目の設問 Explain how the professor's view of communication contrasts with the view expressed in the reading. に答えていく。

エッセイの組み立て方 ※❷は設問からの引用です。

❷ Summarize the main points concerning the development.

① 大きな概念である "pidgin" の定義（一般的概念）：

A pidgin is a language that forms when two groups of people who have different languages need to communicate with each other.

② 大きな概念と主題を結びつける（connecting information）：

Sometimes this communication is needed so that they can trade with each other, but at other times it may be for other needs.

③ この解答の中で言いたいこと（主題）：

The important factor, however, is this need to communicate, because if this does not exist, the two groups will remain isolated even if they live next to each other.

④ 主題に関連するもうひとつの大切な要因：

It is also important that the two groups do not share a third language.

⑤ もうひとつの大切な要因をサポートする理由：

If this is the case, and they want to communicate, then they will most likely use this third language, and a pidgin will probably not develop.

❷ Summarize the main points concerning form of pidgins.

⑥ トピック・センテンス：

A pidgin is a simple language.

⑦ 詳細：

It often has a simple form and relies on vocabulary more than grammar to communicate. This is good in some ways, because one of the main goals of having a language is for people to communicate.

ⓠ Explain the how professor's view of communication contrasts with the view expressed in the reading.

⑧ 教授による反論：

The professor, however, points out that relying too much on simple communication may cause problems.

⑨ 反論をサポートする理由：

Although basic or main ideas may be communicated, there may be problems communicating fine points.

⑩ 具体例により反論を発展させる：

Therefore, where serious negotiations are concerned, groups are most likely to depend on a third language, such as English, to attain full understanding of one another.

読むテクスト

⌈ Summarize the main points concerning the development and form of pidgins. ⌉

A pidgin is a language which is created when two separate language groups live in close proximity to each other. For this reason, pidgins are sometimes referred to as contact languages. In some cases, however, as when different language groups have an economic relationship, the pidgin is used as a means of negotiating business and does not need continuous contact as do other pidgins. Because the nature of a pidgin is to expedite communication, in linguistic form, it often consists of simple grammar patterns, reduced phonology, and is often highly dependent on vocabulary to transmit meaning. But communication is the nature of all language and is generally considered its main role.

⌈ The view expressed in the reading ⌉

In order for pidgins to develop, several factors must be present. The contact between the language groups must be persistent. In other words, contact must prevail for an extended period of time. Secondly, there must be a mutual need for the groups to communicate with each other. Without this need, language groups can live in complete isolation despite living in close physical contact with each other. Thirdly, it is important that the groups do not share some third language. In other words, if two groups living in close proximity and sharing a need to communicate both speak a third language, it is likely that the development of a pidgin will be suppressed by this third language. Pidgins are not generally learned as a first language, however, in the cases where this occurs, it is referred to as creolization.

訳例

　ピジン語とは、異なる2つの言語グループが近接して存在しているときにつくり出される言語である。このため、ピジン語はしばしば接触言語と呼ばれる。しかし、異なった言語を持つ人々が経済関係を持っているような場合、ピジン語はビジネス交渉のための手段として用いられるので、ほかのピジン語のように継続して接触している必要がなくなる。ピジン語の本質はコミュニケーションを効率的にすることであるため、言語形態としては、単純な文法規則や少ない音韻から成り立っており、意味を伝えるために単語に大きく依存していることが多い。しかし、コミュニケーションこそすべての言語の本質であり、一般的には主要な役割であると考えられているのである。

　ピジン語が発展するためには、いくつかの要因が存在しなければならない。言語グループ間の接触は持続的なものでなければならない。つまり、接触が長期間にわたらなければならないのである。第2に、双方のグループに互いにコミュニケーションを取る共通の必要性がなければならない。この必要性がなければ、異なった言語グループは、物理的には近くに存在するにもかかわらず、完全に分離された状態で存続できてしまうからである。第3に、これらのグループが同じ第2の言語を共有していないことが重要である。つまり、もし近接して暮らし、コミュニケーションを取る必要性を共有している2つのグループが、ともに第3の言語を話すのであれば、ピジン語の発展はこの第3の言語により抑圧される可能性が高い。ピジン語は通常、第1言語として学ばれることはないが、これが起こる（第1言語として学ばれる）とクレオール化と呼ばれる。

聴くテクスト

mp3
44

［"Pidgin" の起源について話し始める］

　Now, you've all probably heard the term, Lingua Franca, which literally means "Frankish Language." This term came from the Arab nations which referred to the Europeans as "Franks." The original lingua franca was a trading language composed largely of Italian and mixed with Turkish and other Middle Eastern languages. But I think what's really important to keep in mind is that the main purpose of this kind of language was communication. And when communication is your main goal, then the language that develops will have certain features.

　Well, let me back up a bit and say that we no longer use the term lingua franca in linguistics. We now call languages that develop from frequent trade, or from two language groups living in close contact with each other, **pidgins**. But in order for a pidgin to develop there must be some need among the groups to communicate. Often this need is economic, but not always. And sometimes, the two groups simply are not interested in communicating. I mean, you can see this in the U.S. in immigrant communities. If the community is big enough, it may be self-sufficient. It may have its own stores, newspapers or whatever so that there is no need for the people in the community to learn English. It is not uncommon to find people here who have lived in the U.S. for 10 years or more and only know a few basic English words. The kids of these immigrants go to schools where English is the main language, so they have a need to use English. They have a need to communicate but not everyone does.

> 設問 Summarize the main points concerning the development and form of pidgins. の答えとして、次のパラグラフを要約する

Now, if a pidgin does develop as a language, the form is usually quite simple. Often, for example, there is very little other than the most basic grammar. You will rarely find tense, for instance. The idea of tense will be found in words that may signal tense. I mean, if you wanted to talk about the past, you may throw in a word like "yesterday" rather than change the form of the verb. So I think you can see that in any situation in which communication is important, vocabulary will be the most important way to get your idea across.

> 設問 Explain the how the professor's view of communication contrasts with the view expressed in the reading. の答えとして、次のパラグラフを要約する

Unfortunately, though many linguists stress the importance of communication over form, the problem with relying on communication as the main goal of language is a loss of communicating fine details. You could even say that communication may hurt communication. This may sound strange, but it would be nearly impossible to negotiate a modern business contract in a pidgin. This is why, in many cases, pidgins have been replaced by a third language, and in the case of most of the world, this third language is English.

訳例

　さて、皆さんはたぶん、文字通り「フランク族の言語」を意味するリンガフランカという言葉を聞いたことがあるでしょう。この言葉は、ヨーロッパ人を「フランク族」と呼んでいたアラブの国々から来ています。元のリンガフランカは、大部分がイタリア語とトルコ語にほかの中東の言語が混ざったものから構成された通商言語（取引で使われる言語）でした。しかし、本当に覚えておかなければならない重要なことは、この種の言語の主な目的はコミュニケーションであったということだと思います。そして、コミュニケーションが（その言語の）主な目的である場合、発展した言語はある種の特徴を持つことになるのです。

　もう少し詳しく説明すると、私たちは言語学においてもはやリンガフランカという言葉は使っていません。現在では、頻繁な貿易から、または互いに密接して暮らしている2つの言語グループから発展した言語をピジン語と呼んでいます。しかし、ピジン語が発展するためには、グループ間にコミュニケーションの必要性が存在しなければいけません。この必要性は多くの場合は、経済的なものですが、常にそうとは限りません。ときどき、2つのグループは、コミュニケーションを取ることにまったく興味を持たないこともあります。これは、アメリカの移民コミュニティーにおいて見られます。もしそのコミュニティーが十分に大きければ、コミュニティーは自給自足できるかもしれません。コミュニティーは独自の店や新聞などを持つので、そこに住む人々には英語を学ぶ必要性がないのです。アメリカで10年もしくは、それ以上暮らしているのに、いくつかの基本的な英単語しか知らない人をここで見つけることは珍しいことではありません。これらの移民の子どもたちは、英語が主な言語である学校に行くので、英語を使う必要性があります。彼には、コミュニケーションの必要性がありますが、皆がそうではないのです。

　さて、もしピジン語がひとつの言語として発達するとしたら、その形態は通常、非常に単純なものです。例えば、大抵の場合、基本的な文法以外のものはほとんどありません。時制はめったにないでしょう。時制という概念は、時を表す単語に見られるでしょう。つまり、もし過去のことについて話したいとすれば、動詞の形を変えるのではなく、「昨日」といったような単語を挿入するわけです。従って、コミュニケーションが重要であるような状況においては、考えを伝えるためには語彙が最も大切な手段であることがわかると思います。

　不幸なことに、多くの言語学者は言語の形態よりもコミュニケーションの重要性を強調しますが、コミュニケーションを言語の主な目的としてそれに頼ることは、細かいことを伝える能力の欠如という問題を引き起こすのです。コミュニケーションがコミュニケーションを傷つけるかもしれないとさえいえます。奇妙に聞こえるかもしれませんが、ピジン語を使って現代のビジネス上の契約の交渉を行うことはほとんど不可能でしょう。ですから、多くの場合、ピジン語は第3の言語に取って代わられており、世界中の多くの場所では、この第3の言語は英語なのです。

☐ Arab アラブの

☐ community 共同体、地域社会

☐ complete 完全な、全部の

☐ compose 〜から成る、〜を構成する

☐ consist of ... 〜から成る

☐ contact language 接触用語

☐ economic relationship 経済関係

☐ economic 経済の、経済上の

☐ expedite 促進する、効率よくする、早める

☐ extended period of time 連続した期間、長期間

☐ Frankish フランク族の

☐ immigrant 移民、移住者

☐ isolation 孤立、分離

☐ linguist 言語学者

☐ linguistic 言語の

☐ linguistics 言語学

☐ means 手段、方法

☐ mutual 共通の、相互の

☐ nation 国、国家、国民

☐ negotiate 交渉する、協議する

☐ past 過去（形）、過去時制

☐ persistent 持続性の、永続的な

☐ phonology 音韻論

☐ pidgin ピジン語

☐ prevail 広がる、普及する

☐ proximity 近いこと、接近

☐ rely on ... 〜を当てにする、〜を信頼する

☐ self-sufficient 自給自足できる、自足できる

☐ separate 分かれた、離れた、別個の

☐ share 共有する、共用する

☐ suppress 抑える、抑制する

☐ tense 時制

☐ Turkish トルコ語

☐ uncommon 珍しい、めったに見られない

☐ verb 動詞

2. オンライン投稿文

この課題では、オンラインのディスカッションを読みます。教授が質問を投稿しており、クラスメートがディスカッション掲示板に回答を寄せています。あなたは自分自身の回答を書き、ディスカッションに貢献することが求められています。読むのも含めて 10 分間で自分の意見を書いてください。

指示文と質問・議論の訳

教授が情報科学の授業をしています。教授の質問に答える投稿文を書いてください。

解答では、自分の言葉で意見を述べ、その裏付けをしておきます。

効果的な解答は、最低でも 100 語が必要です。

リー博士

　今週は、情報をデジタル保存するためのさまざまな方法について議論してきました。しかし、私たちが忘れがちなのは、情報の保存が何世紀にもわたって身近なものであり続けているということです。図書館は最初の文明にさえ存在し、これまで、どんな町や都市でも重要な位置を占めてきました。しかし今日、人々は図書館が本当に必要なのかという疑問を抱いています。あまりにも多くの情報がオンラインで手に入るからです。このデジタル時代に、大規模でコストのかかる図書館を維持していく必要が本当にあると思いますか。

アンナ

　私は図書館にはもう、めったに行きません。大学図書館にある資料のほとんどがデジタル化されているので、オンラインでアクセスできます。確かに、図書館に行かないと読めない珍しい本が多少はあるかもしれませんが、どれくらいの頻度で実際にそれらを利用する必要があるのでしょうか。時代は変わってきています。とにかく便利になりました。単に携帯電話を使えばどこからでも必要なものを見つけられるのですから。なので、図書館という場所があるとしても、そこに以前ほど多くのお金を投じていかなくてもいいはずです。

ピーター

　私はアンナさんに同意できません。もちろん、必要な情報のほとんどはオンライン

で入手できますが、図書館には本があるだけではありません。図書館は邪魔されることなく勉強できる静かな場所を提供してくれます。加えて、オンラインでやっているように追加料金を払うことなく、1カ所で電子書籍や映画、音楽が利用できます。これは、地元の図書館に行く労力をはるかに上回る価値があることだと思います。オンラインでどれだけ情報が得られても、図書館は重要であり続けると思います。

模範解答 (一例)

I can understand Anna's viewpoint. It certainly is easier to access information from your own home than by making a trip to the library. That said, I have to wonder if she's been to the library recently. It's not always easy to find the precise information you need online. However, a librarian can tell you at once where to find the information you're looking for. I agree with Peter's assertion that a library is much more than books. It is part of the community. I took advantage of several of the free programs they offer. For example, they give guided walks of the city to teach people about its history. I couldn't get that personal connection online.

訳例

私はアンナさんの意見が理解できます。図書館に出掛けていくよりも自宅から情報にアクセスするほうが間違いなく簡単です。とはいえ、彼女が最近、図書館に行ったかどうかには疑問が残ります。まさに必要としている情報をオンラインで見つけるのは、必ずしも簡単なわけではありません。一方で、図書館員は即座に、探している情報がどこで見つかるのかを教えてくれます。図書館は蔵書をはるかに上回るものだというピーターさんの主張に賛成です。図書館はコミュニティの一部です。私は図書館が提供する無料プログラムをいくつか利用しました。例えば、図書館はガイド付きで市内を歩いて回るイベントを開催しており、人々に市の歴史を伝えてくれます。オンラインでは、そのような個人的な人とのつながりを培うことはできなかったでしょう。

ポイント

ディスカッションには聞き手がいるので、語用論的要素も考えて、発言者は、反対するときにはまず前置きを述べ、感じよく話を始めると良い印象を与えられ、実際の展開により近づけることができる。テンプレートを考えるなら、前置きとして "I can understand Anna's viewpoint." と述べてアンナの考えもいいことを伝え、次に "I have to wonder if she's been to the library recently." とその論点の弱点を指摘する。そのあとに "It's not always easy to find the precise information you need online." と自分の反対意見の論点を大きな概念で述べ、それから、その論点

を裏づける具体例 "However, a librarian can tell you at once where to find the information you're looking for." を挙げている。さらに、これをつなぎの発言とし、別の参加者であるピーターの意見 "a library is much more than books" にも言及し、アンナの意見には同意してないということを "It is part of the community." という大きな概念を出して結論づけ、さらに具体例を加えて裏付けすることで仕上げている。このように、意見を述べるときには、"from general to specific" を常に頭に置いて、まず大きな概念を述べて、そこに説明や具体例を付けていくといい。

大きな枠

1. 前置きとして、A に反対する前に「相手の言うこともわかる」と述べる。
2. それから、それとなく相手の意見の弱点を指摘する。
3. 話を続け、自分の意見を大きな概念で述べる。
4. 自分の意見の裏付けを述べて、相手に納得してもらう。
5. B の意見にも言及するために、それを自分の意見の延長線上に置き、「つなぎ発言」とする。
6. 話をさらにつなげて展開し、結論を出す。

川手 - ミヤジェイエフスカ 恩
（Megumi Kawate-Mierzejewska）

テンプル大学大学院教育学研究科英語教授法博士号取得（専門は中間言語語用論）。テンプル大学日本校大学付属英語研修課程助教授を経て、2000年より、TOEFLなどの標準テストで知られる米国ETS（Educational Testing Service）の日本における公認コンサルタント（TOEFL部門）を務めていた。2012年より2014年2月まで、ETS Authorized Propell Trainer を務めた。現在は、早稲田大学にて英語を教えている。

Steve Mierzejewski

Steve Mierzejewski has worked in English testing and curriculum design in Japan, South Korea, China, Poland, Afghanistan, and the U.S. He has contributed to a number of books on a variety of tests. He used to work as a test developer for Michigan State University. Steve is currently writing fiction and nonfiction from his home in southern Poland.

地球人ネットワークを創る

アルクのシンボル
「地球人マーク」です。

改訂版 完全攻略！ TOEFL iBT®テスト 模試3回分

発 行 日：2024年4月22日 （初版）

著　　　者：川手 - ミヤジェイエフスカ 恩
　　　　　　（Megumi Kawate-Mierzejewska）
　　　　　　Steve Mierzejewski
編　　　集：株式会社オフィスLEPS 岡本茂紀
　　　　　　株式会社アルク 文教編集部
翻　　　訳：高橋良子、飯尾直美、鬼頭和也、
　　　　　　川手 - ミヤジェイエフスカ 恩
校　　　正：Peter Branscombe
表紙デザイン：大村麻紀子
Ｄ　Ｔ　Ｐ：朝日メディアインターナショナル株式会社
音 声 編 集：ジェイルハウス・ミュージック
写 真 協 力：Adam Myers、Christopher Gillyard、
　　　　　　Danielle Locovich、Davey Lagman、
　　　　　　David Bochanski、Jason Zbikowski、
　　　　　　Jesse D. Terzian、Jon Jamieson、
　　　　　　Karla Cruel、Kazuya Kito、Ling Tang、
　　　　　　Marisa Johnson、Ryan Cronrath、
　　　　　　Seiya Vogt、Stephanie Flanagan、
　　　　　　Victoria Song　他
印刷・製本：萩原印刷株式会社
発 行 者：天野智之
発 行 所：株式会社アルク
　　　　　　〒102-0073
　　　　　　東京都千代田区九段北 4-2-6　市ヶ谷ビル
　　　　　　Website　https://www.alc.co.jp/